SOMBREROS AND MOTORCYCLES IN A NEWER SOUTH

SOMBREROS
AND
MOTORCYCLES
IN A NEWER SOUTH

THE POLITICS OF AESTHETICS IN SOUTH CAROLINA'S TOURISM INDUSTRY

P. NICOLE KING

UNIVERSITY PRESS OF MISSISSIPPI / JACKSON

www.upress.state.ms.us

The University Press of Mississippi is a member
of the Association of American University Presses.

Copyright © 2012 by University Press of Mississippi
All rights reserved
Manufactured in the United States of America

First printing 2012

∞

Library of Congress Cataloging-in-Publication Data

King, P. Nicole, 1976–
Sombreros and motorcycles in a newer South : the politics
of aesthetics in South Carolina's tourism industry / P. Nicole
King.
p. cm.
Includes bibliographical references and index.
ISBN 978-1-61703-251-6 (cloth : alk. paper) — ISBN 978-1-
61703-252-3 (ebook) 1. Tourism—Social aspects—South Carolina. 2. Tourism—Political aspects—South Carolina. 3. South
Carolina—Race relations. 4. South Carolina—Politics and government. 5. South Carolina—Social life and customs. I. Title.
G155.U6K56 2012
306.4'81909757—dc23   2011038837

British Library Cataloging-in-Publication Data available

In memory of my father,
Paul Michael King

CONTENTS

ACKNOWLEDGMENTS

Writing this book has been a long but enlightening journey. For me, the project has been a part of leaving home and beginning to see place differently. I saw my home state and the idea of being a "southerner" (something I had rarely ever considered) in a completely new light once I left South Carolina for graduate school out west. But despite this new understanding of place, I felt something was missing. Americans love the drama of the city, the quaint appeal of the rural countryside, and have certainly given enough attention and resources to the suburbs—but, what about those other places, the offbeat places that don't fit neatly into any category? This book was written with all those other places in mind. My career is dedicated to the places we have yet to see fully and to exploring their stories. Whether we drive by them without a second look, or never go through them because they are in a "bad" part of town, those places matter.

My process of learning to see and analyze the complexities of culture and place has benefitted from the wisdom of many great teachers and scholars. My professors at Coastal Carolina University in Conway, South Carolina, pushed me to inquire about the larger world. Randall Wells, Peter Lecouras, Don Millus, Steve Hamelman, and Jill Sessoms all showed me the ways literature expands our worldview. Diana Robin, Beth Bailey, Ruth Salvaggio, Katja Schroeter—and especially the late Gus Blaisdel—opened my eyes to the world of critical theory and media analysis. Gus provided me with a lesson important for any newly minted graduate student: not to take myself too seriously and not to become so enamored with theoretical jargon that my writing no longer makes sense. The two years I spent working towards my master's degree at the University of New Mexico gave me a new understanding of both the physical world and the life of the mind.

I thank the Southwest for broadening my horizons and my time at the University of Maryland for grounding me back on the east coast. I came to the University of Maryland to learn about cultural landscape studies and theories of place. My intellectual and professional development was constantly enhanced by the exemplary mentorship of Mary Corbin Sies, and she continues to be an important advisor to me as I negotiate the academic world. As a student in the Department of American Studies, I encountered a rich and rigorous exploration of place that changed my work and my perspective on American—and southern American—culture. Nancy Struna has assisted my intellectual development since my first semester at the University of Maryland, and I am better for having known her. Angel David Nieves, Leslie Rowland, and Psyche Williams-Forson, were generous with their time and expertise, helping me to develop and focus my interest in place, aesthetics, and identity while at College Park. Joshua Woodfork has been a valued friend and collaborator since the College Park days. Ed Martini and Donald Snyder were helpful mentors in graduate school and (back in the day) good neighbors. Zack Furness has provided both friendship and different ways of thinking about the politics of mobility. Katherine Broadway read this manuscript numerous times, and her skillful edits and support made it a much better book.

Early in the journey Anthony Stanonis saw some merit or, at least, something interesting in my work on South of the Border. By taking part in the *Dixie Emporium* symposium and the book that followed, I met many southern studies scholars. I really began to see the dynamic relationship between insiders and outsiders during a late-night adventure when a scholar from California was inveigled to experience Krispy Kreme doughnuts "in the South" before her presentation on the topic the following day. Through my participation on academic panels with Mary Battle and Andrew Kahrl and conversations with them at conferences, I have gained insight into the bigger picture of tourism, leisure culture, and identity.

My wonderful colleagues in the Department of American Studies at the University of Maryland, Baltimore County (UMBC), have provided an impressive support system—especially for such a small department. I am especially grateful to Pat McDermott, Jason Loviglio, and Warren Belasco, who read and offered feedback on my manuscript. Pat provided both a fine example as a successful professional and a door that was always open. Jason always offered support, a wonderful sense of humor, and the occasional ride home when I was just too tired to brave the Baltimore bus. Ed Orser has pushed me to see the issues surrounding place and community in the Baltimore area in new and interesting ways. My colleagues Tamara Bhalla and Kimberly Moffitt provided essential support during numerous long meetings over coffee. They helped me through the ups and downs of writing this book and negotiating my new role as an assistant professor at UMBC. Kathy Bryan works tirelessly to make the department function, and Carol Harmon has assisted me with travel arrangements and all the day-to-day aspects of my job, making my time at UMBC more productive and enjoyable. UMBC supported the research for this book with a summer faculty fellowship in 2009, and my department gave me a teaching release in spring 2010 to work on the manuscript. My exceptional students at UMBC have inspired me to see things with new eyes every semester. The road I travel with them year after year is one of the most enlightening and enjoyable transits I know.

The employees at the various archives and libraries I visited in South Carolina always made me feel welcome. I sincerely thank the staff at the South Caroliniana Library at the University of South Carolina (especially Beth Bilderback), the Robert Scott Small Library and the Avery Research Center at the College of Charleston (especially Deborah Wright), the South Carolina Historical Society in Charleston, Coastal Carolina University in Conway, Chapin Memorial Library in Myrtle Beach, and the Dillon County Library. Susanne Pelt, who has been gracious and helpful throughout my years researching South of the Border, has gone far beyond the call of duty. She has been one of the warmest and most welcoming people I have met along the way. South of the Border employees Evelyn Hechtkopf and Shirley Jones took time out of their busy summer work schedules to answer my questions about South of the Border's and Alan Schafer's past. Jesse Berger and Nate Mallard made a great film, *S. O. B. and the Legend of Alan Schafer*, and provided me with insight into a younger generation's love of the historic and strange roadside attraction. Laura Koser met with me to discuss South of the Border and provided great insight with her University of South Carolina masters thesis on the topic. Mark Cottingham took the time to provide me with the insights of a Dillon local. I am indebted to Sherry Suttles and the Atlantic Beach Historical Society for beginning the process of collecting the important history of Atlantic Beach, especially the organization's oral history work. I hope the historical society continues to document the fascinating story of South Carolina's Black Pearl—and includes the next generation of black bikers in that narrative. I thank those who have accompanied me and the friends that I made at the Atlantic Beach Bikefests and South of the Border over the years.

My family, especially my mother, Frances Earle King, provided unending love and support that have profoundly influenced my emotional and intellectual life. My grandparents, Earl and Mary Frances Lewis, have always supported me in all I do. My sister Robyn Ward, my brother Paul King, my sister-in-law Lori King, and my nephews Rodney and Lee Ward have all provided love, encouragement, and company. The newest addition to our family, my nephew Dylan Michael King, helps me see the connections between the past and the future. The Woodses, my family through marriage, have been a great source of support, and I sincerely thank John and Martha for much more than producing a wonderful son. My niece and nephews—Rodney, Lee, Dylan, Taylor, and CJ—represent my greatest hopes for the Newer South.

My friend and sounding board down South, Rebecca Snurr—who is now even farther south in Panama—has provided support, entertainment, and a sharp and caustic wit. Rebecca (along with Tommy Crouse, Biff Bolen, and Austin Davis) accompanied me on my early trips to South of the Border and indulged my burgeoning obsession with its mysteries. Damien Ober, Kate Singer, Jeff Lewondowski, Natalie Khala, Charlie Clark, Joanna Osborne, Clay Risen, and Alex Orr have been my good friends since the University of Maryland days, and I am thankful for the stimulating conversations and great times that we are still able to enjoy on trips to the Poconos or the beach. Without such great friends to sustain my sanity (or sometimes to help me embrace insanity) this book would never have been finished.

Walter Biggins at the University Press of Mississippi saw potential in this somewhat strange project on sombreros and motorcycles, and he has skillfully shepherded it into production. It has been a pleasure to work with the entire staff at the press. Lisa Paddock is a gifted copy editor who pushed me to clarify my language, and this book greatly benefits from her edits and her patience.

All mistakes are, or course, mine alone. However, I tried to be as objective as possible and in most cases only included stories that I could verify. There are many other stories about South of the Border and Atlantic Beach that are ripe for investigation and retelling.

I am lucky to be married to the best storyteller I have ever known. My wonderful and considerate husband, Baynard Woods, took the time to read this entire book many, many times. He also patiently listened to my ruminations on the topic and endured my misplaced hostility when I was challenged about the clarity or validity of certain ill-formed ideas. Without traveling the road I have with Bay, I would never have been able to complete this book. He has taken last-minute overnight trips to South of the Border so I could get (another) "thick description" of Pedro's Africa Shop, spent numerous Memorial Day weekends at the motorcycle festival in Atlantic Beach, and endured my spending nearly every joint vacation of our nine years of marriage at some archive, interview, or event associated with this book. His work ethic is an inspiration, and his company is the thing I cherish most in life.

Finally, I thank my father, to whom this work is dedicated, for inspiring wonder in me from an early age. He always encouraged me to seek out knowledge and made me feel as if I could accomplish anything. He was a great man who grew up in a segregated South, but was able to move beyond it. He taught me tolerance and encouraged me to stand up for what I believe in—but he reminded me to never stand so hard that I could not be moved by what was right. He was an educator and an inspiration to many, including his daughter. He read numerous parts of this work early on and was my trusted research partner from the beginning. Even when he was sick and in pain, he accompanied me to make photocopies, visit archives, and engage in serious conversations about this book. He will travel with me in all I do, always.

SOMBREROS AND MOTORCYCLES IN A NEWER SOUTH

INTRODUCTION

Touriscapes in a Newer South

This is a story about two very different places that share deep connections. The original connection that brought me to these places—the South of the Border roadside attraction and the historically black town of Atlantic Beach, both in the state of South Carolina—was the appearance they both had of survival amidst decay. Their histories also concern the collision of identity and place in regional and national culture over the past century. The aesthetics of these tourist sites are tied to their respective social and political pasts.

This book addresses the interplay between politics, aesthetics, and the power of recreational tourism in the US South through an analysis of specific people, places, and stories in South Carolina that illustrate larger cultural trends. Through an intense engagement with these places—as well as with the social, historical, and aesthetic contexts in which they are located—I have developed these concepts: the touriscape, an integrative vision for viewing place, and the Newer South, an approach to southern culture that entails the refashioning of older regional constructions as they moved into the twenty-first century. *Sombreros and Motorcycles in a Newer South* identifies campy but historic tourist sites as important texts for understanding how culture evolves.

Chapter one offers a brief overview of tourism in South Carolina, providing some background for the two place studies (a place-based take on the traditional case study model) that follow. The book primarily focuses on South of the Border and Atlantic Beach, both stalwart places that have weathered the trauma of progress. The crux of my argument appears in the organization of the chapters, which trace how these places were first built and then reshaped over time as the Newer South evolved. These are tales of endurance within transition and mobility. The relevance of studying these historic but overlooked places rests in the encouraging fact that their legacies have been taken up and sustained by generations of young people since the 1970s. In this process of movement and appropriation, certain aspects of history and culture have been discarded, while others have been incorporated and refashioned in ways that engage with both the preservation of the past and the development of the future.

Chapter two, the first chapter on South of the Border, traces the story of Alan Schafer, the roadside attraction's controversial owner. The following chapter analyzes South of the Border as a canvas for Schafer's complex social and aesthetic vision—including the roadside attraction's controversial mascot, Pedro—and how this representation has been received over time. The South of the Border chapters contain a close examination of specific attractions that no longer exist; the Confederateland, USA, historic theme park of the 1960s is juxtaposed with Pedro's Africa Shop of the 1990s in Chapters two and three, respectively.

I begin the story of Atlantic Beach with an analysis of oral histories of early business owners in the town, who advocated local unity and self-reliance. The following chapter analyzes Atlantic Beach's shift, after the desegregation of leisure culture in the South, from a theme of unity to one of individual expression. Integration of public space led to the growth of the Atlantic Beach Bikefest in the 1990s beyond the boundaries of the black town into predominantly white communities. An analysis of black biker subcultures, which advocate individual freedoms and the expressive role of global consumer culture, further illustrates the shift over time from unity to diversification at Atlantic Beach. The remaking of Atlantic Beach by young African Americans on Japanese motorcycles engaged and disrupted the landscape of the entire Grand Strand (the larger region where Atlantic Beach is located) in lasting ways.

The conclusion looks at the ways in which South of the Border and Atlantic Beach may be preserved for future generations while remaining relevant sites of commerce and living history. The cultural histories of these landscapes broaden the conception of what southern tourism was and is about. But the most exciting aspect of this story concerns how younger generations are refashioning these places, which maintain their relevance even as they are transformed into something new.

As the weather warms, travelers who head south on Interstate 95 toward the state of South Carolina will pass numerous billboards advertising South of the Border, an immense, neon roadside tourist attraction with a Mexican border town theme. Many will actually stop there. The sleepy traveler will lodge at the motor inn. The hungry will eat at one of the many restaurants—perhaps the Hot Tamale, the Sombrero Restaurant, or Pedro's Diner. Road-weary truckers will relax at Porky's Truck Stop. RVs

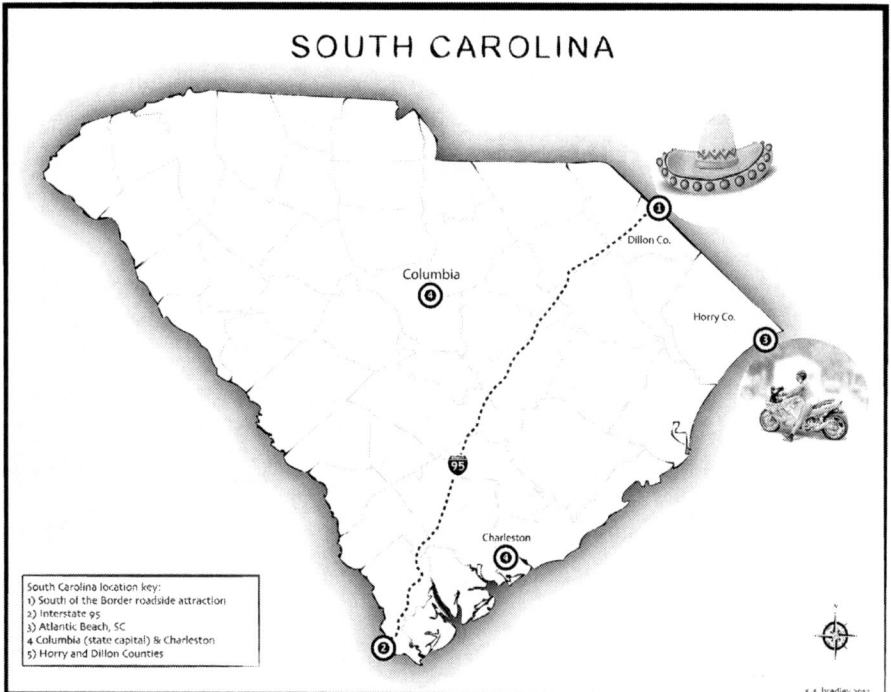

Sombreros and Motorcycles in South Carolina. Map by Steve Bradley.

will fill Pedro's Campground. Shoppers will browse the numerous souvenir shops. The largest shops, Mexico Shop East and West, are on opposite sides of Highway 301, which served as a main north-south route before the construction of the interstate. Few, however, will know that in 1949, along Highway 301, South of the Border began as a tiny cinder-block structure built to sell beer, or that the Jewish southerner who created and owned the place, Alan Schafer, became one of the most powerful and controversial figures in business and behind-the-scenes politics in South Carolina during the late twentieth century. South of the Border is located on the margins and in the borderlands just south of the North Carolina state line in the "other" Carolina.

Restless children, encouraged by flashy billboards to "keep yelling" at their parents to stop at South of the Border, may be allowed to visit the amusement park, play games in the arcade, climb the large animal statues placed throughout the complex, buy fireworks from Fort Pedro, visit the

Reptile Lagoon, or enjoy Pedro's Golf of Mexico, a miniature golf course. Some adults bring their children to the Border out of a sense of nostalgia for those family road trips of the 1950s and 1960s—a passing down of family traditions. Young hipsters are drawn in by the irony of this gaudy "Las Vegas of the South" being dropped in the middle of a dull roadside filled with chain stores and pine trees. Other travelers may be offended by Pedro, the stereotypical, sombrero-wearing mascot of South of the Border, and roll their eyes as they whiz by.

Many of those passing by South of the Border will head south, traveling about an hour to the coast and the state's most popular and lucrative recreational hub, the Grand Strand. This northern region of the South Carolina coast includes sixty miles of beaches and various forms of recreation, and stretches from the North Carolina border down through Horry (Oh-REE) County and into the northern edge of Georgetown County. Most tourists will be headed to Myrtle Beach to enjoy the ocean, the shopping, and the entertainment venues. Few have heard of Atlantic Beach, South Carolina, unless they are traveling to the annual Atlantic Beach Bikefest, a motorcycle festival for African Americans that began to draw tens of thousands of tourists in the mid-1990s.

Atlantic Beach is about seventy miles southeast of South of the Border. Tourists driving alongside the beach on Ocean Boulevard must take a detour bypassing Atlantic Beach. This traffic pattern is a remnant from the time of Jim Crow segregation, when Atlantic Beach was one of the few recreational beaches in the Deep South created by and for African Americans. Today, the traffic patterns and the physical barriers that isolate Atlantic Beach remain because the townspeople see these boundaries as symbols of their history and independence in a county that is still mostly white and sometimes hostile.[1] The small four-block community represents the last bit of undeveloped oceanfront property in the heart of the Grand Strand's tourism empire. If travelers do go out of their way to head into the heart of Atlantic Beach on 31st Avenue, they will pass a tattoo shop, a strip club, and a drug paraphernalia store before ending up at a cul-de-sac near the spot where the old Atlantic Beach pavilion once stood. During the 1950s and 1960s, famous musicians played the patios of Atlantic Beach while people danced beside the sea. Back then, revelers could sleep safely on the strand under a cover of stars as the sounds of beach music blended with waves crashing on the shore to form an enchanting lullaby. Seen from the cul-de-sac, the town's current borders loom in the distance. To either side, dense shrubbery, chain-link fences, and high-rise resorts bespeak the development going on around, but not in, Atlantic Beach. The small town's built environment—the human-made surroundings—includes many aging homes, bars, and motels, but a fascinating history of proud people and an ongoing controversy lie in the shadows of those high-rise resorts.

Millions pass through South of the Border and Atlantic Beach, but few know the complex stories of these tourist sites and their relationships to larger narratives of history and culture. In telling these tales, I employ Jay Mechling's narrative approach to culture, wherein American culture is defined as "those stories that Americans tell one another in order to make sense of their lives."[2] Both of these places and their stories add new perspectives to the history of South Carolina, and to the changing nature of identity, style/aesthetics, global consumer culture, and regional space. These tourist landscapes have survived as havens of independent commerce because they possess the flexibility to move with the flow of social change, while retaining historical continuity and self-determination. Both South of the Border and Atlantic Beach have been shaped by historical and generational shifts in the South. These shifts include: a move beyond *de jure* segregation; the new perspectives of those born after the civil rights movement of the 1950s and 1960s; and the incorporation of a new social and aesthetic vision. All of these changes have resulted in an evolving and more expansive sense of place and identity that welcomes constant mobility.

The South of the Border tourist complex, location of the largest sombrero in the world, and the historically black community of Atlantic Beach, with its annual influx of Japanese motorcycles, function as symbolic icons of the South's changing cultural landscape. Sombreros and motorcycles may not seem especially "southern," but as Tara McPherson argues, we need new directions to expand the contours of what we mean when we study the region. She offers two such directions that move southern studies to new places:

1. We need to move beyond identity politics and fetishizing sameness in Southern studies. It's as crucial to think about difference as about continuity or sameness when thinking about the South, and this means expanding the repertoire of Southern studies to include a variety of subjects and practices (such as Wal-Mart but also the hip-hop group Outkast or a writer such as Minnie Bruce Pratt) that might not, at first glance, seem all that Southern. We needn't preserve the South as much as we need to animate it and move it elsewhere.

2. We need to think of Southernness and Southern geography as at best provisional, relational—as spaces that shift with various border crossings and that are all the stronger for these processes. This also means that we need to reorient Southern studies from an axis of us vs. them or blue vs. grey to think about the South more broadly, allowing us to theorize its status as a hinge point between the Americas. We need to think in terms of transit zones, not closed-off borders.[3]

Both South of the Border and Atlantic Beach have manipulated various aspects of identity—such as race, class, age, and ethnicity—to make money and to make changes in the overarching look and feel of southern culture.

South of the Border and Atlantic Beach fit within southern regional culture as they expand its borders. Both places have histories directly related to the shifting complexities of race and class in the post-World War II South, and they have both maintained independent ownership outside of the increasingly dominant transnational model of corporate tourism development in the South and other regions of the US. The fact that Jewish and black southerners independently owned and constructed these businesses affects their social and political boundaries, their aesthetics, their historical significance, and their sense of place. Furthermore, these places arose from the postwar American development of highways and a recreational car culture that promoted travel from the northeast to the booming Florida coast. South of the Border and Atlantic Beach are both conveniently located halfway between New York City and Miami.[4] They are liminal places located in-between major urban tourist destinations.

On the other hand, the fact that South of the Border and Atlantic Beach do not blend in with the space that surrounds them indicates they have potential as objects of study and points to the benefit of examining them together. Human geographer Tim Cresswell explores events that upset traditional notions of things being "in their place": "Although 'out of place' is logically secondary to 'in place,' it may come first existentially. That is to say, we may have to experience some geographical transgression before we realize that a boundary even existed."[5] It is the physical *differences* of South of the Border and Atlantic Beach, in relation to their surrounding communities, that make the two similar and worthy of parallel analysis. They are products of similar social forces, but they took very different forms as southern tourism emerged as a dominant source of economic power in the twentieth century.

The South of the Border complex draws tourists off the road because its built environment disrupts the monotony of the I-95 corridor. The gaudy tourist attraction, one of the largest employers in Dillon County, brings millions of visitors and millions of dollars every year to an economically depressed area of the state. The area has been referred to as part of the "Corridor of Shame," for its deplorable public education system.[6] In contrast, Atlantic Beach's lack of economic development and facilities for tourists is an abnormality in the Grand Strand region, where the hospitality industry has been booming for decades. Atlantic Beach is a chartered municipality of just under one hundred acres. South of the Border is a private business of just over three hundred acres. The different spatial, organizational, and economic qualities of these two tourist sites express the myriad effects of increased tourism on southern communities. Furthermore, a study of white and black spaces together presents a more comprehensive vision of the South—especially in the case of these two places, which also allude to Mexican, Japanese, Caribbean, and other global signifiers.

The cultural geography of South Carolina began to change during the early twentieth century. Dillon County, home to South of the Border, was formed in 1910. The beaches that make up the Grand Strand, where Atlantic Beach is located, were difficult to reach until the first major road and bridge were built in the 1910s.[7] Early twentieth-century advances in transportation and mobility were catalysts for a refashioned region that began to emerge in the latter part of the twentieth century with the rise of tourism. In his 1991 book, *Dirt Roads to Dixie: Accessibility and Modernization in the South, 1885–1935,* Howard Lawrence Preston presents a familiar refrain: "Dixie has begun to disappear" as the construction of roads and the resulting tourism infrastructure began to replace the "region's cultural identity with a wholesale, predictable sameness."[8] While Preston is correct in some ways, South of the Border and Atlantic Beach serve as exceptions to this rule, functioning as distinct local icons within the constantly evolving tourism industry. Like the complex politics of road construction in the region, these places prove that the power of tourism is not frivolous. Studying tourist landscapes is a way to better understand place and identity—two things deeply intertwined in the US South and beyond.

There has never been a single or monolithic South, but "southerness," in its various forms, still remains an important aspect of identity formation for many.[9] I am primarily interested in what places mean, how that meaning is negotiated over time, and how to use the built environment and material culture as a lens through which to view change and continuity within local, national, and global aspects of place.

The South's tourism industry has flourished because of the region's mild climate, white coastal beaches, low taxes, and a (gender-and-race-based) mythology of southern hospitality.[10] All regional distinctions are far more complex than the surface characteristics and mythologies imply. To offer newer symbols of the South, I turn to South Carolina's number one industry—tourism. In this book, I am analyzing a specific type of southern landscape—the offbeat, independently owned, and local tourist site. These places are products of the early twentieth-century developments of the interstate highway system and American car culture. I bypass the heritage tourism of Charleston, the elite resorts of the southern coast, the endless golf links, and the luxury chain hotels, preferring the "Dirty South," that your momma warned you about—at least mine did. For my examination of tourism and refashioned southern identity, I turn to those peculiar places that you won't find advertised in *Southern Living* magazine.

Southern identity is a constantly changing mode that one wears or subscribes to. In a "homely simile," John Sheldon Reed compares the South to "my favorite pair of blue jeans. It's shrunk some, faded a bit, got a few holes in it. There's always the possibility that it might split at the seams. It doesn't look much like it used to, but it's more comfortable, and there's probably a lot of wear left in it."[11] In a similar vein, southern literary scholar Scott Romine quips, "If one doesn't subscribe to the South of *Southern Living*, then alternative subscriptions are available: the South of the *Oxford American*, the multicultural South often circulating in academic journals, the Dirty South playing on XM radio."[12] Wear and tear and the ability to buy (or buy into) different Souths has made southern identity a more comfortable and available fit for many. Individuals and groups who *claim* southerness give the category its meaning. This process produces many Souths, which can be competing or contradictory. In addition to providing newer symbols of the South, one of the main goals of *Sombreros and Motorcycles in a Newer South* is to push the reader to see the theoretical relevance of the people, places, and aesthetics of recreational tourism. Theory was and is always grounded in the everyday world, even the often strange and gaudy world of southern tourism.

Recent refashionings of southern identity have a certain postmodern tenor. My definition of postmodernism is based on the idea that the world around us is a social construction—always changing, never frozen in time—but one grounded in material things. The postmodern perspective is similar to a never-ending road trip.[13] There is a great freedom in hitting the road, but as David Laderman's work on the road movie shows, in every trip there is a balance between rebellion and conformity, a battle between the open road and the consumer landscape.[14] A Vulgar Marxist, or generally pessimistic, perspective sees the structure of capitalism as the root of all oppression and bad taste. This view is shortsighted in today's market-driven society, where young people often see social entrepreneurship as a way to address the problems they see in society.[15] Cultural studies scholarship that simply celebrates the liberating potential of consumer agency also misses the complex exchange between producers, workers, and consumers in negotiating new spaces and new identities.

The potential to combat the greed, oppression, and homogenizing aspects of global capitalism—the very culprit blamed for a sense of placelessness—can arise from the localized entrepreneurial spirit of capitalism. Preston's study of road construction in the South identifies "good roads progressives" as the "original faction of disgruntled farmers and intellectuals who perceived road improvements as a panacea for improving the downtrodden, rural, impoverished South and as means of restoring a measure of the agrarian values that were losing importance in an increasingly urban industrial society." These Preston contrasts with the "highways progressives," who disguised themselves with progressive ideas even while having the "motivations of capitalists."[16] Movements for social change can benefit from the methods of capitalism if not its (baser) motivations. As alternatives to southern-based chains—like Coca Cola, Kentucky Fried Chicken, Krispy Kreme, and Bojangles' Famous Chicken 'n Biscuits— South of the Border and Atlantic Beach offer an independent rather than corporate and mass-produced model of consumerism as expression while remaining grounded in the "motivations of capitalists." My worry is less with the motivations of those who constructed these commercial venues and more with how these individuals actually worked to make interventions in our understanding of place.

My development of the touriscape and the Newer South were influenced by the theories of scholars investigating the difficulties of moving forward into something new without forgetting the past. My focus on the mobility of "southern" subjectivities advocates a critical tourist consciousness that borrows from complex ideas about the traffic of love and crisis. In *Methodology of the Oppressed*, Chela Sandoval skillfully mines the most valuable aspects of poststructuralist and postmodern theory from iconic figures such as Roland Barthes, Jacques Derrida, and Fredric Jameson.

She then combines these theories with foundational writers on double or oppositional consciousness, writers like W. E. B. DuBois, Audre Lorde, Gloria Anzaldúa, and Franz Fanon.[17] The effect of Sandoval's reimagining of contemporary theory calls for a new consciousness that posits a *tactical subjectivity* with the capacity to de- and recenter, given the forms of power to be moved."[18] This new consciousness is based in mobility as well as a comparative and expansive view of subjectivity; however, the movement towards this newness remains disorienting and painful.

Functioning as a critical tourist, or an "outsider-within," involves a complicated process of creating (and recreating) subjectivity and locating it in the world—a world that has deep structural inequalities that are both found in plain sight and lurking below the surface.[19] The critical tourist undergoes something similar to Linda Pearce's experience of moving from her all-black high school in Wilmington, North Carolina, to a desegregated school. She remembered: "We were in a cocoon bathed in warm fluid, where we were expected to excel. And then something called desegregation punctured it. We went from our own land to being tourists in someone else's."[20] Pearce's punctured cocoon can be seen in Sandoval's expansive and interdisciplinary method, the "hermeneutics of love." Sandoval explains the implications of the concept: "Romantic love provides one kind of entry to a form of being that breaks the citizen-subject from the ties that bind being, to thus enter the differential mode of consciousness, or to enter what Barthes perhaps better describes as 'the gentleness of the abyss,' . . . a utopian nonsite, a no-place where everything is possible—but only in exchange for the pain of crossing."[21] The movement from someplace into this no-place involves breaking through to create somewhere new.[22]

Both South of the Border and Atlantic Beach are environments where such transformations have occurred (and continue to occur). They remain imperfect sites where structural inequalities persist and are refashioned as part of this painful yet productive movement forward. Analyzing marginal tourist sites owned and operated by a Jewish family and a community of African Americans is part of showing the productive potential in seeing and experiencing the world as an outsider, one who travels inside and out, both challenging power and achieving economic success. While these places are not always nice, clean, or innocent, they are challenging and never boring. One of their most important attributes is that, for good or ill, both locales have survived.

The politics of aesthetics, as I employ it, derives from the look of survival as it is written on the landscapes of South of the Border and Atlantic

Beach. To survive, a place must change—but not too much. Both South of the Border and Atlantic Beach—or rather their owners—have resisted buyouts and development deals that would remove these sites from their localized and independent roots and place them within large corporate interests. Such interests are slowly taking over and decimating the "mom and pop" businesses of an earlier roadside landscape in the US. South of the Border and Atlantic Beach do not operate completely outside the corporate tourism industry—to do so would be impossible. However, they evoke a politics of aesthetics located in both survival and the "outsider" ethos they share.

In a *New York Times* article on conceptual artist Glenn Ligon's midcareer retrospective at the Whitney Museum of American Art, "The Inside Story on Outsiderness: Glenn Ligon's Gritty Conceptualism Makes Art Out of Others' Words," Carol Vogel writes that Ligon "generally deals with race, gayness or simply what he calls 'outsiderness'" in his work. The article ends with Ligon's reflections on the literal and metaphoric aspects of being a stranger. "You have to be a bit outside something to see it," Ligon explains. "I think any artist does that. It's an artist's job to always have their antennas up."[23] Whether addressing the politics of aesthetics found in offbeat tourists sites or conceptual art hanging in the Whitney, the issue of taste always arises.

The foremost scholar on taste, Pierre Bourdieu, begins his influential book, *Distinction: A Social Critique of the Judgement of Taste*, by challenging the notion that taste is natural, instead arguing that it is a product of culture and that "cultural needs are the product of upbringing and education."[24] In applying the work of Bourdieu (and slamming more conservative art critics) in her 1989 book, *Primitive Art in Civilized Places*, Sally Price expresses hope about the move to "consider more seriously the cultural factors that influence [aesthetic response] and therefore the relativity of judgments themselves." Using a fitting travel metaphor, Price writes, "As a result, avenues for the investigation of aesthetics in a comprehensively comparative sense are, even if not yet very well traveled, at least open for traffic." Twelve years later, in the afterword to the second edition of her book, Price celebrates the breaking down of barriers and art world hierarchies based on categories such as producers/commentators, elite/popular, and modern/tribal, and the fact that "artworld traffic is now recognized as running along a much busier thoroughfare." Price continues: "We're forced to notice that it's not a one-way route and that it's not just the objects that are traveling." As sites where the politics of aesthetics play out, South of

the Border and Atlantic Beach become places of both commerce and art—
vernacular architecture. "As the 'traffic in culture' continues to erode the
distinctions once segregating first- and third- or fourth- artworld, 'high'
and 'low' genres, producers and critics, and even anthropologists and art
historians," Price explains, "lanes are being opened up in many exciting
directions."[25]

Identifying artistry and patterns in places involves the ability to employ
overlapping spatial and temporal perspectives. In a spatial sense, these
places must be viewed simultaneously from the perspectives of both the
insider and the outsider. In a temporal sense, past, present, and future
deposit meaning as they leave traces on the built environment over time.
Preston writes about the influence of automobility on southern culture in
the early twentieth century: "The natural environment became so intertwined with the material culture of automobility that an entirely new cultural landscape emerged to serve the needs of people who were between
one place and another."[26] The spatial and temporal layers of this new landscape are what these objects—these tourist landscapes—contribute to the
understanding of southern culture as it moves into the twenty-first century.

Back in the 1950s, J. B. Jackson, a founding figure in cultural landscape
studies, was "chronicling the changing American landscape from the highway with both apprehension and enthusiasm, teaching his students to be
tourists in new ways."[27] Because the ties that bind place and identity are
central to southern culture, the tools of cultural landscape studies offer a
chance to view the conjunction of the material and social worlds in context. Focusing on place, as both a concrete, three-dimensional location
and as the process of putting people *in their place* in the social hierar-
chy, must be an integral part of understanding history and culture. People
think about and understand themselves and others in relation to their surroundings and their location within a power structure. I argue that earlier
ideas in cultural landscape studies have produced an emerging interdisciplinary field of place studies, a central way to understand the movement of
culture that is both grounded geographically and connected to our larger
understanding of identity.[28]

To envision how fluid categories of identity intersect and overlap within
the physical and social world of tourist space, I have developed the concept
of the touriscape. The touriscape is more than a simple mash-up of the
words *tourist* and *landscape*; it is a combination of place with a perspective on place. *Tour*, the root of tourist, means "a going round, a travel or a
journey" and evokes the importance of mobility. The root *tour* is related to

turn, "to cause to revolve, transfer, convert, whirl around, change," which is derived from the Greek word for a "carpenter's tool to draw a circle."[29] Sandoval writes: "[Oppositional consciousness] operates as does a technology—a weapon of consciousness that functions like a compass: a pivoting center capable of drawing circles of varying circumference, depending on the setting."[30] The compass is a material object used to locate self in the world. The word *landscape*, derived from a genre of Dutch painting in the sixteenth century, is an "expanse of scenery that can be seen in a single view."[31] Landscape painting is always seen from the perspective of the outsider gazing into a place. J. B. Jackson defines landscape as "a composition of man-made or modified spaces to serve as infrastructure or background to our collective experience; and if *background* seems inappropriately modest, we should remember that in our modern use of the word it means that which underscores not only our identity and presence but also our history."[32] Furthermore, the word *landscape* is fitting because it began as a term to describe art—specifically painting—before it referred to anything "real."[33] Because the image precedes the reality, the term "landscape" illustrates the postmodern focus on the surface, the image, and the aesthetic symbol. A touriscape is a geographic place but also a lens to see the historical, social, and aesthetic aspects embedded in the culture of a place as it strives for something newer.

The touriscape provides an important terrain for viewing the controversies and conflicts of southern culture. A touriscape is a place rooted in a geographic location, but it also possesses the mobility to transcend physical and social boundaries. Visions of the past, the present, and the future are integrated within the touriscape. In addition, touriscapes are created in the space where fluid categories of identity and various views overlap to produce an insider/outsider perspective, a shifting and transformative means of seeing and understanding space and time. This place-based model of analysis is indispensable in tracing the different ways southern places have interacted with southern identity. Touriscapes promote a comprehensive way of seeing the stories embedded in the material world because, as Arjun Appadurai argues, objects have a social life because of the complex ways they embody value.[34] In the early 1980s, Peirce Lewis wrote, "Our human landscape is our unwitting autobiography, reflecting our tastes, our values, our aspirations, and even our fears in tangible form."[35] If the landscape is our autobiography, the touriscape is our travelogue. It tells us not only who we are and where we have been, but where we are going.

Cultural geographer Yi-Fu Tuan sees place as embodying the security, safety, attachment, and certainty of home. However, the very certainty of place can be confining. Space, on the other hand, expresses freedom and openness (for example, the thrill of the open road), while at the same time partaking of the potential for getting lost. For Tuan, space provides movement, while place offers pause (much like a tourist destination, a stop along the roadside during a vacation). He claims that it is impossible to remain in place, because place only derives meaning in relation to movement and change. Tuan points out that space and place need one another for definition. This integrative model for understanding place and space provides a way of seeing the complexities embedded in regional culture— and the changes—such as leaving home for the first time to find your own identity—that result in a productive trauma.[36]

These touriscapes possess complex (colliding and contrasting) built environments and narratives that express both the refashioning of southern culture over time and the emergence of a newer South. The development of the Newer South seeks to move beyond an Old South / New South dichotomy.[37] The Newer South represents a shift into a post-1970s consciousness that has emerged to embrace the increased mobility of southern culture after World War II. The Newer South encompasses an economic shift toward the hospitality industries and the vernacular landscapes of tourism, all of which can portray a refashioned and more inclusive (and complicated) regional identity. My use of the term "newer" does not seek to replace what has come before, but rather to build upon it. There is too much throwing out of the old (in the academy and in everyday life) owing to fashion. Yet in the periodization of southern history, the New South (a period beginning in the late nineteenth century following Reconstruction and encompassing the manufacturing boom, the Good Roads Movement, and the establishment of oppressive Black Codes) needs to be refashioned in order to remain relevant in the twenty-first century. Manufacturing has come and gone (farther south), and racial oppression has eased in certain quarters and gone underground in others. Yet a refashioned boosterism from the New South holds on, and the remnants of the Old South endure as the proliferation of "plantations" floods the landscapes of southern business and tourism.

The Newer South is a hybrid, a synthesis of Old and New Souths blurred by spatiotemporal ways of seeing.[38] The negotiation between the Old and the New South within the continuity versus change dichotomy provides a useful starting point for understanding how the region can be viewed today. Wilbur J. Cash, who was born in Gaffney, South Carolina, wrote *The Mind of the South* in 1941 and argued that the southern mind—the values and way of life of white southerners—had continued largely unchanged from the antebellum period into the twentieth century. In his 1951 book, *Origins of the New South, 1877–1913*, C. Vann Woodward argued that even as the Redeemers and New South boosters pushed for economic modernization and racial segregation, a new order was emerging in the region that broke with the past. From Woodward's perspective, these New South leaders appropriated and manipulated the past to promote their own power and profit.

Moving beyond an either/or dichotomy, historian James C. Cobb integrates the two competing perspectives on southern history and concludes, "The history of southern identity is not a story of continuity *versus* change, but continuity *within* it."[39] From the perspective of southern literary studies, Scott Romine sees southern narratives finding a "home ground" in a liminal space that signals a "double narrative of continuity and rupture."[40] Recent academic work by scholars such as Rebecca Bridges Watts and Tara McPherson, as well as popular culture texts like the Drive-By Truckers' 2001 album, "Southern Rock Opera," the NYC-based black string band, the Ebony Hillbillies, and the films of Ray McKinnon critically engage the "duality of the southern thing" as it is viewed today.[41] Watts explains that if "southernism" is going to continue to be distinct and relevant in the twenty-first century, southerners must learn to "strike a balance between a divisive past, with its ruling order of division, and the present with its ruling order of identification." Contemplating recent work in new southern studies, McPherson responds, ". . . I want new ways of feeling southern that more fully come to terms with the history of racial oppression and racial connection in the South."[42] This duality (the concomitant wonder and the horror of southern culture) is written on the landscapes I analyze.

When breaking down the structure of a Newer South, some key aspects emerge. They include: (1) the dominance of a service-based economy, (2) the self-defining role of consumption, (3) the blending of the local and the global, (4) the synthesis of stability and mobility, (5) the centrality of popular culture and mass media, and (6) the passing of the torch to a post-civil rights generation. Many of these social forces were building long before the period of the Newer South, which I locate in the generations that followed the baby boomers. However, it is the conjunction of these social forces with new ways of seeing regional culture that is central.

These aspects influence the mobile insider/outsider perspective essential to a critical tourist. The concept of the critical tourist certainly can apply beyond the boundaries of the US South, because regions are connected to national and global constructions with growing levels of complexity.

The agricultural roots of the South and even the manufacturing boom of the New South are giving way to service work—especially the hospitality industry—as the defining mode of production (mostly of images and experiences rather than things) and central catalyst for economic development (or lack thereof) in the region. This shift is directly related to the central role of consumption of goods and services in post-World War II America. For good or for ill, Americans define their identities by what, where, and how they consume, and they do so in a far more pervasive and fast-paced manner than ever before.[43] The American mindset is formed by the interplay between the conflicting forces of vast corporations, which can lead to the homogenization and globalization of culture, and local or independent entrepreneurs, who can produce original regional commodities.[44] This synthesis of seemingly divergent modes of production is found in the next aspect of the Newer South: seeing the local in the global. James Peacock describes this synthesis as "grounded globalism." He writes: "With respect to the South, to ground globalism is to fuse a transformative global identity to a sustaining regional identity—a fusion that potentially enhances the strength of both identities and their potential for energizing action."[45] Related to the interplay between the local and the global is the fourth aspect of the Newer South: the ability to ground something in a given place without losing the potential for mobility. And it is also important to remember that place is "often a small and specific piece of territory" located within a larger space.[46]

These first four aspects of the Newer South—a service-based economy, the self-defining role of consumption, the blending of the local and the global, and the synthesis of stability and mobility—all relate to the dominance of popular culture and mass media as central and internalized characteristics of identity formation for post-baby boom generations. These diverse groups of people (born after 1970) are greatly influenced by having come of age after the era of legal segregation and the civil rights movement in the South. The American civil rights movement played out primarily on the terrain and in the mediascapes of the South, but the newer generations of southerners are tourists of the civil rights movement. They travel through it, but they live somewhere else. Escaping the legacy of the past is, of course, easier for some than for others.

Young people inhabit a South framed by a reality that they have rarely if ever seen (except on TV): the "whites only" signs, the lynchings, the water hoses and dogs turned on civil rights workers, the burning crosses. This is not to say that such vehement prejudice simply vanished after the civil rights movement. Prejudice functions in different ways in the Newer South, where a refashioned racism continues to simmer just below the surface. In the Newer South, being a critical tourist means feeling at home in a place, while still possessing the consciousness and vision of an outsider. This vision entails not being too familiar or too detached to see the social structures at work.

The realization that the familiar world is naturalized through social interactions can offer a way to deal with the problems of the South's past, while still possessing hope for the region's future. Applying a postmodern lens to touriscapes can open up the boundaries of southern identity and provide space to move into the Newer South.[47] This space can also allow people to choose—as one chooses a vacation spot—which parts of being southern fit within their own identities and their own personal styles. As the work of Bourdieu illustrates, these personal issues are cultural ones as well.

The places that invite the complexities of vision I have discussed often have an almost indescribable style or look, an energy that comes from the overlapping of time and space. The landscapes of South of the Border and Atlantic Beach possess this look, which is at once complex and simple, old and new, off-putting and alluring. Both places are so dated and tacky that they are beautiful. They possess, in tangible form, the duality of the southern thing.

There is something beautiful in certain cheap, old motels. I used to think it was something about time, age, history. If cheap is a look or even a social statement, rather than an economic pronouncement, then the issue is really aesthetic. Concern with aesthetics and taste separates this work from a straightforward cultural history of specific tourist landscapes. This work examines broad patterns, brush strokes, and shades of neon. It is as much literary, cultural, and aesthetic as it is historical. The neon lights that illuminate South of the Border at night are connected to the neon colors of the Japanese motorcycles that zoom through Atlantic Beach each May.

The aesthetics of a place have a lot to do with class and status—key factors in determining where one vacations. The ability to sustain a profit while constructing a marketable image and sense of place is at the heart of all successful tourism. Touriscapes remind us that we cannot escape the economics of place—not even on vacation.

Sombreros and Motorcycles in a Newer South tells the multi-dimensional stories of two specific touriscapes. The commercialization that some critics—as far back as the Agrarians— see as killing southern distinctiveness actually moves this distinction to new places, engaging new identities in dialogue with old ones. I am not arguing for commercial development and commodification of the South; I am, rather, tracing their inevitable effects on people and places on South Carolina's margins. I am putting a sombrero on the southern belle in a hoop skirt and parking a motorcycle in front of the columns of the plantation home. Like Alan Schafer and the Atlantic Beach bikers, I am splashing neon across the southern landscape.

Chapter One

"SMILING FACES, BEAUTIFUL PLACES"

The Rise of Modern Tourism in South Carolina

Tourism is currently the number one industry in South Carolina, with a more than eighteen billion dollar annual economic impact.[1] South Carolina's hospitality industry has greatly contributed to the ways in which the state is represented and understood by both visitors and residents alike. A recent tourism motto for South Carolina—"Smiling faces. Beautiful places."—evokes both mythologized southern hospitality and the beautiful landscapes that have made tourism so popular in the South.[2] Both South of the Border and Atlantic Beach transgress the stereotypical boundaries of southern tourism—plantation homes, Civil War memorials, gardens, southern belles and cavaliers, mammies and Uncle Moses—often associated with the historic city of Charleston in South Carolina.[3] While Charleston foregrounds heritage tourism centered on an idealized past, South of the Border and Atlantic Beach focus on recreational tourism that refashions another South Carolina out of atypical icons, such as sombreros and motorcycles.

Although South Carolina saw some tourists prior to the twentieth century, the modern tourism infrastructure in the state began to develop sporadically during the 1920s and 1930s. Before tourism could become big business, the region had to embrace the politics of road construction. In *Dirt Roads to Dixie*, Howard Preston claims, "During the 1920s and 1930s, the most visible and tangible signs of change in the rural South were along the highways where the burgeoning new automobile tourist economy first developed."[4] Early on, better roads brought improvements to southern society. A study by the American Road Builders shows that South Carolina's improved road mileage grew from 238 to 1,467 between 1924 and 1930, while one-room schoolhouses (a symbol of poor educational resources and backwardness) dropped from 2,561 to 1,600 during the same period.[5] In the 1920s the fear of traveling down South was assuaged by the construction of better roads and replaced by a "thick, syrupy romanticism," drawn from travel literature and periodicals of the time.[6] The main routes affecting the northeast corner of the state (where South of the Border and Atlantic Beach are now located) were the Capital Route (or Highway)— which connected the nation's capital to the capitals of Virginia, North Carolina, South Carolina, and Georgia—and the Atlantic Coastal Highway, or Ocean Highway, which ran from Quebec City, Canada, down the coast of South Carolina, terminating in Florida. Roads throughout the US were developing in such a rapid and sometimes haphazard way that the Joint Board of State and Federal Highway Officials was created in 1925 and developed the numbered highway system the following year. The Capital Highway became Route 1. Highway 301, which passes the future location of South of the Border, and 301-501, running toward Myrtle Beach, developed as offshoots of Route 1. Ocean Highway (or Highway 17) was advertised as a way to "Go South from Pines to Palms" while avoiding the "congested traffic of large cities."[7] As the roads were built and the tourists came, different communities along divergent routes would compete for traffic: Traffic meant tourists, and tourists meant money.

During the early twentieth century the Upcountry (the Piedmont section of South Carolina, including Greenville-Spartanburg) was still benefiting from the textile industry, but the South Carolina coast was floundering economically. Despite these economic hardships, in 1929 Lowcountry legislators, led by state senator Richard M. Jefferies of Colleton County, proposed legislation that would provide $65 million for state highway construction in the Lowcountry. The measure passed and was signed by the governor, despite opposition from the Upcountry, which had funded its roads through county taxes.[8] The state of South Carolina traditionally opposed raising taxes, which are needed to build roads; however, the Piedmont had more capital and a better location to take advance of big road projects in the South, such as the Bankhead National Highway and the Dixie Highway.[9] Roads have always been politically contentious because of the wealth they can bring to or take away from communities.[10]

While the Lowcountry and the Piedmont did not see eye to eye on development and promotion, in 1934 businessmen with interests along the coast of South Carolina joined forces with North Carolina resort owners to form The Carolinas Inc. The organization's primary goal was to build tourist travel as part of a "comprehensive economic vision" and, with a similar geography, the coastal regions of both Carolinas found common ground in tourism marketing. A 1935 advertisement explained the organization's "purpose of bringing facts about the Carolinas before their people, that they may be better informed as to the resources, history, and industrial importance of the Carolinas, and that they may know how they can assist in the broad movement to advertise to the world the advantages of this favored section."[11] Convincing local residents of the importance of tourism was a central aspect of the organization's plan. The advertisement explained that Americans spent $5 billion annually on tourism, and that the Carolinas, despite their tourism potential, bring in an "insignificant share of those tourist dollars." The advertisement promoted the desirability of tourists owing to their spending power and pointed out that tourists would later invest and buy homes in the region.[12] The seeds of a critical awareness of tourism's potential—seeing how outsiders could be used to improve the state—were planted early in modern tourism promotion. Carolinas Inc. implores all residents of the Carolinas to "do their share" and "awaken to our tourist possibilities."[13] This meant be ready to pay taxes, and know and advertise your state to visitors in whatever way possible. Unifying efforts like Carolinas Inc. and Governor Thomas McLeod's 1923 "Boost South Carolina" conference, which tried to formulate a statewide plan for tourism promotion, were not huge successes. However, individuals and localities began to cobble together a burgeoning tourism infrastructure. Tourism promotion, like southern identity, is strongest at the local level.

With the organization of better roads, key areas along the coast began to develop lodging other than private boarding houses and haphazard tourist camps alongside the road. Businessman John T. Woodside, a successful textile industrialist from Greenville, South Carolina, bought 64,488 acres of land from Myrtle Beach Farms (a land company established by Simeon B. Chapin of Wisconsin and Edwin and D.M. Burroughs of Conway, South Carolina) for $950,000 and planned to organize a resort for the wealthy along the undeveloped northern section of the South Carolina coast. The Depression thwarted Woodside's plans. Yet, before defaulting and returning the land back to Myrtle Beach Farms, Woodside paid to organize the roads and basic layout of Myrtle Beach and built both the illustrious Ocean Forest Hotel and Pine Lakes International Country Club. These two properties were only part of a more extensive plan drawn up by Raymond M. Hood, a famed architect from Rhode Island who designed the Tribune Tower in Chicago. The "castle-like estates to be called *Arcady*, the very name to be reminiscent of a section of ancient Greece in which peace and contentment were found in undisturbed natural surroundings" never fully materialized because of the Great Depression, but their infrastructure and ground work were laid.[14] Even Charleston, with its long and well-known history, lacked modern accommodations for tourists until the

Fort Sumter Hotel opened in 1923 and the elegant Francis Marion Hotel followed in 1924. Before the 1920s, Charleston's older hotels were "little more than flop houses."[15] A built environment for tourism development was forming, but larger economic and social trends intervened.

The Great Depression and World War II temporarily interrupted tourism development. But as soon as the war ended, consumption became an integral part of American identity, including the pursuit of "smiling faces and beautiful places."[16] The rapid growth of the tourism industry in the postwar era led to major changes in South Carolina's cultural landscape.[17] During the postwar period, South Carolina truly began to develop a distinct and profitable tourism industry that went beyond the construction of highways and sporadic developments for the wealthy. Tourism was no longer the exclusive privilege of the elite, but an essential social activity for average Americans.

The "first stirrings of recognition that South Carolina might become a tourist state" occurred in 1945, when the newly formed State Research, Planning and Development Board began to advertise in national publications. In 1950, the board created a department of public relations. In 1951, after the South Carolina Chamber of Commerce produced a comprehensive study entitled "Dollars in Flight: A Manual Showing Why and How South Carolina Should Promote Tourist Trade," which detailed the revenue lost owing to lack of travel promotion, the state legislature approved meager funds for publications to attract visitors to South Carolina. These included such pieces as the colloquially titled "Nothin' Could be Finah Than to See South Carolina."[18] The investment was necessary because South Carolina "ranked last in the southern states and near the bottom nationally in obtaining tourist dollars." Only North Dakota and Rhode Island had less income from tourism. This first large-scale distribution of tourism literature was limited to the nineteen neighboring states that South Carolina considered its market at the time. In 1951, tourists spent $67 million in South Carolina and contributed $2 million in state taxes. In an attempt to leverage the potential economic impact of tourism, the South Carolina Chamber of Commerce began a project to survey five thousand motorists in 1954.[19] The chamber wanted to know how to lure the emerging market of tourists hitting the road to their state. Thus began the first model of tourism promotion for the state: Ask the tourists, and provide an organization that can directly answer their questions about tourism in South Carolina.

This model shows that tourism development began as a conversation and an exchange between South Carolina and its visitors.

The state did not make enough of an economic investment to handle tourist demand. South Carolina received so many requests from potential tourists in 1955 that the state ran out of money three-quarters of the way through the year and could not respond An article in the *(Columbia, South Carolina) State* newspaper reported, "Tourism Advertising Program Almost Too Successful in SC." S. W. Gable, the acting director of the State Development Board, proclaimed "requests were the highest in history" and that the organization was "embarrassed for lack of funds to answer inquires."[20] The State Development Board asked the state legislature for an increase in funds to handle the growth in tourist demand and to facilitate a conversation that would educate surrounding states about the tourism potential of South Carolina—especially its previously untapped coastal zone. More than a decade passed before South Carolina was actually ready to fund tourism promotions fully.

Tourism truly emerged as a modern industry in South Carolina in 1967, when Governor Robert McNair merged the travel and information division of the State Development Board and the outdoor recreation division of the State Forestry Commission into the South Carolina Department of Parks, Recreation and Tourism (SCPRT), a cabinet level agency.[21] McNair, who was governor from 1965 until 1971, led South Carolina through the tumultuous time of school desegregation in 1970 and shepherded pro-business recruitment of new industries and jobs for the state.[22] Tourism was one of McNair's main interests while governor. Robert Hickman, a former reporter and press secretary for Governor McNair, became the executive director of SCPRT.[23] A study by Lewis C. Copeland of the University of Tennessee showed that tourists spent $285 million in South Carolina in 1966, which was a 9 percent increase from 1965 and 119 percent from 1954, and the increase in tourist spending produced $25 million in state taxes. While these figures were promising, South Carolina's take was still less than 1 percent of the national figure. "And that's the reason for our existence," said Hickman. "We were begun [sic] to make South Carolina an attractive place to visit and to live. If we can't convince our own people of this, there's no need to go any further."[24] Tourism was framed as an industry that could benefit both visitors and residents through a reciprocal relationship. Now that tourism was emerging as an important industry in South Carolina, the state had to up its game and enter an era of intense competition for tourism dollars on a regional, national— and later—an international scale.

It was not the job of businessmen and politicians alone to promote
the state's burgeoning tourism industry; residents were also advised to be
educated promoters of South Carolina, much like they were asked to offer
"southern hospitality" to potential industrial investments from abroad.[25]
Tourism boosters sought to replace locals' indifference and, at times, hostility towards outsiders with a romanticized southern cordiality. With hard
work, business boosters and local residents provided the "smiling faces."
South Carolinians were encouraged by the tourism industry and the local
media to promote their home state to visitors. A journalist writing for the
Columbia Record warned readers that a "careless 'I dunno' may mean the
loss of hundreds of dollars when a tourist has the inclination to look around
before hurrying on." During World War II, citizens were told to conserve
and contribute, but after the war, those duties were amended to promote
and consume. The state's developing tourism industry organizations sponsored a "series of courtesy clinics."[26] Clearly, southern hospitality and "smiling faces" were not innate southern traits; South Carolinians needed to be
convinced to be hospitable if they wanted a piece of the tourism pie.

Southern women were expected to serve that pie. Southern tourism
developers merged the relative freedom the Second World War offered
women in the workplace with women's' traditional roles in the domestic
sphere. In the South, white women functioned as symbols of southern
hospitality and therefore had a public role in promoting the hospitality
industry. The tourism industry offered white women a certain level of
power and participation—but within the confines of demure southern
womanhood. Women welcomed travelers and tourists into their "home,"
meaning their home state of South Carolina. In 1968, the first of eight
tourist welcome centers planned for South Carolina opened in Little River,
at the northernmost edge of the Grand Strand region along Highway 17.
The welcome center was strategically placed by the less-traveled Ocean
Highway (17) to lure tourists to visit the South Carolina beaches, rather
than quickly zooming down the highly traveled route through the middle
of the state (Highway 301) to Florida. The rest area blended a modern glass
facade with Old South-style columns. Barbara McAden, executive "wom-
en's editor" for the *State* newspaper, covered the opening of the center.
She explained, "They [tourists] will be more like guests who get the warm,
cordial welcome that a Southern homemaker offers when she says, 'Won't
you come in the living room?'" The employees at the welcome center, all of
them female, were referred to as "Southern Belle hostesses." These southern belles traded in their hoop skirts for "custom-designed ensembles of

blue skimmer dresses, white boots, large rimmed white hats banded in blue and blue and blue and red coats." The outfits were made from South Carolina textiles and included white gloves.[27] The refashioned southern belle wore feminine but modern attire and worked for a living.

While those in charge of the state's hospitality industries used updated southern belles decked out in red, white, and blue to welcome the white middle-class visitor to their state, exclusion of black residents and tourists was still a tenet of the state's tourism industry. During the postwar boom, African Americans were not welcome to inhabit the emerging tourist sites in the state except as workers in the service industry, or as visitors to the few black-owned tourist spots. An ad in the 1956 edition of *Holiday* magazine shows a white man and woman looking off into the distance in front of a South Carolina plantation and garden. A line in the ad copy— "Here you'll find roving minstrels singing spirituals of the Old South, as only they can"—presents black South Carolinians as exotic figures from a romanticized past, not as active participants in the postwar tourism development of their state. No African Americans are represented in the ad, though perhaps they are supposed to be objects of the tourists' gaze.[28] Employing a "wait-and-see" tactic promoted by tourism boosters and businessmen, South Carolina avoided becoming a major media hot spot of the civil rights movement, but it was not a plausible place for African American workers or business owners to enter the emerging tourism industry.[29] Tensions attending racially integrated leisure were illustrated by the (at the time) under-publicized Orangeburg Massacre of 1968, in which three South Carolina State College (now University) students were killed during an altercation with police amid protests designed to desegregate a local bowling alley.[30] African Americans in South Carolina's tourist industry were romanticized in the moonlight and magnolias of the plantation South, but they were mostly absent from the tourism marketing of the Grand Strand area, which touted white beaches and Coney Island-style amusements.

The southern coast of South Carolina, with its Revolutionary and Civil War pedigree and plantation legacy, contrasts with its northern neighbor, the "Independent Republic" of Horry County, where the Grand Strand's recreational hub is located. Geography cast Horry County as an outsider within its own state. Bounded by the Atlantic Ocean and isolated by rivers, swamps, and a border shared with North Carolina, much of Horry County was secluded and difficult to reach until advances in road and bridge construction in the early twentieth century provided a conduit. Because of isolation and poor soil, the area did not develop a plantation economy or culture and was dominated by small-scale farmers, who were often portrayed as outsiders themselves. The Independent Republic of Horry wanted to stay out of the Civil War, until South Carolina seceded and war was inevitable. In the words of Coastal Carolina University distinguished professor emeritus of history Charles Joyner, Horry County has "stood off to the edge of South Carolina—both literally and figuratively." This "little-d democratic society of small farms" has grown into a little-d democratic land of leisure.[31]

The beaches were the primary "beautiful places" that drew tourists to both Atlantic Beach and South of the Border (though those traveling to and through were often headed further south to the Florida beaches). In the 1970s, the more "democratic" Grand Strand outranked all other South Carolina destinations, commanding over half of the tourist market. The more elite tourist destinations of Charleston (with 18 percent) and Hilton Head (with 6 percent) followed. The top three destinations for tourists were all on the South Carolina coast, and coastal tourism constituted almost 80 percent of the tourist trade in the state.[32] While Myrtle Beach, the heart of the Grand Strand, was the most profitable of the South Carolina beaches, different resort areas catered to different taste and class levels. The more elite beaches are all located south of Myrtle Beach, surrounding the pinnacle of South Carolina high culture—the city of Charleston. The places people vacation—like the cars they drive, the clothes they wear, and the places they shop—signify important aspects of identity. Where one vacations is not always a choice and aspects of a place's identity often change over time, but some generalized regional distinctions endure.

In 1941, George S. Bliss of West Lynn, Massachusetts, took part in a group trip by train and motor coach from Boston to Charleston, South Carolina. Bliss later presented the dividing line between the northern (Grand Strand) and southern (Charleston and the Lowcountry) coast in stark terms: "All unanimous in saying this place [Myrtle Beach] is punk—too much like Revere Beach." Revere Beach, which opened in Massachusetts in 1895, was the first public beach in America. Bliss described his tour group's trek through twenty miles of "God-forsaken country, low lands, hovels, signs for sea fishing, then through a heavy pine forest with swamps as we turn off the main road too soon come to a very narrow brick gateway which the driver skillfully navigates—and we get a glimpse of paradise—Brookgreen Gardens!" Bliss frames this shift as coming out of a "durned old swamp into a beautiful garden."[33] From four former rice plantations, Archer and Anna Hyatt Huntington built Brookgreen Gardens, the first public sculpture garden in the United States, in 1931.[34] Anna Hyatt Huntington, an accomplished sculptor from Massachusetts, and her husband, a member of a wealthy New York family, were major benefactors of the arts. It is noteworthy that seventy years ago a traveler from Boston delighted in an area of the South refashioned by northerners using a "southern plantation" model.

Fifty years later, in 2001, Richard N. Coté, a self- proclaimed "northern-born writer who embraced the South," described the same dividing line in his novel, *The Redneck Riviera*, set in Myrtle Beach: "A two-hour drive north of Charleston, South Carolina's Redneck Riviera is a forty-mile-long strip of coastline that ran south from the North Carolina state line and includes Little River, North Myrtle Beach, Myrtle Beach, and ends at Murrell's Inlet, ten miles south of Myrtle Beach."[35] Coté writes about the northern coast in highly charged language: "Civilization—as most traditional South Carolinians conceive of it, anyway—starts a couple of miles south of Murrell's Inlet at Brookgreen Gardens. The historic former rice plantation and its magnificent outdoor statuary is the first pearl in an unbroken chain of natural beauty that lies to the south of the neon, plastic, and T-shirt shops of the Redneck Riviera."[36] The equation of "civilization" with "plantation" shows the enduring history of the southern plantation as a romanticized place. Yet Coté contrasts the "natural" beauty of the Lowcountry with the "cultural" landscape of consumerism along the Grand Strand. These stark distinctions present a false dichotomy that does not exist along the South Carolina coast—especially today, when everything from hotels and golf courses to track subdivisions and trailer parks utilize the term "plantation" as a marketing keyword for "luxury" in their titles.[37]

There are areas of extreme poverty and dilapidated buildings in Charleston, and Myrtle Beach has some luxury accommodations and wealthy enclaves, but the tourism industries of these two areas remain culturally divergent in many ways. The lack of an illustrious history and the *right* type of culture on the Grand Strand is what makes these class distinctions from 1941 to 2001 so similar. Myrtle Beach's tourism leaders had an "unwillingness to create or embellish a made-up past," instead choosing to "revel in [Myrtle Beach's] newness."[38] In South Carolina, the Lowcountry is high culture, and the Grand Strand is low class.

In the early 1970s, when Myrtle Beach dominated the take of of tourist dollars spent in the state (over half), SCPRT began to study the return on their (and taxpayers') investment in tourism. A study compiled by the

South Carolina Division of Tourism in Columbia reported that in 1973, for every dollar invested by SCPRT on tourism marketing, $32 came back to South Carolina, and that over 60 percent of persons responding to advertising actually visited the state that year.[39] Despite troubling economic issues in the United States—such as the gas crisis resulting from the 1973 oil embargo and related stock market crash—tourism still emerged as a national economic strategy. In 1977, a subcommittee of the United States Senate formed to develop a national tourism policy. Fragmentation and lack of planning were cited as problems exacerbated by the falling availability and rising price of gasoline. The travel and tourism industry accounted for an estimated 10 percent of US petroleum consumption. Even as tourism brought money into communities in the 1970s, the national study noted "popular opposition to further tourism development" owing to environmental issues, troubling competition between government and private business, and—most crucially—citizens' belief that "out-of-state travelers come into their community, use up the local resources, decimate the environment, and leave without having made any valuable contribution."[40] While the US Senate studied the positive and negative connotations of tourism, South Carolina was recognized as a potential "national model" for tourism promotion. A national travel newsletter, "The Travel Advisor," ranked South Carolina's state tourism office—which provided free travel literature and a trip kit upon request—as the "most helpful" such office in the United States. In 1976, 33 million people came to or through South Carolina, spending $1.113 million while in the state. SCPRT director Fred P. Brinkman, Jr. reported there were 265,000 requests for information about tourism in the state during 1976. Brinkman stated that to best deal with budget limitations, the organization needed to answer these central questions: "What can we do with the money we've got?" and "What does the traveler want?"[41] By the end of the 1970s, the general assembly had removed the $600,000 ceiling on tourism promotional funds from the state admissions tax. Tourism officials could now spend what their endeavors brought in, which, despite gas crises and recessions, was a great deal.

With increased competition for tourist dollars, rankings and economic impact studies—in addition to the consumer inquiry and education programs of past decades—were essential to gauging success. Comparing SCPRT's 1978 economic impact studies with a national ranking study completed the same year by the Business Research Division at the University of Colorado, tourism experts promoted pursuing regional cooperation and, because of the bad economy, also pushed an appeal to in-state residents. The $1.7 billion spent annually by tourists in South Carolina in 1978, a 215 percent increase from 1973, produced jobs for 59,300 South Carolinians and $430 million in wages. While South Carolina now ranked an impressive sixth in tourism advertising expenditures in the nation, it ranked twentieth nationally in total number of tourists, and a low forty-third in the nation in average spending per tourist per day.[42] The relatively low cost of a trip to South Carolina—especially to the inexpensive and popular Grand Strand region—led to the continued growth of South Carolina's tourism industry despite gas shortages and national economic downturns.[43] However, as South Carolina spent more money wooing tourists and building up the image of "smiling faces and beautiful places," state officials wanted to see higher returns for promoting an industry that was quickly becoming an important element of American consumer culture.

As Karen McPherson pointed out in an article in the *State* in 1980, Americans were still traveling during tight economic times because they saw "vacations as a right"—they simply travelled in a "different style." In addition, McPherson claimed that people were seeking to "immerse themselves in a whirlwind of activities in an effort to leave their worries behind." The recession helped recreational tourist destinations that were sites of various amusements, but it hindered "more thoughtful" vacations that involved history or heritage tourism. Economic issues also pushed tourism boosters to focus more intently on in-state tourists. Pushed by the gasoline shortages of 1974 and 1979, the University of South Carolina began to study home state travel. The major purpose of vacations for the in-state traveler was "rest and relaxation." After analyzing local travelers—whose demographic profile was a middle-aged couple with some college education and an average annual income of $12,000 to $30,000 traveling with children—the study promoted a low-cost vacation package of three to five nights at the coast, stressing "personal benefits" first and "family togetherness" second. According to the study, "educational benefits" and "unique experiences" should not be factors in promoting the product, a vacation in South Carolina. A slogan likely to appeal is not "see South Carolina first," but "Relax—You're at a South Carolina beach."[44] Even as economic recession resulted in shorter and cheaper trips, the tourism market continued to grow in South Carolina during the 1980s. This decade produced soaring profits, new taxes to benefit tourism, and a shift in the state's marketing strategy, including more aggressive competition and a broader focus on global markets.

In 1980, tourism spending cracked the $2 billion mark for the first time in South Carolina's history. Douglas P. Wendel, former city manager of North Myrtle Beach and former Horry County manager and executive director of the 260-member Congressional Travel and Tourism Caucus, complained about national tourism policy—including the Carter administration's attempt to cut the United States Travel Service, which helps draw foreign visitors to the United States, and the paltry $4.1 million for tourism in the Commerce Department's International Trade Association as well as the Reagan administration's budget cuts to tourism spending. Wendel stated, "Tourism and travel is the most untapped (financial) resource we have in the United States. It simply has been ignored."[45] Tourism was developing a social and political reach encompassing local, regional, national, and global markets.

As the 1980s progressed, tourism began to rival textiles as South Carolina's number one industry, and state tax laws bent to accommodate this growth. In 1984 a new "sleeping tax," a 2 percent state accommodations tax, was levied on hotels, motels, campsites, and other transient lodgings to assist with tourism development and marketing. In the 1984 to 1985 season alone, the accommodations tax brought in $8.5 million in revenue (in 2009–10 the tax brought in almost $39 million).[46] In 1986, a 2 percent gasoline tax brought in $38 million dollars, also a boon to tourism.[47] In 1986, Governor Richard W. Riley proclaimed May 19–25 South Carolina tourism week and made May tourism month for the state. In 1985, tourism was bringing in $3 million annually, more than 80,000 jobs, and $179 million in state and local taxes.[48] Because of this increase in visitors and a steadily growing economic impact, South Carolina's tourism promoters changed the focus of their advertising strategy.

Gone were the days of direct ads and dialogue requiring individualized responses. These tactics were no longer "economically practical," given high demand. The use of television and print campaigns that "seek to immediately influence" was on the rise.[49] Rather than request the opinion of tourists, South Carolina used advertising and marketing to convince and persuade tourists that what the state had to offer would appeal to them. This shift reflects a more organized and powerful tourism industry, where the producers defined the market—a break from the original model that focused on consumer opinion.

As tourism grew, so too did competition. In 1985, "aggressive tourism ads" attempted to "take a bite out of Florida's orange." Advertisements boasted that South Carolina was less crowded, cleaner, and two states nearer than Florida for northeastern travelers. But by the end of the 1980s, slightly over half of South Carolina's tourists were still passing through on their way to Florida.[50] Tourism promoters wanted South Carolina to be a final destination, rather than a stop along the way. Along with increased competition, the market for South Carolina's tourism industry grew beyond US borders. The state began to market to European vacationers—mostly in Western Europe, including Germany, the United Kingdom, and Switzerland—in 1981.[51] That year, a meager 17,000 overseas travelers visited South Carolina, but by 1987, 45,500 Western Europeans traveled to South Carolina, where they spent $12.7 million annually. By the 1990s, the state was beginning to extend its international appeals to include such markets as Japan.[52] In 1961, the city of Myrtle Beach developed a small festival—Canadian American Days or Can-Am Days—for Canadians vacationing in the United States for their spring break.[53] "Myrtle Beach business leaders developed the festival to entice Canadian tourists to stay along the Grand Strand instead of traveling on to Florida," said Ashby Ward of the Myrtle Beach Chamber of Commerce. He pointed out that 40,000 to 45,000 Canadians visited Myrtle Beach in 1981 (10,000 more than had done so the previous year). Ward added, "This whole festival is worth $15 to 20 million of business in the Myrtle Beach area."[54] In 2009, nearly 900,000 Canadians visited South Carolina. According to SCPRT, in 2009, at least 66,555 overseas travelers, excluding Canadians and Mexicans, indicated South Carolina was the first or primary destination on their US trip (the comparable figure for calendar year 2008 was 80,697). Historical data indicates that Germany and the UK are two of the primary overseas sources of visitors to South Carolina.[55] While South Carolina is clearly not a top destination for international tourists, in the final decades of the twentieth century the state has slowly begun to market itself on a global stage in hopes that it one day may achieve that status.

International festivals emerging in the 1960s and 1970s became big business in South Carolina by the end of the twentieth century. In 1977, Charleston, South Carolina, began to host the Spoleto USA festival, a performing arts festival established by esteemed composer Gian Carlo Menotti as a counterpart to The Festival of Two Worlds (Festival dei Due Mondi) held in Spoleto, Italy. By 1987, Charleston's Spoleto festival had contributed $300 million to South Carolina's economy over ten years of operation. By the 1990s, conserving the folk culture of South Carolina had become a focus for academics and tourism boosters alike. The 1991 Cultural Conservation Conference held at Hickory Knob State Park focused on the "challenge of saving small town traditions while promoting tourism and economic development." Dr. Alan Jabbour, director of the American Folklife Center at the Library of Congress, and local historians such as Dr. Charles Joyner, spoke at the conference, advocating for cultural tourism that highlights preservation.[56]

Tourism became an industry in the late-1960s and blossomed into big business for South Carolina during the 1980s, but unhinged development caused problems, especially along the coast. By the 1990s, pollution from overdevelopment, swelling summer populations, and overfishing ravaged the delicate coastal area. The corruption of water supplies and beach erosion were also becoming problems. In 1988, the South Carolina legislature passed the Beachfront Management Act to regulate development, but a lawsuit caused the legislation to lift its ban on new beachfront construction. The South Carolina Coastal Management Council was forced to turn to erosion control methods, such as shipping in sand to the areas most in danger. But erosion problems were further exacerbated on September 21, 1989, when Hurricane Hugo, a category-four storm, hit the region. The storm affected the entire South Carolina coast, from the Grand Strand south to the Lowcountry, with 135 miles per hour winds and a twenty-foot storm surge. Twenty-nine people were killed, damage to property totaled almost $6 billion, and sixteen state parks along the coast were closed. The state immediately began to rebuild. SCPRT held a brainstorming forum in October of 1989 to create a plan to deal with Hurricane Hugo's impact on the state's almost $5 billion tourism industry. South Carolina joined with the federal government in an over $9 million beach replenishment project—which rebuilt the worst hit beaches on the Grand Strand—and the largest dune revegetation project in the nation's history, costing $1.5 million. All visible remnants of the storm's wrath were gone in just a couple of years.[57]

The recovery from Hurricane Hugo demonstrates both the strength of the tourism industry heading into the 1990s, and a refashioning of the destroyed landscape of the Grand Strand into a placeless corporate model of tourism redevelopment. The rebuilding effort following Hurricane Hugo helped the economics of tourism in the state, but it hindered the cultural and environmental balance needed to sustain the South Carolina coast's distinct identity. Rather than reflecting important issues of cultural conservation, much of the Grand Strand's restoration followed the corporate tourism model of high-rise condominiums, emphasizing "bigger is better." Legislation and public outcry intended to prevent such rebuilding could not withstand the economic impact of tourism, which was becoming

South Carolina's most lucrative and influential industry. According to Jack Hall Maquire's analysis of leisure business districts in Myrtle Beach, major hurricanes such as Hazel (October 1954), and especially Hugo (September 1989), led to the area's growth. "These severe storms served developers and tourists alike. Each assisted the long-term development of the area by destroying many small beach side structures. Constructed on those sites were new buildings, usually larger and more expensive . . . This post-hurricane rebuilding resulted in significant new investment, new publicity and eventually new tourists."[58] However, the local culture and environment benefited from neither cookie-cutter condominiums nor the corporate model of tourism development, which often gives money to national and international corporations, not local entrepreneurs.

By 1990, tourism's economic impact had reached $5 billion in South Carolina, and tourism promotion adopted the model of those identical condos. In the early 1990s, tourism advertising again shifted its focus to "panoramic images" in "high visibility" magazines, such as *Family Circle* and *Southern Living*. This "bold new direction" into the world of glossy promotions followed from the fact that the state "ha[d] to begin to plan early to remain competitive in the fierce fight for tourism dollars."[59] In 1990, the new chairman of SCPRT, William J. Sigmon, Sr., wrote an article for *South Carolina Business* titled, "The Lure of the Palmetto State: Cooperative Efforts to Keep Tourism Going." Sigmon argued that the state's travel and tourism would only grow "through a strong cooperative effort and innovative, aggressive marketing."[60] Moving into the final decade of the twentieth century, South Carolina's tourism promoters wanted to blend internal cooperation with intense marketing on a national and international scale. Essentially, South Carolina's tourism officials wanted to diversify their market and their product. The expansion of the market included working with a constituency and a market long ignored: African Americans. The assistant director of community development for SCPRT was working to "extend tourism to all areas of South Carolina, which included working with the Gullah residents of St. Helena Island to increase business opportunities for the native islanders."[61] The Grand Strand's high-rise condos stood in contrast to the growing investment in heritage tourism along the southern coast of South Carolina. The northern and southern coasts took different approaches towards refashioning themselves after the storm.

South Carolina's rich but complicated narrative of African American history proved difficult to market until black South Carolinians were included in the process. In 1992, SCPRT and the South Carolina State Museum produced the "state's first comprehensive directory on African-American culture," called *To Walk the Whole Journey: African American Cultural Resources in South Carolina, a Directory.* John William Lawrence, executive director of SCPRT at the time, explained: "SCPRT supported this project from the beginning, seeing that it met the agency's primary goal to help spread the benefits of tourism throughout the state, reaching all areas, embracing all traditions." Dr. Leo F. Twiggs and Emma Singleton, two African American commissioners for the South Carolina State Museum, worked with SCPRT on the directory. In the introduction, they explain: "South Carolina is a unique place for African-Americans. It is the place where great numbers of our ancestors were brought up from holds of ships to begin a long and agonizing journey in a new and unfamiliar place . . . . In another sense, it is a documentation of the resiliency and perseverance of our African-American spirit."[62] This new direction in tourism promotion reflects both an interest in the multifaceted history of the state of South Carolina and the importance of an emerging market. In promoting the Palmetto State, good conscience and good business do occasionally collide.

By the mid-1990s, African Americans were spending $34 billion annually on domestic travel, with half of that amount spent on visits to historical or cultural sites. Heritage tourism dominated the high culture tourism model prevalent in the South Carolina Lowcountry. "We are seeing a long overdue realization of the potential and complexity of the African-American market," said Marion Edmunds, director of marketing for SCPRT. African Americans travel to the South more than to any other region in America. According to Cynthia Legette, who owns a Columbia, South Carolina, firm specializing in ethnic marketing, "The South is home for most African Americans in this country. . . . When African-Americans left the South to escape racism and social struggles, they found that sort of thing everywhere. So, they look back to their base in the South as their real home."[63] It is difficult to market this sense of place—this feeling of being at home in a state that fought for slavery and against civil rights for African Americans—using the simple clichés often found in tourist promotions.

Eddy L. Harris echoed the sentiment of "returning home" in his 1993 reflections on a road trip down South. Harris left his home in St. Louis to undertake a personal journey to the South on his motorcycle: "And so I headed south. I did not travel to Africa to find my roots. I traveled to the South to find them. For the South, not Africa, is home to Blackamericans, and Blackamericans as a race are essentially southerners." As Harris explained, "Without realizing it at the time, I was going home."[64] This concept of "going home" drives the large market for African American tourism, as well as and a deeper and more general desire to travel. American studies scholar Psyche Williams-Forson writes:

> From the moment that African people reached these shores until well into the period of the Great Migration and then the early civil rights movement, African American people had to measure their freedom of movement by someone else's authority. Once freedom was realized, women, men, and children traveled for days, months, and sometimes years. Some searched for a new existence, while others simply searched, not wanting to be confined to any permanent space.[65]

The eloquence of Harris and Williams-Forson is often lost amid the lingo of tourism promotion in South Carolina.

In the early-1990s, African Americans spent an estimated $280 million annually in South Carolina, more than was spent in all but a dozen other states, but the state lagged behind most other parts of the South in attracting black tourists. The marketing of South Carolina's African American history was not appealing to African Americans. In 1997, SCPRT produced a "Report on African-American Travel and Tourism in South Carolina." Perhaps one reason the promotions were unsuccessful lies in a skewed comparison in the report, which declared: "Sullivan's Island in Charleston is to African Americans what Ellis Island is to European immigrants; 70–80 percent of their ancestors passed through it."[66] Describing blacks' experience of the horrors of the Middle Passage and slavery as simply "passing through" presented a serious problem. This uncritical equation of the slave trade with European immigration to the United States was corrected in the 2005 "African-American Heritage Guide," a brochure produced by the state to advertise a new Heritage Corridor in South Carolina. The brochure estimated that 40 percent of African Americans could trace their (American) roots to Sullivan's Island. Furthermore, it stated: "Although some have referred to Sullivan's Island was to Africans [sic] as Ellis Island was to European immigrants, the comparison seems misleading since European immigrants came to America by choice and Africans came by force."[67] The lack of social and historical context in the 1997 statement and the awkward attempt to correct it—without actually owning the mistake—in 2005 are representative of the difficulties South Carolina's predominantly white tourism officials have experienced in trying to market the state's African American history. The use of the phrase "their ancestors" in the 1997 report presents African American history and the history of slavery as "their history" instead of "our history." This awkwardness and segmentation derives from a long tradition of white governance and power in the region—a reality that is slowly changing, even in South Carolina.

A moment of potential transformation for tourism development in South Carolina occurred in 2006 when a bill, introduced by South Carolina Representative James Clyburn, was passed by Congress and signed into law by President George W. Bush. The bill authorized $1 million in annual funding for a period of ten years to establish the Gullah/Geechee Heritage Corridor. The Gullah/Geechee culture spans the sea islands from Wilmington, North Carolina, to Jacksonville, Florida. This culture, which is disappearing in part because of resorts and luxury seaside tourism development, possesses a creole language that blends African grammar with English vocabulary. Geographic isolation has helped preserve African folk cultures and traditions among the Gullah/Geechee. Clyburn professed, "I cannot sit idly by and watch an entire culture disappear that represents my heritage and the heritage of those that look like me." According to Clyburn, establishing a Gullah/Geechee Heritage Corridor will serve to "preserve the culture while tapping into the growing interest in heritage tourism."[68] In a way, this model tries to fight bad tourism with good tourism.

Clyburn's efforts show the potential for African American politicians to influence the state's tourism industry in positive ways while bringing the state's leisure industries productively into the twenty-first century. Michael Allen, coordinator of the Gullah/Geechee Heritage Corridor for the National Parks Service (NPS), stated that Clyburn wanted the concerns of the Gullah people in the affected communities taken into account in developing the heritage corridor. Allen, a South Carolina native of Gullah heritage, wanted to assure that the "light was shining in the right way" and to avoid "sins of the past" in developing the heritage corridor. He has worked closely with the communities within the corridor in formulating a comprehensive management plan, and as the corridor was being planned over the past few years, there have been numerous public meetings (which are videotaped and transcribed) held in the Gullah/Geechee communities to get essential feedback about corridor design. Under Allen's guidance, the NPS is leading the way for a truly community-based public history project and tourism development strategy. In addition to the Gullah/Geechee Heritage Corridor, the "African Passages" exhibit at the Fort Moultrie Visitor's Center on Sullivan's Island opened in early 2009. The exhibit includes history, art, stories, and material culture, all representing the complex history of African Americans and the slave trade in South Carolina. When Michael Allen graduated from South Carolina State University and came to work for the NPS at Fort Moultrie in 1980, nothing there represented the "dark part of the fort's past." The "African Passages" exhibit took ten years to design and plan and is the product of "grass roots support." Discussing the exhibit, Allen said, "We can have a dialogue about history, a dialogue about race, about ethnicity, man's inhumane treatment of man and about moral issues. Things that we shy away from."[69] The Gullah/Geechee Heritage Corridor and the "African Passages" exhibit are positive steps for tourism development in South Carolina. Yet without a comprehensive vision and a cooperative and community-based tourism strategy grounded in social engagement as well as in profit, South Carolina's tourism industry, like the Confederate flag that still flies on the statehouse grounds, will continue to represent an inability to move productively into the future.

The marketing of South Carolina's African American history was harmed by the Confederate flag controversy, which gained national notoriety in the late-1990s. In South Carolina, the Confederate flag was placed atop the statehouse in 1962; depending on which story you believe, this act represented either a memorial to the centennial of the Civil War, or a protest against civil rights and attempts to desegregate southern society. The fact that the Confederate flag flew atop the statehouse along with the American flag caused an intense controversy that ultimately played out in the state's tourism industry.[70] During the summer of 1999, the NAACP called for a boycott of the state to begin early in 2000. This goal of the boycott was to damage South Carolina's billion-dollar tourism economy. During the summer of 2000, the South Carolina legislature voted on a compromise. The Confederate flag was to be removed from atop the statehouse and placed on a flagpole by the Confederate Memorial, which is located in a prominent spot on the statehouse grounds. Because the flag remains in a prominent place on public property, the NAACP continues its boycott to this day. The civil rights organization has stated that the boycott will end once the flag is removed from the statehouse grounds and placed in a fitting context, such as a museum. The NAACP reported that between January and September of 2000 alone, South Carolina lost an estimated $100 million in potential tourist income. Marion Edmons, spokesman for SCPRT stated, "Exactly how big the impact [of the boycott] has been difficult, if not impossible, to determine, but there has been an impact." Because of the boycott, in 2009 the Atlantic Coast Conference (ACC) pulled out of a deal to hold its 2011 through 2013 conference baseball tournaments in Myrtle Beach, and state leaders worry about how the boycott will affect the 2010–15 sesquicentennial of the Civil War, which is expected to be a "financial boon for the state."[71] The state's tourism industry is the virtual battleground where the Confederate flag is being flown. This divisive symbol still flies on public land in South Carolina, but with continued loss of tourist dollars and a new generation of southerners emerging, we might ask: How long will the flag stand its ground?

In 1951, with South Carolina's tourism marketing reaching only nineteen states, tourists spent $67 million and generated $2 million in taxes. The market for tourism in South Carolina now reaches across the globe, and tourists spend more than $18 billion and generate more than $1 billion in state and local taxes. These economic figures demonstrate the growth of tourism as a powerful industry, with the ability to influence the history and culture of the state of South Carolina. However, the real stories are found in the specific people and places that both influence and are influenced by the growth of a tourism industry in South Carolina. When economic figures and cultural theories are grounded in real people and real places, we can see and feel the movement of culture much more deeply. South Carolina has now entered a contemporary and complex era of tourism that has left behind the legal exclusion of African Americans and dressing "southern belle hostesses" in silly costumes to welcome visitors to the state. However, the over-development of the coastal region, the poverty of the rural midlands, and a continued shadow of discrimination still haunt the South Carolina of "beautiful places and smiling faces." The stories of South of the Border and Atlantic Beach represent the diverse ways that economics and culture affect the people on the ground, demonstrating that the past cannot be forgotten even as we move into the complex terrain of the future. Tourism may one day go the way of South Carolina's textile industry, but the stories and the places involved will remain in the memories of people and as traces on the touriscape, ruins of a different time and place.

South Carolina's Confederate flag controversy was not located only in the state's capital. In 2000, there were protests at South of the Border. These protests were not aimed against South of the Border specifically, but against the entire state of South Carolina. South of the Border happens to be located at the state line. With Interstate 95's role as the main thoroughfare for moving from the northeast to the southeast, South of the Border was an important symbol of South Carolina. Atlantic Beach was caught in an untenable situation during the controversy. The Atlantic Beach Bikefest, which draws primarily black bikers and tourists, provided much needed revenue for the struggling town. In 2000, the NAACP wrote to various African American bike clubs, asking them to support the boycott of South Carolina and not attend the motorcycle festival. The small black town, which made an official statement against the flag, was caught in a dilemma. How could the residents of Atlantic Beach—as well as South Carolinians and those with relatives in the state—boycott themselves, their own homes, or their families? This dilemma raises larger questions: How can we draw a line and separate such allegiances? How much of our identity derives from place?

The case studies that follow move beyond the Confederate flag controversy into newer territory that is no less controversial. There are many fascinating complexities that emerge in analyzing these tourist landscapes. So, sit back and enjoy the ride into the Newer South. There's plenty to love and hate, but it is certainly not a boring journey. Furthermore, it is a trip that never ends, because the Newer South is being constantly refashioned in ways that will make you want to pull over and take a closer look.

PLACE ONE

SOUTH OF THE BORDER

Chapter Two

BEHIND THE NEON SOMBRERO

Alan Schafer's South of the Border, 1949–2001

A neon sombrero rises in the darkness. The two-hundred-foot Sombrero Tower welcomes visitors; it is the first sign of South Carolina. Beneath the shadow of the world's largest sombrero lies a fascinating story about the changing nature of space and identity in the US South. This story begins in the New South and veers back to the Old South as it journeys forward. Alan Schafer (1915–2001) was *the* man behind the sombrero at South of the Border. On bucolic farmland in rural Dillon County, Schafer constructed a preliminary vision—a monument—of a Newer South.

Expanding the often-simplistic dichotomy of race relations in the South, South of the Border functions as a complex borderland where real and imagined identities mingle and clash. The constantly changing tourist complex both engages and challenges traditional notions of what it means to be southern. South of the Border grew with America's postwar consumer culture, and Schafer astutely took advantage of—and in Dillon County led—the shift toward a service-based economy and a new global outlook. From the time he opened his roadside business in 1949 until his death in 2001, Schafer made all the major decisions concerning the construction of South of the Border, from designing its aesthetic to defining its political role. The availability of cheap products from around the world allowed Schafer to bring the globe—or a commodified vision of it—into Dillon County. Schafer constructed South of the Border to engage outsiders who were simply passing through. However, he had to negotiate the social and political strictures of his local community, a conglomerate of old farming and railroad towns. He constructed his tourist spot as he constructed his own identity—as a constantly shifting landscape of contrasts and contradictions.

The name "South of the Border" denotes the physical border between the states of North and South Carolina and evokes the cross-cultural consumerism of a Mexican border town. The borders of the roadside attraction

Alan Schafer in his office at South of the Border, circa 1958. Carolina Studio Collection, South of the Border. Courtesy of the South Caroliniana Library, University of South Carolina, Columbia.

are social as well as physical. South of the Border has often pushed the boundaries of what is considered acceptable within the tourism industry of South Carolina. Its location on the border, as well as alongside the road, evokes a sense of place that is at once stable and constantly moving. Its built environment is always changing, and tourists are constantly passing through. Yet, despite all the changes, South of the Border has maintained a singular style and aesthetic for over half a century.

Critically analyzing South of the Border's social and built environment over time highlights the hybrid identities that emerged from the increased prosperity, mobility, and commodification that rapidly evolved in the United States following World War II. Dillon is a predominantly rural county, with a racial composition that has remained primarily split between white and black with a slight white majority.[1] Yet this black/white dichotomy is an oversimplification of the diversity of the South of the Border community. Locals who work at South of the Border come from both sides of the border. Just across the state line in North Carolina is Robeson County, which possesses a large American Indian population—primarily the Lumbee, a tribe that has constituted over 20 percent of the population since 1940 and is currently the largest racial group in the county, at 38 percent.[2] The Latino population in Robeson County is slightly greater than 8 percent and triple that of Dillon County. Both counties exceed their respective states' poverty averages, with more than 20 percent of residents below the poverty line in each area.[3] The community of South of the Border is also made more diverse by the constant flow of travelers passing through.

The tale of South of the Border is mainly Schafer's story, because he obtained the power to construct the physical and rhetorical space of his tourist empire through his innovative business practices, accrued wealth, and political connections. In an article on South of the Border's fiftieth anniversary, reporter Anna Griffith wrote, "Schafer is as big a character as the 97-foot-tall sombrero-wearing Pedro that guards over his kingdom. He's as much a study in contrast as the clashing shades of pink, aqua, and fuchsia his designs favor."[4]

Schafer was a political powerhouse as well as a successful businessman. He described himself to a journalist as a "knee-jerk liberal, bleeding-heart Democrat."[5] He served as chair of the Dillon County Democratic Party from 1965 to 1981. In 1968, Schafer served as a delegate for Dillon County at the Democratic convention in Chicago. While most South Carolina delegates supported Hubert Humphrey and young Americans rioted in the streets in protest against the Vietnam War, Schafer sat in the front row of the South Carolina delegation wearing a "Draft Ted [Kennedy]" hat and holding a banner that carried the same sentiment. In 1980, at the height of his political career, Schafer attended a cocktail party for Democratic delegates wearing a white suit and a "J.R. for president button." Schafer and the fictional powerhouse of the 1980s television show *Dallas* shared a penchant for business, wealth, power, and controversy. Schafer blended his colorful political opinions with South of the Border's advertising. One upside-down billboard erected during the Reagan era read, "South of the Border—sign planned in Washington. Pedro feex later OK?"[6]

Schafer's South of the Border exemplified trends in mid-century American roadside culture and tourism, such as bright billboards, gigantic designs, and "modern" attractions.[7] More apposite to my argument, however, his travel spot challenged the demure and conservative façade of rural southern culture and thereby undermined the dominance of the entrenched local power structure, the institutional segregation prevalent in the region, and stereotypes of a homogenous and conservative southern culture. The tactics and the motivation behind Schafer's challenges are complicated and far from innocent; however, his history and his roadside wonderland offer clues for better understanding the complexities of the burgeoning Newer South.

In the tumultuous period following the Civil War, Alan Schafer's German-born grandfather, Abraham, immigrated to the United States and then moved from New York to South Carolina. Issac Iseman of Darlington, South Carolina, sponsored Abraham Schafer's immigration. Abraham worked for Iseman in Darlington and later married his daughter Rebecca and moved to nearby Little Rock to establish a mercantile business. Researchers believe that Abraham Schafer "may have been the earliest Jew to settle in the area."[8] By the time Alan Schafer's father, Samuel, was born in 1888, Irishman James W. Dillon had assisted in the procurement of land for a railroad station and a small town. The new town of Dillon thrived owing to the railroad traffic, and development of the area led the state legislature to carve Dillon County out of the northern part of Marion County in 1910.[9] Samuel Schafer and his first wife, Wilhelmina (Heller) Schafer, had two children, including Alan. Alan Schafer was born in Baltimore, his mother's hometown, in 1915, but he was raised in South Carolina. His mother died in the 1918 flu epidemic, and Schafer claimed that Mag Hines, a black woman who worked for and lived with the Schafer family, raised him.[10]

Dillon County experienced its share of economic hardships in the early twentieth century, and Alan Schafer claimed to have learned from them. "The bank took the farm in the 1920s and that's why I hate banks. And that's why I've never borrowed any money," Schafer told a journalist.[11] During the 1930s, one-third of South Carolina's farms were foreclosed, and almost three-fourths of the state's farmers survived on borrowed money.[12] However, during the 1930s Dillon County also experienced some hope in connection with the construction of a new road. Highway 301 became known as Dillon's "Gold Coast" because, as Durward T. Stokes writes in his study of the county, a "new era in transportation had begun which proved to be profitable in many ways for the county and its citizens."[13] The railroad led to the establishment of the town and county of Dillon at the beginning of the twentieth century, and advances in transportation continued to contribute to changes in the area. It is believed that James Dillon "used a little home brew to convince Atlantic Coastline railroad officials to route their tracks through his land." Schafer followed the tradition and used the sale of beer to build his business empire in Dillon County.[14]

To tap the market brought by the highway and the legal sale of alcohol after the repeal of Prohibition in 1933, the Schafer family created the Schafer Distribution Company in 1934, turning the business into one of the region's most successful beer distribution operations. Only one semester shy of graduation, Alan Schafer returned home from the University of South Carolina in 1933 because his grandfather was ill. After Abraham Schafer's death, Samuel asked his son to go into business with him. The young Schafer convinced his father to sell the family's country store and concentrate on the beer business Samuel had recently begun. At the Schafer's store, patrons could buy groceries on credit but had to pay cash for beer, which Samuel Schafer would periodically deliver from Baltimore, Maryland. As a young and observant entrepreneur-in-training, Alan Schafer noticed that even during tight times, beer brought money. Beer, not tourism, was his first business venture. The family business expanded beyond the old family store because mobility and new markets offered increasing profitability in a modernizing South.[15]

As Jews, the Schafer family skirted the cultural stigma associated with selling alcohol that would have impacted the Southern Baptists and other religious conservatives who dominated the area. Controversy surrounding the sale and consumption of alcohol ran deep. Even as late as 1960, the *Dillon Herald* reported that during the previous year seventy-four liquor stills had been destroyed. The sheriff at the time, Pete Rogers, stated that this fact was indicative of "an active and constant warfare against moonshining in the county."[16] Those involved in the legal sale of alcohol still had to convince the public that alcohol had a place in polite society. In the 1950s, the South Carolina Division of the US Brewer's Foundation ran ads in the *Dillon Herald* promoting beer as the "beverage of moderation." The organization pledged to work "constantly to encourage maintenance of wholesome conditions wherever beer and ale are sold."[17] The divisive nature of Alan Schafer's first business venture would set the standard for his business and political dealings in years to come.

Schafer later attributed the success of his distribution business to "loyalty in the black accounts," pointing to possible coalitions between the area's small Jewish community and its large African American population.[18] According to Stokes, with the "hard work and the managerial genius of the younger Schafer," the distribution business flourished, and by 1950 its territory had expanded from the Carolinas as far south as Miami, Florida.[19] As the business grew, so too did the Schafer family's cultural and political influence in the area.

Samuel Schafer was a well-respected member of the local Jewish community. The Schafers remained one of the few Jewish families in Little Rock during most of Alan's childhood. However, in the 1930s the populations of Jewish communities in neighboring Dillon and Latta reached their peak, with 159 Jews living in the two towns. Samuel Schafer helped build the first synagogue in the area in 1942. In the early part of the twentieth century, Dillon County had a small but vibrant Jewish community, but the Jewish population dropped to around fifty by the end of the 1970s. By the 1990s, few Jewish families were left in the area due to migration, intermarriage, conversion, and assimilation. The synagogue Samuel Schafer helped found was sold in 1993, and Dillon County's Jewish community now worships in neighboring Florence.[20] The Jewish population of the early twentieth century left its mark on Dillon County, South of the Border being the most outstanding example of the community's influence. Ben Bernanke, the current chair of the Federal Reserve, worked at South of the Border throughout high school and college and is another product of Dillon County's once tight-knit Jewish community.

In addition to establishing himself as a leader in the Jewish community, Samuel Schafer proudly served as a member of the Democratic Party's executive committee. The Democratic Party was the only viable political party in the South during the early and mid-twentieth century. After his father became ill, however, Alan Schafer felt that the local Democrats failed to honor his father's contributions. "When the election came up in 1944, Dad had gone to Sloan-Kettering [Memorial Hospital]. I asked a guy I thought was a friend of his to elect Dad an honorary committeeman [of the Democratic Party]. The guy promised he would, but they didn't. And it damn near broke my father's heart." Alan Schafer saw this slight as unforgivable: "Early on I made up my mind if I ever got a chance to cut those bastards' throats, I would."[21] Samuel Schafer died in 1945; his son's vendetta against Dillon's political establishment did not.

Schafer created a personal story to justify his challenge to the political machinery of Dillon County, a tactic he often employed (during the few interviews he granted) to support his actions in politics and business. Schafer's construction of personal narratives to defend his motives often obscured the actual political and social forces that informed his choices. This was an astute way to negotiate the delicate insider/outsider position that Schafer continually worked to his advantage. In 1939, Schafer married Helen Swinson, who was not Jewish. The marriage pushed Schafer farther outside the relatively insular Jewish community and farther into the new hybridity emerging in southern culture.

The postwar period marked both the rise of Alan Schafer on the local scene and a larger shift in southern life. Schafer entered the armed services in 1943, where he served military police duty on the east coast until 1945.[22] Not stationed abroad as part of the war effort, Schafer witnessed firsthand the dramatic changes in the region wrought by war. In 1940, for example, more than three-quarters of South Carolina's population lived in rural areas or in towns with fewer than twenty-five hundred residents, and the state had the lowest population of foreign-born residents in the country.[23] As service men and women returned home, they found that the war had "challenged provincialism, offered employment, and reshaped society" in important ways. After the war, soldiers "could not fit their experiences or expectations back into the South of the 1930s." The desire of the young to facilitate changes in race relations or pursue innovative means of economic progress was often thwarted by an older generation not keen on relinquishing the yoke of power or the old southern traditions that came with it.[24]

Wartime opportunities for employment and service by African Americans, along with the rumblings of civil rights activism, began to erode white supremacy even in provincial Dillon County. In 1948, taking advantage of the postwar South's changing nature, Schafer embarked on two progressive campaigns in politics and business: registering black voters and a "two-dollar campaign" to flaunt his economic power in the region. As a consequence of a recent United States Supreme Court decision, Democratic primaries, the "real elections" in the South at the time, opened to blacks in 1948.[25] But few white South Carolinians warmed to the idea of black voters.[26] Schafer often discussed his involvement in the 1948 primary. "I went out and registered every black citizen in the Little Rock precinct," Schafer explained. "Then I took control of that nucleus of 140 to 150 voters and I've had it ever since." As a result of these actions, Schafer was at the center of local tensions over political and racial power. "With that black base, I took over the county machine," claimed Schafer. "The Ku Klux Klan used to follow the trucks of my beer distributing company around. I was a pariah in the white community."[27] Although Schafer was white, he was not quite "lily-white," as he described his political enemies.[28]

Schafer used his outsider social status with both blacks and whites in the area as a way to travel between these communities. His comments frame his 1948 political endeavor as seizing control of the emerging black vote, rather than helping blacks gain their own voices or political power. Schafer's language—"I took control" and "I took over the county machine"— leads to the question of whether he was co-opting the emerging African American vote for personal political power or forming a coalition based on shared power. His motivations were likely a mixture of both.

To local conservative whites, the distinction mattered little. Black voting meant black empowerment. Schafer's alliance with African Americans thus spurred a backlash. He explained the situation in 1948: "Boycotts against my beer company were organized. Crosses were burned in front of my home. Groups of Klansmen began following my beer trucks around, urging white retailers to not buy beer from that 'nigger lover' Schafer." According to Schafer, "The Klan continued this harassment through the years, holding rallies aimed at me just 3 miles south of South of the Border and then driving in a Cavalcade through S.O.B. premises as a warning."[29] Such efforts at intimidation were not surprising, considering many white southerners' fervent opposition to desegregation at the time. Schafer's work with local blacks was not a one-time occurrence. "I continued to work with the blacks, in getting them registered and holding church meetings to help them get around all the pressures that they ran into at the polls," Schafer explained. "When the politicians at last realized that the black vote was becoming a force to be reckoned with, the open hate and discrimination went underground. Still, by flagrant gerrymandering, blacks were kept from winning any political office, even though they are about 40 percent of the county's population."[30] While white southerners had diverse reactions to civil rights, Schafer's work with the African American community placed him solidly outside the norm for white southerners of his generation.[31] Schafer, however, was not one to be confined by the norms of southern society or the "lily-white" elite.

In October 1948, just a month after the primary, Schafer paid every employee of his beer distribution business (which had a four thousand dollar per week payroll at the time) in rare two-dollar bills to show "that legally controlled alcoholic beverages contribute a vital share to the prosperity and well-being of the Town, County, and State."[32] These bills flooded the area and made an impression. In addition to illustrating the vital role of legal alcohol, Schafer wanted to show that he was an economic and political force not easily silenced through boycotts or threats. Schafer promoted the sale and consumption of alcohol and crossed the color line to work with the black community at the moment of its emergence on the political scene. Schafer's status as a Jewish southerner gave him the currency to inhabit these social borderlands. In addition, the wealth and upward mobility he acquired through his business acumen offered him additional possibilities for building powerful coalitions. The two-dollar bills flowing through the local economy of Dillon County were physical symbols of Schafer's power to inhabit a fluid position within the area's social, political, and business arenas.

Schafer skillfully used his marginal identity to create and to combat criticism to fit his agenda. When the Jewish Anti-Defamation League sent him a letter of complaint concerning the "almost-Kosher" Virginia ham he advertised at South of the Border, he replied, "I'm almost Kosher myself." Schafer joked, "There is a power to being Jewish—you hear about persecution, but most people think you're a lot smarter than you are. It's a nation-wide syndrome." Journalist Rudy Maxa clarified: "Schafer is a southerner when it suits him. He is also Jewish when it suits him."[33]

Some Jews in the South negotiated their "delicate situation"—their livelihood often depended on not rocking the boat—by attempting to be accepted by whites in the dominant white supremacist culture.[34] The other choice was to challenge white supremacy and risk retribution. As a businessman and political figure, Schafer had to negotiate this social borderland even as he opened and operated South of the Border. Both Schafer's wealth and his whiteness endowed him with a certain degree of mobility socially and politically.

Schafer's understanding of the importance of manipulating physical as well as social borderlands came into play when he selected the location for South of the Border. He opened the small business when Robeson County, in "bordering" North Carolina, went dry; no alcohol could be bought or sold there. In 1948, Robeson was the first county to vote in large numbers to abolish the sale of alcohol, taking advantage of a 1947 local option law approved by the general assembly.[35] No longer able to distribute beer in the area, Schafer decided to attract beer drinkers to come to him. The new laws concerning the sale of alcohol added a greater significance to the North Carolina-South Carolina border. In negotiating this situation, Schafer had to ground his once mobile distribution business in a specific location. At times, being grounded in place actually offers more freedom from social and legal regulations than mobility. Furthermore, the regulation of alcohol opened an entirely new space for its sale. In 1949, Schafer procured a piece of land in Hamer, South Carolina, an unincorporated area seven miles north of Dillon. In the 1991 film *South of the Border* (directed by Lisa

Napoli), Schafer explained how he procured the land: "So I came out here and talked to a black lady, who is still living, by the way. She's ninety-three or four years old. She's one of my—I don't know what you call her. But I take care of her just like she's a relative. I paid her five hundred dollars for three acres of land, which was more than it was worth. And put up a beer depot."[36] Schafer's story conveys a sense of his paternalistic relationship with the local black community.

The simple spatial placement of the "South of the Border Beer Depot" on the southern side of the state line gave South of the Border its name and contributed to its lasting identity. The Mexican border town theme came later.[37] The location of the store was directly tied to Schafer's attempt to circumvent local alcohol laws. The name and location of the business also evoke Schafer's own identity, established on the borders of acceptable southern society. Both Dillon County Sherriff Dixon Lee and Governor Strom Thurmond advised Schafer to serve food in addition to beer to avoid conflict with those who disapproved of the sale of alcohol.[38] Schafer eventually changed the name from "beer depot" to "drive-in" and added a ten-seat grill. A December 1949 South of the Border ad in the *Dillon Herald* announced "a new kind of drive-in restaurant," where patrons could "eat, drink," and "be merry." The establishment now served "deliciously toasted sandwiches, made to order while you wait. Every sandwich a meal in itself. Sliced chicken, corned beef. Pastrami—plus all regular style sandwiches." Lest patrons forget the establishment's primary purpose, however, large bold letters proclaimed, "Beer by the case," and the store ran a promotion whereby the first one thousand cars would receive a free bottle of wine. Schafer later remembered the offerings less flatteringly, as grilled ham, grilled cheese, or peanut butter and jelly. "That was the whole menu, except for soda and coffee—and beer, of course," he told a journalist.[39] Selling food did not automatically make South of the Border a socially acceptable place, but the veneer of food helped mask the socially unacceptable beer market. Schafer manipulated the built environment of South of the Border and its border businesses, just as he manipulated his identity and the social and political boundaries of Dillon and Robeson Counties. Schafer became skilled at maximizing or minimizing controversy according to his needs.

The success of the beer-depot turned drive-in permitted Schafer to do more advertising for the alcohol trade at South of the Border in 1951, when he added the Champagne Room onto the original structure.[40] An ad that appeared the same year showed the expanded South of the Border

South of the Border Restaurant and Motel, circa 1958. Carolina Studio Collection, South of the Border. Courtesy of the South Caroliniana Library, University of South Carolina, Columbia.

and touted the fact that the business was open twenty-four hours a day. This is another example of how Schafer's business functioned in the gap between the constraints of local law and the demands of travelers. In 1949, the city of Dillon instituted a curfew on beer sales from midnight to sunrise.[41] Because South of the Border was outside the city limits, it was able to circumvent this rule. South of the Border benefited from local prohibition and the freedom of the open road, which carried travelers through at all hours. Time as well as space led to the expansion and success of Schafer's border business. In addition to facilitating an alcohol trade unpopular with many locals during the 1950s, South of the Border soon began to offer accommodations to tourists. During the 1950s, South of the Border grew from a small beer-depot to include a grill, a lounge, a gas station, a souvenir shop, and an eighty-room motel.[42]

When Schafer opened his first motel, he hung a large South Carolina flag (not a Confederate flag) to welcome tourists to the Palmetto State. The South Carolina state flag is dark blue with a palmetto tree in the middle and a crescent moon in the left corner. The palmetto tree, because of its use at Charleston's Fort Moultrie during the Revolutionary War, is the state tree. When tourists, often on their way to palm-filled Florida, began asking about the tree on the flag, Schafer bought one hundred palmettos to plant at South of the Border.[43] Palmetto trees flourish in the tropical and coastal regions of the southeast but are rarely found very far inland. People thought the trees would die along the roadside in Dillon County, but most remain today. Playing with natural, social, and geographical boundaries, Schafer remade the landscape of South of the Border in various ways.

Schafer opened his first motel in 1954, the same year the United States Supreme Court handed down the *Brown v. Board of Education* decision banning public school segregation, thereby polarizing the nation on issues of integrated spaces.[44] Motels, which were considered to be racy at the time, already challenged the public/private dichotomy in American culture and were not integrated in the South in the 1950s. As more motels sprouted up across the American landscape, motel referral organizations, consisting of "independently owned motels whose owners adhere to set standards and aid one another by supporting national advertising and a reservation and referral system," emerged.[45] According to Schafer, because of the racial politics of the time this system did not fit the progressive nature of his emerging tourist empire. He wrote to journalist Rudy Maxa, "In 1954, we were admitted to what was then a mutual referral organization [of motel owners] . . . but within 18 months were asked to resign, which we did. The reason (never stated openly, but told to us personally by the top brass) was that we accepted Negroes on equal basis with anyone else who had the $$$." Schafer defended his progressivism regarding race: "Of course, we were the first major motel/restaurant south of Washington who *from the start* always had an open door policy—first come, first served. And also we checked only the color of their money, not their skins."[46] This statement—"we checked only the color of their money, not their skins"—was Schafer's public pronouncement on what he saw as the equalizing power of the dollar.

In the early 1980s, Schafer's lawyer stated in a court of law that even before the federal government demanded integration in public accommodations, Schafer served blacks at South of the Border: "There was never a sit in at South of the Border. There was a demonstration conducted by the Ku Klux Klan in retaliation for [Schafer's] opening these facilities to black people."[47] At that same time, Gloria Blackwell, a professor and civil rights activist who had grown up with Schafer in Little Rock, described his efforts on behalf of African Americans. Blackwell thought of Schafer "almost like a brother." The two had worked together to educate and register black

South of the Border Employees, circa 1958. Carolina Studio Collection, South of the Border.
Courtesy of the South Caroliniana Library, University of South Carolina, Columbia.

voters. When Blackwell tried to restart a defunct chapter of the NAACP
in Dillon County, Schafer became a member. According to Blackwell, "I
can speak for the citizens—for the black citizens in Little Rock and Dillon County, and we have always seen him as, first a friend, for things that
had to do with civil rights, education, health, welfare, any of those efforts;
in those efforts we worked together." Blackwell likewise noted that both
she and Schafer stood on the margins of white southern society. She com-
mented, "We knew of course what race was all about since we were both
victims, but our relationship had nothing to do with white and black. And
I have seen him all of his life working as a person who worked out of a
philosophy . . . Everything he has ever done has been consistent with a
philosophy of dedication to the improvement of human rights."[48]

Despite such public encomia, little physical evidence survives to substantiate Schafer's claim that South of the Border was an integrated space
from the beginning. The ads and articles in the *Dillon Herald* from the
1950s and 1960s do not mention African American patrons, and the
Carolina Studio photographic collection at the University of South Carolina's South Caroliniana Library show images of black workers, not black
patrons.[49]

Ads run by Schafer during this era offer no evidence that South of the
Border welcomed African Americans, and African American travel guides

do not mention South of the Border. Schafer's sweeping claim that his was the first decent restaurant open to African Americans between Washington, D.C., and Miami ignored the existence of black-owned businesses in the region. Furthermore, with the stridency of opposition to desegregation in the South during this time, it seems almost unthinkable that an integrated bar, restaurant, and motel located in a conservative rural county would have flourished as South of the Border did during the 1950s and 1960s.

Evelyn Hechtkopf, Alan Schafer's half-sister and a current South of the Border employee, discussed how having a religious and open-minded family life and growing up in a small town may have influenced Alan Schafer to bend the color line. "They [his parents] were very good and Alan grew up with that," she explained. "There was no color. I'm not saying there was no separation, but there was not much we could do about it."[50] Shirley Jones is from Robeson County, North Carolina, and having worked at South of the Border since 1965, has the longest tenure of any current employee. When asked about South of the Border's status as integrated space, she replied:

> Really there was no problem when I started to work with any race, you know. All three races in the area worked here at that time. There was the American Indians—the Lumbees, the whites, and the blacks. We functioned really well. And as far as the tourists we had no problems with them. We all got along fine. There were no problems with eating, with black patrons or the Lumbee patrons.[51]

When asked if all patrons sat wherever they wanted and if every space was open to every race, Jones indicated that such was the case. Mark Cottingham, who lived down the road from the Schafer family and became close friends with Schafer's youngest son while growing up, recalled that most businesses in Dillon County were segregated into the 1970s, with the exception of South of the Border. When I asked him why, he responded:

> I think because it was mostly tourists. It was visited by northern people headed down south or northern people headed back north. It was nothing uncommon to them. They were accustomed to it, in the North. But in the South it was something slow to take on and it still is.[52]

South of the Border was not a radical space for civil rights activism, but a commercial business that challenged the stark color line present in the borderlands of the Carolinas during the 1950s and 1960s.

Even if he catered to blacks in some way, Schafer was not brave (or foolish) enough to publicly advertise his stance during the 1950s and 1960s in South Carolina—the last state to desegregate its public schools (beginning with higher education in 1963) and public spaces (a much longer battle). Economic tactics, often referred to as "the squeeze," were used to punish black or white South Carolinians who supported integration. Segregationists applied "social ostracism, economic boycott, and political pressure" to enforce their way of life in South Carolina.[53] Schafer claimed that South of the Border "accepted" black patrons, but he did not explain the conditions of that acceptance. Integrating leisure space could be a dangerous and even deadly undertaking in South Carolina during the 1950s and 1960s. In 1950, the Ku Klux Klan experienced a revival in the region led by Grand Dragon Thomas L. Hamilton. Horace Carter founded the *Tabor City (North Carolina) Tribune* and won a Pulitzer Prize for Meritorious Public Service in journalism for his coverage challenging the local Ku Klux Klan in the early 1950s. Tabor City is 43 miles from South of the Border (and just 32 miles from Atlantic Beach, South Carolina). Like South of the Border, Tabor City is located right on the North Carolina-South Carolina Border. In his 1991 book *Virus of Fear*, Carter explained: "Located on the South Carolina border, [Tabor City] was widely hailed as 'Border Town' and 'Razor City' because of its record of violence." Carter's columns directly challenged the Ku Klux Klan led by Grand Dragon Hamilton, who, along with ninety-seven other Klan members, was convicted of various crimes (kidnappings, floggings, and conspiracy) in 1953. Carter pointed out that the local Klan harassed African Americans, Jews, and Catholics, and attacked whites they thought were acting immorally.[54]

The region surrounding South of the Border was notorious for its Ku Klux Klan activities. Beginning in the 1950s, "Catfish" Cole organized a revival of the Klan in the borderlands of the Carolinas. Cole hailed from Marion County, South Carolina, which borders Dillon County. One of Cole's targets was the large Lumbee population in Robeson County, North Carolina. The famous Battle of Hayes Pond occurred in 1958, when a Klan rally, organized by Cole, provoked a massive protest by the county's Lumbee Indians. The Lumbee surrounded and greatly outnumbered the Klansmen, who eventually fled in fear into the surrounding swamps. This was a well-publicized victory for the Lumbee Indians. The incident made the cover of *Life* magazine in 1958. Cole was also arrested and served time in prison for the violence he perpetrated via the Klan.[55] Racial tension continued to build in the region during the 1960s. In 1968, a tragic incident referred to as the Orangeburg Massacre occurred. Three black South Carolina State College (now University) students were killed, and twenty-seven others injured by police when racial tensions resulted from efforts to desegregate the only bowling alley in Orangeburg.[56] The push to desegregate public space, as well as the harassment of the Lumbee population surrounding South of the Border, speaks to the dangerous nature of Schafer's creation of a more mobile and open public space in 1949.

While the Lumbee were harassed by white supremacists, they were welcome at South of the Border. Karen Blu's book on the Lumbee states that in the 1960s the Lumbee "proclaimed, whether correct[ly] or not, 'You can get anything [at South of the Border].' When it was illegal to sell beer, wine, and liquor in Robeson," Blu writes, "Indians seeking to purchase any of these items legally often drove to this South Carolina tourist center, where they could also be entertained by the passing of, to them, strange people with strange ways."[57] For groups marginalized by segregation laws, South of the Border clearly supplied a place where the rules of the racial caste system could be bent, if not broken. South of the Border was not a center of civil rights protest, but a Jewish-owned roadside business on the outskirts of town trying to keep profits high and appeal to as broad a customer base as possible. Early on South of the Border was broken up into sections—the main grill and the "Champagne Room"—and kept open around the clock, providing the time and the space for diverse races to use the business. South Carolinians, in large part, supported segregation during the 1950s and 1960s; however, South of the Border's customers were not just locals.

In 1957, further establishing an outsider position within the conservative culture of the area, Schafer opened a liquor store at South of the Border. In South Carolina liquor laws were quite strict at the time. Liquor was sold at a store separate from the one that sold beer and wine and could not be consumed where it was purchased. The location of South of the Border originally derived from a desire to sell beer to locals living in a neighboring dry county. However, Schafer's venture into liquor was framed as a service for motel guests, reflecting the shift of South of the Border's primary consumer base from locals to tourists. Each South of the Border motel room had a minibar installed after the liquor store opened. Schafer characterized the liquor trade as a service provided to outside travelers, but of course, nothing prevented locals from buying liquor from South of the Border, or from escaping the restrictions of home or the prying eyes of neighbors by using the motel and its minibar.

The fact that Schafer sold beer and liquor, had nightclubs, and had a motel with private entrances and minibars added to the risqué nature of South of the Border's built environment. In 1958, one of the souvenir shops began featuring a "men only—ladies keep out" section, which lasted until 2010 in the form of "Pedro's Dirty Old Man Shop" in Mexico Shop West. Yet, South of the Border also offered numerous attractions, such as rides, arcades, playgrounds, swimming pools, and miniature golf courses that fell under the rubric of "family fun." South of the Border presented itself as a place that appealed to locals as well as travelers. It was both controversial and family-friendly. It welcomed all who possessed purchasing power. In attempting to make the most money by appealing to the most consumers, Schafer created a fascinatingly layered tourist landscape, one that led to more integrated notions of space and social interaction.

The Interstate Highway Act of 1956 further changed the nature of the American roadside and strengthened Schafer's hand within Dillon County. Many have expressed the strong suspicion that Schafer somehow "finagled" the construction plans to ensure that South of the Border not only came within view of drivers but that the federal highway included two exits that poured customers directly into the tourist complex. Schafer publically denied that his money and power somehow influenced the location of the exits, explaining that in 1957, when the Eisenhower administration first issued the interstate map, " . . . I went with Rep. [John] McMillan to see the Bureau of Public Roads. We had 60 rooms at that time, and I said. 'Should we expand or not?' Every map they had showed the interstate would cross the border right at our point, so we went ahead and expanded."[58] In an interview in 1982, South Carolina governor Robert McNair admitted that he worked with officials in North Carolina to make sure the interstate crossed by South of the Border because Dillon County depended on South of the Border for economic survival.[59]

Some argue that the US Interstate system was instrumental in destroying independently owned mom-and-pop roadside businesses, leading to a general sense of "placelessness" in American travel.[60] When interstate highway construction concluded in South Carolina in 1969, South of the Border not only survived, it flourished.[61] South of the Border showed that an independently owned business with political connections, wealth, and tenacity could not only survive the shift to super-highways, it could prosper. The continued success of Schafer's roadside empire illustrates the ability of a touriscape to integrate newer forms of commerce by embracing a future of heightened speed and mobility.

The interstate pushed Schafer to embellish and further expand the built environment of South of the Border.[62] To lure speedy travelers off the interstate, South of the Border became bigger, brighter, and more garish. Schafer made sure travelers would notice his roadside attraction, elaborating numerous eye-catching and often off-color billboards with outlandish catch phrases. One billboard advertising the motel featured a stereotypical image of an American Indian holding a knife and making smoke signals and included the phrase "Don't be lost injun! Get a Reservation."[63] Schafer, like his tourist complex, became bigger and more outlandish as the 1960s led to major shifts in southern and American culture.

The 1960s are known for the rise of the counterculture, the Vietnam War, various movements for equal rights for women and African Americans, a new left-leaning political culture, diversification, and change. Looking through the *Dillon Herald* from the 1960s, it is clear that those writing to express the local perspective were fond of progress in the sense of new roads and businesses. However, the type of progress associated with desegregation and the civil rights movement was not so welcome. Dillon County—with the motto "quietly progressive"—was typical of small towns in South Carolina during the 1960s.

A 1960 *Dillon Herald* editorial, "South's Racial 'Problems' Are In The Minds Of Northerners With Troubles Of Their Own," took the familiar position that the problem of racial unrest in the South was a creation of "outsiders" from the North—where, according to the editorial, "such problems really do exist." The editorial cited numerous black on white crimes in northern cities as proof. For example, "Negro muggings" of nurses at Johns Hopkins Hospital were especially disconcerting because, lacking geographic acumen, the author found Baltimore "practically a Southern city, being just *above* the Mason-Dixon Line" [emphasis mine]. In the editorial "Proving Case Against Themselves," the paper's editors lamented the "current rash of lunch counter raids." Those involved in civil rights protests were characterized as "not endowed with the dignity and refinement that would entitle them to the acceptance they demand . . . One of the first marks of gentility is an abhorrence of intruding where one is not wanted."[64] The civil rights movement was presented as a tasteless affront—as if equality made Emily Post weak at the knees.

Given this milieu, it is not surprising that, in an attempt to win favor with the local elites and play up to stereotypes tourists may have held about the South, Schafer opened the ironically named Confederateland, USA in 1961. The grand opening of Confederateland, USA, which was timed to memorialize the Civil War centennial, was announced in the first "Pedro's Borderlines" on August 6, 1961. "Borderlines" consisted of advertisements thinly disguised as news reports that Schafer ran during the 1960s in the *Dillon Herald*. They advertised new additions to the tourist complex, announced visiting dignitaries, delivered news about employees, and printed letters from tourists to Pedro. The advent of weekly "Borderlines" represents Schafer's continued attempt to appeal to locals as well as the tourists passing through.

Confederateland, USA added another layer of meaning to South of the Border's history and landscape. South of the Border employee Shirley Jones described the attraction: "It was a small amusement park. That's where the Fort was. It was back over here near Fort Pedro. It had cannons and stuff. It was quite Confederate."[65] This 1960s "historical theme park" demonstrated Schafer's ability to utilize the "authentic" history of the Confederacy, while also maintaining an ironic distance in an attempt to present the Civil War as (inoffensive) modern entertainment. Furthermore, Confederateland, USA smoothed over regional hostilities using Schafer's own brand of humor: the politically incorrect spoof.

Essentially, Schafer understood how to play it both ways. As he built his roadside tourist complex, he understood the importance of northern tourists' money in sustaining the southern tourist market. Appealing to various consumers traveling along the highway created an odd North-South amalgamation at South of the Border. From a 1952 ad that announced "Confederate Cooking!! (Yankee Style)," to various Yankee/Confederate jokes scattered throughout "Pedro's Borderlines" and the South of the Border complex, it is clear that early on Schafer was playing up Yankee/Confederate distinctions, while literally making these differences laughable.[66] A billboard from the early 1960s illustrated Schafer's view of the Yankee, refashioned as a northern tourist: "Pedro never shot a Yankee . . . (but maybe Robbed a few?")[67] Schafer's joke plays upon South of the Border's ability to "rob" northern travelers on vacation in the South of their dollars—a reversal of the carpetbagger stereotype of the past. Schafer's humorous take on Confederate/Yankee distinctions did not prevent him from profiting from the serious glorification of the "Lost Cause" at Confederateland, USA.

Schafer procured "authentic" Civil War cannons, a replica of a Civil War stagecoach, and the remains of the *Pee Dee*, a Confederate gunboat, before the grand opening of Confederateland, USA. The announcement of the replica Confederate stagecoach in "Pedro's Borderlines" evoked both the fictional marshal of the radio and TV show *Gunsmoke* and real-life Confederate guerilla leader William Clarke Quantrill, further illustrating Schafer's penchant for blending history and popular culture, reality and farce. "Yippee! Shades of Marshall Dillon and Cantrell's Raiders—pedro just completed negotiations with N.B.C. (That's National Broadcasting, not Biscuit, Co.) for an exact replica of a Confederate Stage Coach."[68] In addition, the *Pee Dee* Confederate States Cruiser, which sank in the Pee Dee River to avoid capture by Sherman, found a "final resting place" at Confederateland, USA. According to the article, the *Pee Dee* "will join a growing collection of authentic Confederate War relics which will be permanently and carefully preserved" at South of the Border's new historic theme park. Furthermore, Schafer promised historians that the ship would be preserved in a "dignified manner." "We are not going to make a circus of it," Schafer stated. "It will be a reminder of this area's last gallant effort in the Civil War."[69]

The serious side of Confederateland, USA signifies Schafer's nascent move inside the power structure of 1960s southern politics—a structure that was beginning to bend, while still holding on to a certain version of the past. A photo on the front page of the *Dillon Herald* depicts Schafer in a Confederate soldier's uniform, with his leg propped up on one of the "authentic" Confederate cannons and the "modernist" Confederateland Tower looming in the background. The caption refers to him as "Kunnel Pedro." Like Schafer's billboards, the image seems like a playful lark or joke. Nonetheless, the Confederateland, USA grand opening and dedication were serious business.[70] A reported six thousand people attended the dedication and formal opening of Confederateland, USA on Monday, August 28, 1961. In keeping with the USA part of the new attraction, the National Anthem was played to begin the ceremony. Afterwards, Reverend James F. Dickenson gave the invocation and Dillon mayor Rudolph Jones welcomed the crowd and "spoke warmly of Mr. Schafer's great contribution to the economy of the section through his development of the tourist center and his unfailing cooperation in every community enterprise." John C. Seller, president of the Dillon County Chamber of Commerce, was master of ceremonies and announced the guests of honor, including members of the South Carolina Confederate Centennial Commission, University of South Carolina historian Dr. Daniel Hollis, and various local politicians and businessmen. The band played, "Are You From Dixie?" and the speaker, Hon. John A. Mays, chairman of the South Carolina Confederate Centennial Commission, was introduced. During his remarks, Mays

Schafer (far right) looks on during the dedication of Confederateland, USA, 1961. Carolina Studio Collection, South of the Border. Courtesy of the South Caroliniana Library, University of South Carolina, Columbia.

praised Schafer: "All of this vast and beautiful development, and this Confederateland designed to foster and preserve the traditions we Southerners hold dear, are the realization of the dream of Alan Schafer, who had the courage and the talent to make his dream come true." Mays, an aide, and Schafer placed a bronze plaque at the base of the Confederateland Tower, dedicating it to "noble men who gave their lives and fortunes for a cause they believed right." Then Schafer presented a "Pedro-sized" (meaning large) Confederate flag to Helen Culp and her state champion Dillon High School Band. The band marched behind the flag and played "Dixie" as the crowd applauded. Later that evening, an extravagant fireworks display continued the celebrations.[71]

The landscape of Confederateland, USA was both historic and modern. It included the ninety-six-foot tall Confederateland Tower, which was "of modernistic design and topped with a rotosphere star that measures 41 feet from tip to tip of its neon-lighted points that aim in every direction." Likewise, Fort Pedro, "a large log structure fashioned on the forts of frontier days" on the outside, and with "an air-conditioned museum and Confederate souvenir bazaar with a green-tinted glass roof," blended "authentic" Confederate documents and memorabilia with souvenirs. There was also a "corral where Pedro's Camel Corps of live camels and burros live in a simulated desert complete with palm fringed oasis," a Confederate miniature railroad, and the Confederateland golf course. Just a little over a week after the dedication, Schafer added a pair of buffalo to Confederateland, USA. He insisted that the "entire Confederate Army—west of the Mississippi—virtually subsisted on Buffalo meat for the duration of the war," and that many Confederate men became famous buffalo hunters after the war.[72] Schafer must have gotten a good deal on buffalo.

Many of the western motifs, such as the frontier fort, buffalo—and of course, sombreros—served to dislocate a monolithic southern theme at South of the Border, while also playing into the exoticization of Mexico common in US leisure culture at the time.[73] The new roads throughout the South brought a "host of new motorists, many of whom had traveled in the West . . . what the South had to offer paled in comparison," and Schafer sought to blend the Old West and Mexican border town allure with a "southern" attraction. During the era of Confederateland, USA, South of the Border also featured Pedro's Plantation, where tourists could engage in the experience of picking cotton. Tourists on vacation could assume the role of slaves on a plantation as a recreational activity. Entering South of the Border's constantly changing land of leisure often involved a disconnection from reality and a host of strange contradictions.

After the Confederateland, USA dedication, Schafer received more respect and positive press from the local community. Boycotts and Ku Klux Klan rallies against South of the Border were replaced with praise and acceptance. Schafer's performance as a "Confederate" further glossed over the transgressive nature of his border businesses and his political alliances with the local black community. On September 1, 1961, the *Dillon Herald* ran an editorial entitled, "Confederateland And South of the Border Are Tremendous Assets To Dillon County." The editorial begins by quoting Schafer's remarks during the dedication: "This is Confederateland, and most of us here are Confederates. But if you should see any Yankees wandering around, don't treat them too rough. *Somebody's* got to pay for all this!" The paper's editors felt that this "whimsically humorous remark," which fit with Schafer's "clever" advertisements, still had "more than a dash of truth." The editorial celebrated the fact that the millions of dollars coming into South of the Border and therefore Dillon County were brought in "on wheels from distant points." The editors explained, "Few local people patronize the world-famous South of the Border restaurant except when they want to 'put on the dog' in entertaining very special guests, or when some club they belong to puts on an especially 'swanky' party. And naturally but few local people ever have occasion to use any of the 200 deluxe motel units." While the editorial claimed few locals patronized South of the Border, it pointed out that the payroll at South of the Border, "one of the largest, if not the largest, in the county," went directly to the residents of Dillon County. "Thus, in every sense of the word, South of the Border is an industry that brings outside wealth into Dillon County." Finally, the editorial "commends and lauds [Schafer] and rejoices, without the faintest tinge of envy, in his tremendous success."[74]

Yet through the years there was residual—and mutual—resentment between Schafer and the town of Dillon. Mark Cottingham described this lingering animosity:

He [Schafer] never needed Dillon. He never needed anything Dillon had to offer. And I think he kind of resented a lot of the people of Dillon, I think. And that's just my opinion. I think he resented a lot of them because they felt that way about him. They felt like, "well, we don't want his money." [Because it was made from beer and tourists.] People will say that in one breath, but then they are receiving a paycheck from him every week. He was the biggest employer.[75]

In 2009, public relations director Susanne Pelt took pride in the fact that a group of Scottish tourism officials visited South of the Border. The Scots, she said, remarked that Dillon had nothing to teach South of the Border, but that South of the Border could teach the town of Dillon about marketing and drawing visitors.[76] Schafer's and South of the Border's successes did inspire envy in some, because Schafer did things his own way—rather than the way they had been done in the past. His use of ironic humor and his ability to play things both ways—while never fully locating himself or his tourist attraction in a stable category—baffled many locals, but his successes sometimes angered them.

Like most things Schafer accomplished at South of the Border, the Confederateland, USA dedication and surrounding hubbub seemed pseudoserious and carried an ironic undertone. When Schafer stated, "Most of us here are Confederates" and donned the Confederate uniform, he expanded the boundaries of southern identity. Schafer, in a certain way, was dislocating Confederate identity—or rather, southern identity—from the experience of the Civil War and adding a Jewish vaudeville performance to the mix. He constructed hidden layers of meaning that lurked below the surface of his seemingly silly (and often offensive) jokes. Furthermore, he played down his risqué and oppositional nature (and business venture) to gain further power with insiders. Evoking Pedro's "good buddy" A. W. "Red" Bethea—a local populist politician and farmer, who was also a harsh segregationist—in a 1961 edition of "Borderlines" may have been as farcical as Schafer's loyalty to the cause of the Confederacy— or his new insider status itself.

While using the Civil War as a marketing ploy, Schafer was fighting real political battles behind the scenes. In addition to referencing Bethea (and Bethea's unsuccessful 1962 run for governor), Schafer mentioned his arch nemesis, the politician Roger Scott in a "Borderline" that appeared following the Confederateland, USA dedication. Schafer wrote that Pedro's "old friend" Roger Scott was an "honored guest" at the dedication.[77] Leading up to the 1960 election, Scott had been attacking Schafer as a crime lord and South of the Border as a space for illegal and immoral activity. Schafer used an economic argument to combat Scott's moral assault on Schafer's business and his character. There was clearly a power struggle going on in Dillon County between Scott, a career politician who served or ran for just about every office in the state, and Schafer, a local entrepreneur who never ran for public office. When Scott condemned South of the Border, Schafer counter-attacked with a full-page ad in the *Dillon Herald*.

The ad's enormous headline yelled, "You Can't Eat Mud!" and was signed with a large "South of the Border" and much smaller "By Alan Schafer" at the bottom. Schafer berated the "mud-slinging" of one of the candidates for sheriff, Roger Scott, who was not named but was described. Schafer explained that South of the Border was one of the largest businesses in Dillon County, with more than three hundred employees. In addition, Schafer mentioned that South of the Border pumped over $10 million into the county annually. Schafer also touted the fact that South of the Border was a "home-grown industry" spending $100,000 annually on "bringing out-of-state people, who would not stop in the county if South of the Border were not here." Finally, he wrote in bold that South of the Border had paid over $1 million in taxes to the state and county. In addition to pointing out the economic contributions of South of the Border to the region, Schafer argued, "[W]e must obtain industry to replace dwindling farm jobs" in Dillon County, and that can only be done with a "calm political climate." Schafer claimed Scott was "shouting to the world at large that Dillon County was overrun with gangsters, dope peddlers, thugs, drug addicts, houses of prostitution, teenage criminals, illegal liquor, and drunken public officials." Scott had leveled many of these claims directly at Schafer and South of the Border. Schafer wrote that these were clearly the "hallucinations of a sick man," and that "outsiders" who did not know the true Dillon County had become "alarmed." Schafer felt that, in addition to mud slinging, the unnamed candidate (Scott) was "trying to stir up racial and religious troubles in Dillon County, where none exist."[78] Pete Rogers, the incumbent who had been sheriff since the early 1950s, eventually beat Roger Scott in 1960. Sheriff Rogers was Schafer's ally during the 1960s, even though political allegiances—like the landscape of South of the Border—changed with the times.

During the election of June 1962, Schafer devoted an entire "Pedro's Borderlines" to a "personal letter to the people of Dillon County," explaining why he was taking part in the political campaign and moving in on the big political powerbrokers in the county. While Schafer claimed he had no political ambitions and wished to stay out of politics, he felt the attacks on his businesses again necessitated his political involvement. He specifically referenced attacks Senator Dixon Lee had made on him and his businesses, even after Schafer helped Lee in the 1958 campaign. Schafer also criticized the special treatment and gifts given to "NORTHERN OWNED PLANTS" (Schafer's capitalization). He pointed out that all of his businesses were locally owned, with profits reinvested back into Dillon County. Schafer also wrote that "visitors" often asked him, "Why is Dillon County so much against Jews?" He informed the "visitors" that this was not true, adding that "several of our best manufacturing plants" were Jewish owned. Schafer felt these attacks gave the county a reputation "for being against all Jews," which was a reputation it could "ill afford." Schafer concluded by praising the lofty ideals of free speech and liberty. These political arguments were influenced by the fact that tourist attractions depend for their success on public perception and political favor.

The lively political landscape of Dillon County politics was constantly changing, much like the recreational landscape at South of the Border.[79] Following the 1962 election, Schafer announced he was bringing back an old Dillon County tradition, harness racing, at South of the Border. The expansion into harness racing reflected Schafer's shift to political insider status, and emphasized that Schafer's rise to power was innately intertwined with South of the Border's landscape. A front-page article announced Schafer's new business venture:

> Dillon County was an enthusiastic center of harness horse racing during the first third of this century, with mostly local gentlemen owners and drivers in spirited competition in several meets each year at the sand-clay oval on the eastern outskirts of town . . . the era came to a close when the Dillon racetrack became a residential sub-division about 25 years ago.[80]

Interestingly, the advisory board for South of the Border's newest attraction—evoking gentlemanly leisure of the past—included big political movers and shakers in Dillon County, such as Red Bethea, Pete Rogers, Gene Carmichael, Jr., and even Roger Scott. South of the Border changed as Schafer moved further inside power structures. Yet shared business interests did not equal a political truce. Schafer remained a maverick in political battles even as he moved further inside the local power structure.

In 1964, politicians again leveled familiar attacks at Schafer and South of the Border. Schafer responded with "You Can't Eat Mud! (Continued)." Sheriff Pete Rogers was again being challenged and maligned by Dixon Lee and Senator Roger Scott.[81] As the election was gearing up, a fire caused $200,000 worth of damages at South of the Border. The *Dillon Herald* reported on May 15, 1964: "Mr. Schafer was inclined to suspect that the fire was not an accident, and he requested an arson expert from the State Law Enforcement Division." Essentially, the money from Schafer's business ventures gave him the power to become a local political player. Therefore, it would make sense that his enemies would attack both the source and the symbol of this wealth—his South of the Border empire. The fire, which was never officially declared arson, did not intimidate Schafer sufficiently to make him leave politics. Instead, it spurred him on. Schafer began to try his hand in national as well as state and local politics.

As his power, money, and insider status grew, Schafer's political maneuvers entered questionable territory. Schafer remained a staunch Democrat even as many in the region began to defect to the national Republican Party, because the Democratic candidate for president, Lyndon B. Johnson, had ties to the 1964 Civil Rights Act, and Barry Goldwater, a foe of civil rights legislation, was a new kind of Republican. Schafer campaigned hard for LBJ and even hatched a plan to smear Goldwater. Schafer's correspondence with United States Senator Olin D. Johnston describes a plan to obtain Goldwater's NAACP membership card and print up one hundred thousand copies to distribute in South Carolina. Schafer wrote that he could "get a great many of the South Carolina Negro leaders to go along with this (bragging about Goldwater's NAACP Membership) without a thought of them deserting the party." The senator replied that he needed time to check on Goldwater's NAACP membership, and that he would get back in touch with Schafer.[82] Nothing ever came of this smear tactic; however, this letter provides a rare archival example of the expanding nature of Schafer's political machinations.[83] This incident also shows that despite Schafer's move towards insider status within the whites-only local power structure, he continued to envision local blacks as part of his political coalition.

Schafer claimed to have entered politics in 1948, when he "took over" the recently enfranchised black voters in the area. Emerging from the shadows of behind-the-scenes political maneuvers, Schafer became the chairman of the Dillon County Democratic Party in 1965. A Jewish man tangentially aligned with the African American community taking over as head of the Democratic Party in a rural southern county did show some 1960s-style progress, and Schafer was admittedly more progressive on racial issues than many of his local political contemporaries.[84] Buoyed by the wealth from his business endeavors, Schafer began shifting from a renegade politician of the people to an opportunistic and powerful politician within the Democratic machine (which still held sway in local elections at the time). By the end of the 1960s, Schafer no longer needed to pander to political insiders in Dillon County, the old "lily-white" elite, because he had established credentials as a political powerhouse in his own right. His pandering to the "lily-whites" at an end, Confederateland, USA had served its purpose. Like many attractions at South of the Border, Confederateland, USA was history by the end of the 1960s. At this time, Schafer expanded his transgressive border business into fireworks. The ammunition at Fort Pedro shifted from authentic Civil War cannons to bottle rockets and a host of other pyrotechnics. Fireworks were (and still are) illegal in North Carolina and most neighboring states, and Schafer made far more money from hawking firecrackers (still a big seller today) than outdated visions of the Old South.

Confederateland, USA and its strange rise during the 1960s brings into question Schafer's claim that South of the Border was open to all races from the beginning. Would African American patrons have wanted to go anywhere near Confederateland, USA in 1961? Schafer's 1948 registration of black voters and his 1954 motel that accepted people based on the "color of their money not their skins" are complicated by his later glorification of the Confederate cause and pandering to the local white elite. These factors all speak to the whirlwind of contradictory forces leading tumultuously toward a Newer South.

With the expansion of his political power as chairman of the local Democratic Party and the proximity of Interstate 95, by the 1970s Schafer was successful enough to build the largest and most lasting symbol of his of his tourist empire's power: the iconic (and phallic) sombrero tower.[85] The two-hundred-and-twenty-foot tower has an elevator that brings visitors up to the sombrero observation deck to view Schafer's neon empire. The "largest sombrero in the world" fits in with classic examples of gigantism in vernacular roadside architecture, but below the surface it also functions as a material symbol of Schafer's economic and political influence in the region—his larger-than-life status. One newspaper went so far as to describe Schafer, who had never won election to any public office, "as one of the most powerful politicians in South Carolina."[86] Another referred to him as the "enigmatic millionaire" of Dillon County.[87]

As Schafer gained political power, the southern political system was itself changing. In February 1980, Schafer gained a position on the South Carolina Highway and Public Transportation Commission, his first "official" public appointment in South Carolina government and the peak of his political power.[88] While Schafer's Sombrero Tower still stands as a symbol of his influence, he was quickly unseated from his new perch on the Public Transportation Commission by a scandal that arose just months after his appointment.

Schafer was accused (and later convicted) of buying votes during the 1980 Democratic primary for sheriff of Dillon County. Schafer directly tied the controversial sheriff's race in 1980 to his racially progressive political leanings. The candidates for sheriff were Roy Lee (the incumbent and a Schafer ally), who—according to Schafer—appointed the first black deputies in Dillon County's history at Schafer's request, and challenger Greg Rogers, whose major backer was his father, Pete Rogers, a local judge and a major political force in the area who had also previously been Schafer's political ally. The investigation into vote fraud focused on the absentee ballots: Lee received 1,265 absentees votes (many from voters able to make it to the polls), compared to Rogers's eighty-one.

In the beginning, Schafer remained defiant, claiming that the absentee ballot box, which was removed by South Carolina law enforcement from

South of the Border, had allowed African Americans to vote without harassment. But absentee ballots—many proven to be fraudulent—were sent through the mail, and tampering with them was a federal offense.[89] Eventually, thirty individuals—from both sides of the ticket—were found guilty in the vote buying scandal. A 1981 article in the *State* newspaper reported that the verdicts and the stiff penalties handed down in these cases "have sent shock waves across Dillon County, the state of South Carolina and even the United States of America."[90] In typical Alan Schafer fashion, the controversial millionaire got married to long-time South of the Border employee Patricia Francis Campbell just a few days after he entered a guilty plea to one count of conspiracy and two counts of mail fraud.[91]

An editorial in the *Dillon Herald* entitled "Get Off Our Backs" complained that the vote buying scandal in Dillon County was part of a "political vendetta" that used the county "as an example" in punishing offenses (vote buying) that have "been virtually traditional in South Carolina politics." Schafer was referred to as a "political kingpin" who "has done much more good in his life than bad." The editorial expressed the sentiment that Schafer "would be much more valuable to Dillon County with his efforts in industrial development and philanthropies if he were at home and not in prison." Schafer's years of making economic arguments for himself and his business ventures resonated within his local community—or at least with the local newspaper editors. The *Dillon Herald* editorial praised Schafer's general character as well as his business and civic contributions, but it also pointed out that "his days as a political powerhouse are finished."[92]

Schafer continued to oversee his tourist complex and to defend himself publicly from his cell in the federal prison at Eglin Air Force Base in Florida. In a letter to the *Dillon Herald*, printed April 29, 1982, Schafer claimed that vote buying had been "business as usual" in Dillon County for years, and that the racist underpinnings of the election and the history of disenfranchising the county's black voters made Schafer feel that "the rightness of my motives justified the means."[93] Dillon County elections had long been contentious and back-door dealings were not new occurrences.[94]

Schafer did show regret and remorse at the conclusion to his open letter. "I do not condone what I did. I am deeply ashamed for myself; for my family; for the Democratic Party and for the many friends I feel I have let down. My transgressions were not for personal profit nor for political power nor political gain," Schafer wrote. "They were motivated by what I believed to be the best of reasons—love of the underdog, a fear of the concentration of power."[95] Repentance did not equal submission, however. Although he pledged that such offenses "will never happen again," he also vowed:

> [A]s long as God gives me strength, [to] fight for the poor, the under-privileged, and against the concentration of power in any man. This is what my life has stood for. I seek no recognition for it. I have never sought wealth for its own sake, but for what good I could do with it for my fellow man. Whatever may happen to me, these feelings will go with me to the grave.[96]

By 1994, Schafer had become less apologetic and sentimental, and he again began to maintain his innocence. "I did absolutely nothing wrong, I just had a chicken shit bunch of lawyers," he claimed. Although Schafer was "officially" out of politics, he declared it "doesn't mean I can't give the sons of bitches who are still in it hell."[97]

The vote-buying scandal pulled Schafer away from politics and back to a focus on South of the Border, which provided the money that led to his political rise in the first place. Schafer refused to let a stint in federal prison stop the expansion of his constantly evolving land of neon. In 1988, he added a fifteen-thousand-square-foot convention center to South of the Border's numerous attractions.[98] He also went into the soda business in 1993, saving Blenheim Ginger Ale, South Carolina's entry in the regional soda business.[99] It was probably both local pride and wise business acumen that caused Schafer to buy the bottling company. After relocating the Blenheim bottling company to the South of the Border complex (and turning the old facility into a museum), Schafer's next big business expansion greatly changed the landscape of South of the Border and pushed Schafer back into behind-the-scenes politics.

In the mid-1980s, the South Carolina Legislature quietly and without debate passed a measure, sponsored by state senator (and Schafer's friend) Jack Lindsay, making video gambling legal in the state.[100] Between 1996 and 1999, Schafer added the Silver Slipper and then four more video gambling establishments to South of the Border.[101] The issue of video gambling played an important role in South Carolina's 1998 gubernatorial race, which pitted Republican incumbent David Beasley, an opponent of video gambling, against Democrat Jim Hodges, who largely dodged the issue. Operators of video gambling establishments, including Schafer, poured a great deal of money into the Hodges campaign and ran negative advertisements against

Beasley. The 1998 race was one of the most costly and nastiest gubernatorial races in modern South Carolina history, but Schafer and video gambling appeared to have triumphed with a Hodges victory.[102]

But Schafer had only won the battle, not the video gambling war. Owing to complex political maneuvering, video gambling became illegal in South Carolina as of July 1, 2000, and the video gambling parlors closed.[103] The flashy Silver Slipper was converted into the Silver Arcade. The rest of the video gambling parlors down Highway 301 were left derelict and later converted into car dealerships and other random businesses. As South Carolina's most visible icon of tourism on the busy Interstate 95 corridor, South of the Border also suffered because of the South Carolina tourism boycott launched in 2000 by the NAACP in response to the state's refusal to remove the Confederate flag from the statehouse grounds.[104] The abandoned video gambling parlors added to the retro ghost town feel South of the Border had acquired by the end of the twentieth century.

Despite these setbacks, Schafer's unflagging dedication to his business resulted in continued growth and national publicity—South of the Border was moving from a regional to a national icon. In 1986, *Roadside America*, "the modern traveler's guide to the wild and wonderful world of America's tourist attractions," featured the site. In the 1992 "new and revised" edition of *Roadside America*, then the definitive guide to hip and off-beat US roadside icons, South of the Border's status was elevated to one of the seven wonders of roadside America.[105] Yet by the 1990s, public perception of the tourist attraction began to shift from that of a "swanky" roadside attraction to a "campy" and ironic throwback to an earlier era. In 1996, the *Washington Post* named South of the Border the tackiest place in the Mid-Atlantic.[106] This event prompted the *State* newspaper in South Carolina to respond, "Aside from quibbling over the *Post*'s geographical acumen (just where does the South begin these days?) we'd have to say this award seems long overdue."[107] In 2001, *American Heritage* dubbed South of the Border one of America's best roadside attractions.[108] The travel site made its big screen debut in the critically panned 1999 film *The Forces of Nature*, directed by Bronwen Hughes and starring Ben Afleck and Sandra Bullock. Ten years later, in 2009, the documentary *S. O. B. and the Legend of Alan Schafer* (directed by Jesse Berger and Nate Mallard) premiered at the Charleston International Film Festival and won the festival's audience choice award.

By the end of the twentieth century, selling beer was no longer controversial, and the dry county had gone wet. The empire built on beer, like its owner, was beginning to age, growing into its ragged, retro image. In 2000, the remaining bar at South of the Border, The Cancun Saloon, was reinvented as Pedro's Antique Shop. Like Schafer, South of the Border had aged and weathered many changes in southern and American culture. No hard liquor could be bought at South of the Border after the saloon closed. The antique shop—which, like most things at South of the Border, was Schafer's idea—represented an appreciation of the material objects and memories of the past. The white and blue antique shop stands out among the bright tones of yellow, red, fuchsia, orange, and pink that color most of South of the Border. As Schafer mellowed with age, so too did his roadside attraction.

Schafer ran his tourist empire until right before his death in 2001, often putting in twelve-hour days, seven days a week, even while battling prostate cancer and leukemia. At the time of Schafer's death, eight million travelers per year visited South of the Border, and he employed over seven hundred workers in the rural and economically depressed area of Dillon County. His business empire was valued at more than $50 million.[109]

Schafer worked behind the scenes and sometimes beyond the law to "give those bastards hell"—referring to the ruling white elite of Dillon County or anyone else who got in his way. He developed an insider's perspective while maintaining the outsider edge of a maverick. His power came from his qualified whiteness, his wealth, his connections, and his ability to play things both ways. The fact that he was not "lily white" and did not completely defer to the local elite and white supremacy made him an outsider and a threat to a long-standing (white) southern way of life. His realization that his beer distribution business succeeded because of "loyalty in the black accounts" led to his professed focus on "the color of their money, not their skin" at South of the Border. Schafer took risks, but ultimately he understood the complexities of his consumers' identities, tastes, and preferences. He understood that constant change creates a vibrant space for commerce, as well as the occasional crossing of societal boundaries. He understood that places and people must constantly move and be remade to remain relevant. His biggest mistake—represented by his 1980s stint in federal prison—was becoming too much of an insider and abandoning his democratic ideals.

Schafer often presented the story of South of the Border as a place that almost built itself. He once told a journalist, "All an accident. We didn't anticipate the tourists." Schafer was pushed into the food service business in order to attain social acceptability. He claimed his souvenir trade began when a northern salesman stopped at South of the Border without enough money to get home. "He had a station wagon filled with plush toys—bears, elephants. So I bought them. I took about a five-times markup, and I put these animals on all the shelves, and in three weeks they were gone. And I said, 'Jesus.'" Schafer also declared that travelers' demands pushed him into the motel business. "They'd aim for South of the Border after seeing our signs, thinking that we had a motel here," Schafer says. "For a while, we had them sleeping on the floor in the dining room. Then I thought, 'Well, this is silly, to have them staying here for free.'"[110] Schafer soon opened his first motel rooms. When asked by Lisa Napoli how Pedro came about, Schafer responded: "From the tourists. They'd ask, 'Where's the Mexican that runs this place?' So we had to invent him."[111]

These supposed "accidents" and "inventions" imply that consumers (primarily tourists) played an important role in South of the Border's evolution. The story of Alan Schafer is important, but it must be examined in the context of the ways people perceive, interact with, and consume South of the Border. The reasons that people stop at South of the Border are not incidental; they are an important part of the roadside attraction's history and current campy cachet.

One reason that people do not stop at South of the Border is the ethnic stereotype and racist underpinnings of the "Mexican that runs the place," Pedro. Pedro is clearly a problematic image, but like Alan Schafer, he calls for deeper analysis. Analysis does not make Pedro an acceptable image, but breaking down his story helps illustrate the shifting nature of race, ethnicity, and identity as tourism became a dominant industry in South Carolina.

In the 1950s, Pedro emerged from the sombrero and serape iconography as a persona intended to represent South of the Border. Does the current campy look of South of the Border take the bite out of Pedro's inherent offensiveness? Can an ethnic stereotype survive as the mascot for a roadside attraction as we move into the twenty-first century and into the Newer South? The answers to these questions lie with the current generation of Schafers who run South of the Border, and with the consumers—even the ones who find Pedro offensive and unacceptable—who continue to stop and spend money at this campy roadside emporium of commercial kitsch.

Chapter Three

"CAMP WEETH PEDRO"

Politics and Aesthetics Reshape the Borders of Taste at SOB

Over a decade ago, when I first began researching South of the Border, I asked my mother if she ever took me there when I was a kid. It is just an hour from my hometown of Conway, South Carolina, and I wondered if my fascination with the place had roots in childhood memories. She replied with a resolute, "No. I never would have taken you there as a child. That place is tacky. Locals don't go there." She then added derisively, "Except for you." In general, my mother and I have very different tastes.

Before I even knew who Alan Schafer was, South of the Border presented a fascinating story through its garish built environment and its innovatively retro—with all the irony that phrase entails—style. There was also something mysterious about it. When I walked into Pedro's Diner, one of my favorite South of the Border spots, I would hear the music from David Lynch's early-1990s TV show *Twin Peaks* in my head. Like that show, South of the Border exuded a strange and alluring aesthetic. South of the Border was dangerous and controversial. Under its bright façade lurked a dark complexity and devious allure. South of the Border pulled me in because it just looked and felt so transgressive, so different from the cookie-cutter chains and high-rise condos littering Myrtle Beach. I was drawn to South of the Border and have spent well over a decade trying to figure out why. While its history has fascinated me and—although I never met him—Alan Schafer strikes me as an enthralling and complex character, it is really the look and the feel of the complex itself, as I came to know it in the 1990s, that haunts me. South of the Border is a mesmerizingly beautiful yet flawed landscape.

Recalling J. B. Jackson's definition of landscape, cited in the introduction, it is important to remember that landscapes are by nature synthetic, not natural. They are made or modified by humans and express our history and our identity. The English word *landscape* is interesting because it began as a term used to describe art—specifically landscape painting—before it referred to anything "real."[1] The evolution of "landscape" is an example of life imitating art. South of the Border can be read as a work of art—perhaps, one of the great installations of the twentieth century.

In 1949, the same year South of the Border was founded, Joseph Downs, a curator for the Metropolitan Museum of Art spoke to a group of art and antique collectors and made the claim, "little of artistic merit was made south of Baltimore." This statement angered some in the art world and is the introductory moment in Maurie McInnis' 2005 article, "Little of Artistic Merit? The Problem and Promise of Southern Art History" in *American Art*. McInnis writes, "[M]ore than fifty years later, the southern and Caribbean colonies have received little attention from art historians."[2] The definition of art must both move outside traditional boundaries and into the vernacular, as it grapples with the problem and promise of southern art. For as McInnis argues, overlooked artistic endeavors in the South and the Caribbean have a great deal to offer to our understanding of "aesthetic taste but also about conceptions of race, place, and society that await further exploration."[3] Reading the built environment of South of the Border as a twentieth-century work of art brings to light the ways in which taste and aesthetics influence our understanding of both history and culture as we move into the Newer South.

In the 1960s, South of the Border was "swanky" because of its "more is more" ornamented look, but today the word *tacky* is often used to describe the roadside attraction. Behind the tacky and flamboyant look of South of the Border lurk layers of meaning. The look of the roadside tourist attraction is a reflection of its place outside of both the political system of "good old boy" southern politics in the rural South and the dominant "moonlight and magnolias" model of southern tourism. Schafer lived his entire life in Dillon County. With his fiery politics and his gaudy travel stop, he was the prototypical insider/outsider—occupying a position that enabled his success as an entrepreneur and his ability to create an original aesthetic statement with his border businesses. Schafer's history and social position hint at a new way to look at the material culture of the US roadside. As Schafer's canvas, the South of the Border landscape represents a sensibility more than a style, because South of the Border's landscape is a bricolage of so many different styles.

The definition and application of the term *tacky* has changed (and will continue to change) over time. As Barbara Kirshenblatt-Gimblett points out, "Bad taste could be said to be bad timing."[4] South of the Border was originally tacky because it pushed booze and, in some ways, catered to all races in a segregated society. Today, the travel complex is tacky because of its neon palette, dated look, and stereotypical depiction of Mexicans. In a 1993 article, "Under the Big Sombrero," a journalist explains why some people find South of the Border distasteful: "For them South of the Border is emblematic of the New South, a monument to greed and bad taste, a place Elvis might have loved in his later years."[5] South of the Border functions as a symbol of the Newer South—a refashioned region where history and consumer culture collide in fascinating ways.

It would be easy to call South of the Border tacky or racist and to discount the place and its history as irrelevant, to zoom by without a second glance. Yet, as David Grimsted writes of popular culture theory, the "value of any cultural analysis" is directly related to the "thoughtful intensity given to the artifact."[6] This "thoughtful intensity given to the artifact" of South of the Border has pushed me to deal with the thorny issue of taste—including distinctions between camp and kitsch, why they matter, and how they have manifested in the built environment of South of the Border.

South of the Border is a campy landscape of commercial kitsch. I am not conflating camp and kitsch with this declaration. While camp and kitsch certainly have common characteristics, they also have important distinctions. The overall landscape and aesthetic statement made by South of the Border is camp, expressing an exaggerated and stylized artifice as a form of commentary. South of the Border is not kitsch, because it is not innocent or overly sentimental; it is improper, humorous, and ironic. In Milan Kundera's reading of kitsch, difficulties, contradictions, and complexities are sanitized. Camp requires thoughtful intensity because it carries a deeper meaning—numerous deeper meanings, actually. Kitsch tries to gloss over complexities with whopping doses of sentimentality. Camp is intellectual. Kitsch is emotional. Camp expresses sentiment. Kitsch is sentimental. In Marita Sturken's *Tourists of History*, kitsch objects—such as teddy bears and snow globes associated with tragedies like the Oklahoma City bombing or the terrorist attacks of 9/11—are read as attempts to reclaim an innocence and simplicity America never really possessed.[7] Kitsch can be found within the landscape of South of the Border in the form of gift shop souvenirs; however, the aesthetic statement of South of the Border's landscape is based in a camp sensibility. "SOB" (as Schafer abbreviated South of the Border's name in advertising, on products, and throughout the complex) hides its cultural critique within a fantasy landscape devoted to amusement. SOB may appear to be a collection of commercial kitsch on its surface or to the passing motorist; however, close reading reveals a complex visual statement worthy of reconsideration.

Susan Sontag's iconic 1964 essay, "Notes on Camp," offers an early and enduring take on camp. My main point of contention with Sontag is her claim that camp is apolitical. This claim has been effectively challenged in recent scholarship, especially in gay and queer theory.[8] Camp is a stylized performance involving artifice and exaggeration. Such exaggeration calls attention to itself, just as South of the Border's incongruity draws attention to itself—and to the constructed nature of what is normal or expected of the American roadside, southern tourism, and the South. Contemporary camp performances convey a critique of normative notions of taste and can therefore challenge the status quo. From the beginning, when Schafer turned beer signs kitty-corner and painted them purple, and covered his cinderblock beer-depot in bright pink paint, he was formulating the style of South of the Border in stark contrast to its natural and social surroundings, as if to say, "I'm here. I'm SOB. Get used to it."[9] In a practical sense, this look drew people from the neighboring dry counties and off the road, but it also was a statement of South of the Border's "outsider" social situation. Schafer provided products deemed poor in taste—booze, fireworks, gambling, pornography—to a colorful clientele in a conservative society traditionally thought of in stark terms of black and white. But instead of creating a gray area, Schafer created a liminal zone of neon.

Camp, as exemplified in the films of John Waters, the Blaxploitation movie genre of the 1970s, or Larry Flynt's *Hustler* magazine, is often an over-the-top expression unconcerned with political correctness.[10] "Political correctness" or "PC" are much maligned terms in contemporary discourse. Essentially, PC is the sometimes over-vigilant desire not to offend. SOB subscribes to a philosophy that it is better to address difference by make fun of it than to pretend not to see difference—or to commit the worse offense of making fun of cultural differences behind closed doors (mostly with friends who are just like you). SOB. and places like it enter the fray of cultural controversy head on, employing loud and brash material culture positioned in public spaces specifically to get attention and make money.

Schafer was *the* SOB behind South of the Border's camp commentary. Sontag drew a distinction between naïve and deliberate camp and argued that pure camp is always naïve.[11] Schafer was a sly promoter and knew what he was doing—even if he did not always let on that he did. South of the Border was deliberate camp masking itself in naivety. With camp,

Schafer was both expressing and trying to deflect the transgressive nature of his business. A bright exterior, a witty name, and humor were utilized to distract attention from the fact that he was selling booze to anyone with money on the border of a dry county in the Bible Belt during the 1950s and 1960s. The look of South of the Border challenged the social mores of Dillon County, but this appearance also assuaged the tensions of this challenge by claiming it was all one big joke. If consumers did not get it, it was their fault, not Schafer's.

The point of camp is to "dethrone the serious," according to Sontag. We think enjoyment and entertainment, not serious issues like politics and power, should define leisure and tourism. However, Schafer's transgressive border businesses were serious business in the South at mid-century. Before Schafer, Mrs. E. D. King owned the last store where alcohol could be purchased before entering dry Robeson County. Just a few months before Schafer opened South of the Border, King's store was blown up when dynamite was thrown through its window.[12] In such dangerous conditions, Schafer needed humor to distance his business from its controversial product. Camp "involves a complex relation to 'the serious.'" Within the realm of camp things get turned on their heads, and one can be "serious about the frivolous, frivolous about the serious."[13] This complex relationship was illustrated by Schafer's use of "Pedro's Borderlines" to advertise his tourist complex through witty jokes blended with serious political commentary. The economic impact of South of the Border in Dillon County was quite serious, but the attraction's landscape of leisure emphasized entertainment, escapism, and fun. The ability to blur the strict color line of the postwar South derived both from South of the Border's main audience of transient travelers, and from its place as a frivolous tourist trap for duped Yankees. Schafer was able to negotiate the line between the serious and the frivolous by presenting a "comic vision of the world," one of the key aspects of camp.[14]

Schafer's uncanny sense of humor is a central aspect of South of the Border's landscape. The constant word play—Pedro's Golf of Mexico, ad slogans like "I never sausage a place: You're always a wiener at Pedros," "Pedro's weather report: chili today, hot tamale," and, of course, Confederateland, USA—presents Schafer's humorous world view, one that welcomed language games and irony.[15] As a man who came of age during the Depression, lived through World War II and the Vietnam War, and lost mother, father, wife, and son early in life, Schafer always used South of the Border to express his love of embellishment and bawdy humor. Life was too short to play it straight all the time. Schafer was not afraid of the risqué and could turn an insult into an attack on the nature of insults.

Sontag wrote that camp taste is above all "a mode of enjoyment, of appreciation—not judgment. Camp is generous. It wants to enjoy. It only seems like malice, cynicism." Schafer worked long hours, often seven days a week, on South of the Border. He was a man in love—perhaps obsessed—with his work. He told filmmaker Lisa Napoli:

> I can't sleep at night. I keep a legal pad and three or four felt tip pens by the bed at night and very often I wake up at three or four o'clock in the morning and get an idea in my head—like a great billboard. I take them and drop them on that table over there and in the cold light of day about twenty out of twenty one are ridiculous. But every now and then, something comes up.[16]

Schafer reinvested his profits back into the business and constantly changed the landscape to express his own vision and address the needs of consumers. As his long-time employee Shirley Jones said, "He took the responsibility of South of the Border to his heart. This was really his heart, South of the Border."[17] Alan Schafer built his camp empire out of love, as is apparent in South of the Border's aesthetic and its sensibility. SOB is not just about making a profit—it is also about making a statement.

Absence of love often produces kitsch. Sentimentality, the basis of kitsch, is quite different from love. Camp taste is a "kind of love, love for human nature. It relishes, rather than judges, the little triumphs and awkward intensities of 'character.'"[18] Schafer loved the flourishes of Las Vegas, the vibrant commercial trade of Mexican border towns, the exaggerated roadside architecture of the 1920s, and the populuxe design of the postwar period. His love of place in and of itself explains why he merged these aesthetic visions, added his sense of humor and personal flair, and built them all on a space of unincorporated land on the border of South Carolina. Schafer deeply loved South Carolina and Dillon County, but he wanted to refashion the landscape he knew and loved in his own way. There is a sense of power in taking a space and claiming it as your territory by creating a place in your image. SOB is "on the border" in so many ways.

The design and construction of buildings at South of the Border were costly and continual. Schafer's vision was never static but changed with the times and business trends. Architecture itself is an art innately connected with the business of taste. In the essay "Is Space Politic?" Frederic Jameson writes, "Architecture is business as well as culture, and outright value fully as much as ideal representation: the seam architecture shares with economics also has no parallel in the other arts."[19] Dell Upton further explored the issue, explaining, "Taste was manifested as architectural decorum, the knowledge of what to do in which settings, the ability to chart the right path between too much and too little . . . In short, the discipline of architecture was to be socially defined and socially exercised."[20] Much recent attention has been paid to vernacular architecture (especially from the 1950s and 1960s) and its essential role in understanding important aspects of our culture's past and present.[21] It is important to note that it was primarily places like Las Vegas (far away in the desert of the West), NASCAR (the Darlington track is right down the road from South of the Border), and Mexican border towns that influenced Alan Schafer—not cultural critics like Clement Greenberg, Herman Broch, Milan Kundera, or even Susan Sontag. "I like Las Vegas because it gives me a lot of ideas," Schafer once told a journalist. "They're always ahead of the country in showmanship."[22]

Schafer's life runs in tandem with the shift towards new and more democratic monuments to taste. Important and influential landscapes were located not just in big cities, but in the small towns and along the roadsides of places (like Hamer, South Carolina) few people have ever heard of. In 1965, as Schafer was just taking over the local Democratic Party in Dillon County, Tom Wolfe analyzed this shift to a more democratized notion of taste in the United States. "The war created money. It made massive infusions of money into every level of society," Wolfe explained. "Suddenly classes of people whose styles of life had been practically invisible had money to build monuments to their own style."[23] Wolfe observed this phenomenon in gangsters' creation of Las Vegas and in the development of stock car racing by southern "outlaws" with war money and without extensive education or exposure to "culture." Similarly, South of the Border's postwar emergence and subsequent development by a self-made man is just the kind of monument to which Wolfe referred, one which reflects the tumultuous historical forces and ruptures that aided its creation. Wolfe claimed, "The educated classes in this country, as in every country, the people who grew up to control visual and printed communication media, are all plugged into what is, when one gets down to it, an ancient, aristocratic aesthetic." Wolfe continues:

Stock cars racing, custom cars—and for that matter, the jerk, the monkey, rock music—still seem beneath serious consideration, still the preserve of ratty people with ratty hair and dermatitis and corroded thoracic boxes and so forth. Yet all these rancid people are creating new styles all the time and changing the whole life of the country in ways no one seems to bother to record, much less analyze.[24]

Schafer was not a part of the elite; however, he was far from being "ratty" and "rancid," even by the standards of a quasi-dandy like Wolfe. Schafer had the politician's skill to play up or downplay his class status and could identify with both elite politicians and the average man or woman. Schafer was indeed rich for most of his life, but he was never part of the cultural elite.

Schafer's over-the-top camp aesthetic, on display at South of the Border, did not fully extend into his well-guarded private life. Schafer was not enamored of self-promotion and granted few interviews in a career that spanned many decades. He gave a great deal to his local community and asked for little recognition in return. Alan Schafer was a walking contradiction. An article by Brett Bursey, entitled "Meet Alan Schafer: Grandmaster of Tack," detailed the author's introduction to the mastermind behind South of the Border. "When Schafer wheels up to his office in a shiny red Porsche 944, I expect him to be as brash and in-your-face as his road-side empire. Surprise! No sombrero and red crushed velvet; no gold chains and cigar. The slight and soft-spoken gentleman is in running shoes and matching gray casual wear."[25] Camp can be the modus operandi of a private and kind Jewish guy from the rural South—an outward expression of internal contradictions.

Along with South of the Border, the postwar period saw the emergence of many new (and campy) modes of entertainment, including stock car racing and rock 'n roll, described by historian Pete Daniel as emerging from between the fissures that were beginning to appear in the white supremacist and conservative perspectives that dominated the South. Daniel transforms "low culture," sometimes referred to as "working-class culture," into "lowdown" culture, because he considers the latter a better label, one that is an "ambivalent term edged with pride and denigration."[26] In "More is Better: Mass Consumption, Gender, and Class Identity in Postwar America," Shelley Nickles found the same trends in the kitchens of working-class women, who rejected the simplicity of art deco design promoted by design specialists and tastemakers of the period. Nickles argues, "[W]orking-class women's preference for shiny ornamental rosebuds was not about bad taste, fashion, or status seeking but about social identity."[27] The assertion of aesthetic preference was also about claiming

Pedro, South of the Border's controversial mascot.
Photo by author, 2008.

agency and power. Schafer understood the expressive role of consumption. In the language of modern advertising, he sold a lifestyle—along with beer, fireworks, tacos, and souvenirs.

South of the Border's lampooning of various cultures and identities intensified its aesthetic of tackiness. This tightrope of taste—tacky in a good way, versus tacky in a bad way—becomes most complicated in dealing with the strange career of Pedro, Schafer's alter ego and South of the Border's patron saint. Love him or hate him, Pedro is a complex symbol of SOB's camp aesthetic.

On the surface, South of the Border's illusive Pedro figure and the souvenir trade at South of the Border both illustrate the commodification of identities that simplify and essentialize the complexities of cultures. Pedro and South of the Border do not represent the "authentic" or the "real," yet the mindset and emotions they represent are legitimate and worthy of analysis. Examining the strange career of Pedro during South of the

Border's rise as a roadside empire reveals how the politics surrounding identity have expanded from the realm of physical occupancy to representation. Alan Schafer's use of Pedro in the context of South of the Border's larger history, culture, and aesthetic is one indication that the postmodern shift from truth and reality to representation and simulation is not only the province of privileged intellectuals, but has been gaining momentum in the provinces all along.

Pedro most obviously embodies the ways in which people in the South can imagine and exoticize Mexico and Mexicans, or simplify various Latino identities into a singular "Mexican" construct. Deborah Wyrick, who edited *Jouvert: A Journal of Postcolonial Studies*, explains the general criticism of Pedro:

> SOB apparently subscribes to a certain pan-exoticism, with "Mexico" covering every region of the world beyond North and South Carolina. When I pumped overpriced gas into my car, it occurred to me that SOB's totalizing material culture may be more than an oversized remnant of the cheerfully tacky Eisenhower era . . . It may also be a symptom of a continuing xenophobia in this part of the United States. . . .[28]

Criticism of Pedro is often tied to its location in the southern region of the United States.

South of the Border's name originally derived from the need to call attention to the geographical location of the business south of the state line, where alcohol could be purchased legally. In the 1950s, as South of the Border's business expanded beyond selling beer, a more extensive Mexican border town theme developed. South of the Border has a carnivalesque built environment full of over-the-top embellishment that pushes beyond the normal bounds of what people expect to see in South Carolina.[29] Pedro also illustrates a more pervasive and long-standing approach to Mexican culture in the United States of America. In the early twentieth century, Mexican culture became popular in the United States, and romantic notions about the exotic nature of "authentic" Mexican culture became quite the vogue. The roadside architecture of the period often used faux-Mexican motifs to represent the "exotic" nature of domestic travel.[30] Similar trends exoticizing Latinos can be found in postwar American popular culture: in the "Latin Lover" personae of actors such as Ricardo Montalban and Cesar Romero, the "Brazilian Bombshell" epitomized by Carmen Miranda, the popularity of Desi Arnaz, and in the cartoon character

Speedy Gonzales. The Pedro character resembles Speedy Gonzales (they came on the scene at around the same time) because his image is cartoon-like; both figures wear similar attire topped off with oversized sombreros, and both speak with an over-played accent.

In 1999, when The Cartoon Network (owned by AOL-Time Warner) pulled Speedy Gonzales off the air to avoid offending its viewers, a back-lash against the removal was led by the League of United Latin American Citizens (LULAC), "the nation's oldest Hispanic-American rights orga-nization." In 2002, LULAC, along with other Latino organizations, suc-cessfully argued that Speedy Gonzales was a positive cultural icon loved throughout Latin America and by Latinos in the United States, and the network returned him to rotation. Rather than viewing Speedy Gonzales as a negative stereotype, some viewers saw him as a clever and capable figure who, like the trickster of African American and Jewish folklore, out-smarts his opponents.[31] Controversial figures, like Speedy Gonzales and South of the Border's Pedro, shed light on the constantly changing import of identity and on the diverse ways to claim agency or to offend others in the seemingly frivolous realm of popular culture.

The use of Pedro and the Mexican theme also expands the context of the geographic term *south* beyond the southern region of the United States of America, complicating the meaning of southern culture.[32] The legal and political complexities of borders—both real and fictive—at SOB challenge the notion of a singular South. These many "Souths" play with travelers' spatial bearings and complicate the notion of any one "authentic South" being a fixed geographic location.[33]

A recent South of the Border brochure features "Pedro's Map," a ren-dering of I-95 beginning in Washington, D.C., and ending in Orlando, Florida—with, of course, South of the Border prominently featured in the middle. The brochure juxtaposes a single small image of a plantation home—a traditional cultural representation of the South—designating Charleston with seven much larger images of Pedro. The plantation home functions as a foil for the carnivalesque landscape of South of the Border. In the largest image on the brochure, Pedro is leaning against a cactus nap-ping, with his sombrero down over his face, and his hands crossed over a large, serape-draped belly—the classic stereotype of the "lazy Mexican." Next to this image are the words, "South of the Border—Where the Real South begins!" This statement mocks the very idea of a "real" South in the context of both the United States and Mexico, while using a familiar ethnic stereotype.[34]

The claim that South of the Border represents anything "real" has drawn criticism from those who take the figure seriously, rather than engaging in the sense of play and humor Schafer claimed motivated his creation of Pedro. "Once, a Mexican embassy guy wrote to a senator from New Mexico saying the embassy was hot, that we gave employers a bad image of Mexicans," Schafer flippantly explained during a 1979 interview. "I told the senator we had 100 good-paying jobs, above the minimum wage, with chances for advancement, and he should send some Mexicans down. I never heard from him again. They lost a chance to give jobs to 100 Mexicans."[35] Here Schafer oversimplified the distinction between representations and actual people, and uses his own wealth and power to deflect criticism of his tourist complex. Schafer's statement exhibits a belief in the American meritocracy, where an individual only needs a "good-paying job, above the minimum wage, with a chance for advancement" to achieve the American dream. Here again we see that, for Schafer, the power of money could erase cultural and racial differences.

Reading South of the Border as a "real" representation of the US South has also drawn criticism. When Maureen Duffin-Ward wrote a piece on the American road trip for the *(Charlotte, North Carolina) News and Observer,* she received a response signed by B. E.: "Even if you had not stated that you were from Philadelphia, I would have known that you are 'not from around here' when you said that South of the Border is the 'real South.' I think anyone from the real South who has been to South of the Border will disagree with your view and just might be kind of offended." B. E. offers an "insiders take" on Schafer's roadside attraction: "South of the Border is just an eyesore and junky place to take the money of Yankees from up North (including Philadelphia) who are speeding back and forth to Florida. I don't think anyone from the real South will stop there more than one time, unless they are loading up on fireworks. I think you need to get out more often and see some more of the real South—it certainly is not South of the Border!"[36] B. E. never does offer suggestions for finding this "real South," stating only that it is decidedly not South of the Border and that people from this "real South" have a penchant for fireworks. While Pedro and South of the Border do not represent the "real South" of either Mexico or the southern United States, they do play with the ways people think about these places or place in general. The idea of the "real" South is as much a myth as Pedro and can be as offensive. Things need not be real or authentic to matter.

Artist and photographer Ruben Ortiz Torres exhibited a photo depicting South of the Border's Sombrero Tower in a 1998 art show in California.

The artist compared the photograph of the Sombrero Tower to one taken in Guatemala. He elaborated, "In Guatemala they do this dance which is called the Dance of the Mexicans, and a Guatemalan guy dresses as a Mexican guy. He wears the same iconography, the big hat, the gun—they've seen Mexican films from the 1930s—so there's the gun, the tequila, whatever." The artist believed the photos and their subjects "convey more information about Guatemala and South Carolina than they do about Mexico." He explained, "So for me, what all this means is that whenever we see any representation—no matter how objective or scientific—it's always telling us more about who's doing it than what's being represented."[37] In *White on Black: Images of Africa and Blacks in Western Popular Culture*, Jan Nederveen Pieterse agrees with Ortiz Torres. Pieterse writes, "Representations of otherness are therefore also indirectly representations of self."[38] According to this logic, South of the Border's built environment speaks most clearly of Alan Schafer's culture and identity, and the perspectives he gained living in the South from his birth in 1915 until his death in 2001. Analyzing the discourse surrounding Pedro's origins offers a better understanding of what this image and the landscape of South of the Border may represent in a larger context.

In Napoli's 1991 video, "South of the Border," Schafer claims that it was customers' questions—"Where's the Mexican that runs this place?"—that inspired the addition of Pedro to South of the Border's Mexican theme. "South of the Border (A Short History)," a 2000 public relations document, provided a different answer to the question of Pedro's origins. In an informal style, the document explains: "Well, Mr. Schafer went to Mexico to establish import connections and met two young men. He helped them get admitted to the United States, and they went to work at the motel office as bellboys for several years. People started calling them Pedro and Pancho, and eventually just Pedro." Schafer's lawyer used the story of the two young men from Mexico at Schafer's 1982 sentencing hearing as evidence of the impresario's magnanimous nature.[39] When I asked Shirley Jones, who has worked at South of the Border since 1965, about Pedro, she affirmed that there was an actual Pedro. "That is true," Jones explained. "He worked over at the motel when I started. We also had this Mexican mariachi band that stayed for several months and played over in the restaurant at night. That was exciting."[40]

At first Schafer only used sombreros and serapes to advertise South of the Border. As the business grew, so too did the mascot. Following World War II, branding became an important aspect of marketing products in an expanding consumer culture. Mascots added personality and friendly, inviting imagery, which was especially important to the business of tourism. While numerous brand mascots evoke a homespun or down-home feel, Schafer wanted to blend the ordinary with "sometheeng deefferent," as an SOB billboard puts it. Schafer created Pedro as an "exotic" good old boy—perhaps made in his own image, but with enough of a twist to still possess an ironic distance. In a way, Pedro is a southern Jewish guy in brown face.

Minstrel performances were still relished in Dillon County in the 1960s, as a 1960 headline on the front page of the *Dillon Herald*, "Lions Club Annual Minstrel Show at 8pm Tonight," corroborates. The show must have generated some complaints, because a scathing and defensive editorial, "Lions Club Annual Minstrel Show Preserved Only Truly American Theatrical Art Form," attacked detractors: "It is a little sad, and a little odd that resentment should smolder, in some quarters, against this form of entertainment. Any such resentment must be based on some kind of complex." The editors pointed out that no one complained about the white ethnic stereotypes that abound, the "rednecks" and "white trash" that some misguidedly claim constitute the last groups that can be mocked and demeaned.[41] The editorial in the *Dillon Herald* concluded, "In the purlieus of Broadway the blackface comedian may be taboo, but there happily are places left where 'Hambone ain't dead.'"[42] Dillon County was obviously one of those places.

There is a tinge of minstrelsy in the content and form of Schafer's narrative in "Pedro Presents South of the Border's Award Weening Billboards," a short Schafer publication containing images of SOB's early billboards.

In 1950, pedro, hitch-hiking down U.S. 301, on his way back to Mexico, got lost. Arriving at a place called Hamer, S.C., almost starving, he stopped at a farm, scrounged some bread and cheese and went back to the road to catch a ride.

A Hungry Yankee saw him, hit the brakes, and offered him $5 for the sandwich. pedro immediately decided that at $5 for a nickel's worth of cheese and a slice of bread, this was the place for him!

So pedro bought a wheel of cheese, 3 loaves of bread, borrowed a tobacco crate, and set up business by the side of the road. Sadly, no one stopped.

Desperate, pedro grabbed a board and wrote on it: sanweech $5. The Yankees still kept whizzing by. A day later, the bread getting stale, pedro changed the sign: sanweech $1. Six or eight people stopped. pedro was in business. Soon, he changed the sign again: sanweech 50 cents. Business Boomed! pedro sent for hees brother, pancho. They added another crate, and wrote two more signs, reading sanweech 10 cents. They were mobbed!

In the Mad Rush, pancho was run over by a New York Cab Driver who had no insurance. pedro decided queek, he better get off the road. Off the road, not so many Yankees pulled in to buy the Sanweech. So, pedro put up more Signs, and More, and More. An' pedro leev happily Ever Seence! Hope you are the same.[43]

This publication offers an absurd revisionist history of South of the Border, changing its origins from a beer store operated by the shrewd, controversial Schafer to a sandwich stand operated by a disarmingly cartoonish Pedro. "Pedroisms"—verbal representations of the sound of Spanish vowels used in English words, with awkward grammatical constructions—appear throughout this "heestory," as well as in other advertisements for South of the Border. Pedro is depicted as the owner and creator of South of the Border throughout the site and in its official publications, including literature welcoming visitors and asking for their opinions of the services on offer. Pedro functions as the public performance of Schafer's alter ego, an outsider and trickster who has exploited "hungry Yankees" for economic gain and empowerment.[44] South of the Border is the archetype of the ad hoc roadside stand. Even with all its modern luxuries, South of the Border is still about highway hucksterism. Pedro is the public symbol of a huge operation, one that operates on the fringes of corporate tourism.

In the beginning, South of the Border "drew unhappiness because it was a peddler of beer; no one cared about it being a peddler of stereotypes."[45] "Pedro's Borderlines" dating from the 1960s show a lack of concern with ethnic stereotyping. A "Borderline" from 1965 announces that "Zee International Club of Dillon High School" came to South of the Border and "enjoyed a real Mexican dinner in the Acapulco Room this past week as part of their study program."[46] A couple from Fort Dodge, Iowa, wrote a letter asking Pedro to send a few copies of the menus "so that we might show our children your wonderful sense of humor."[47] Even Ben Bernanke, chairman of the Federal Reserve under two presidents and a Dillon County native, dressed as Pedro—complete with sombrero and serape—when he worked at South of the Border during the summers while attending Harvard.

Pedro has been interpreted in various and contradictory ways by those writing on South of the Border. In a 1987 article in South Carolina's *State* newspaper, Dan Lackey wrote, "'Pedro will show you to your room,' says the desk clerk in the lobby of Pedro's Motel. I turn, expecting a bona fide Mexican bellboy, but Pedro is any of several distinctly gringo guys in blue knit shirts labeled 'staff.'"[48] In 1990, Lawrence Toppman wrote of a run-in with a number of "Pedros/employees," whom he described as "bicycle-riding male and female bellhops who dress in orange SOB shirts and sombreros associated with the line, 'Badges? We don't got no stinking badges.'"[49] In a 2000 article on South of the Border in the Myrtle Beach newspaper the *Sun News*, Anna Griffin wrote, "Today, South of the Border staff refer to male teen-age youth who work in the motel, many Lumbee Indians from nearby Pembroke, as 'Pedros.'"[50] An online article on the tourist attraction at roadsideamerica.com discusses the usage of "Pedro": "Today, all SOB workers, regardless of race, creed or color, are called pedro [*sic*]."[51] These descriptions of Pedro intensify, confuse, and erase racial difference. Evelyn Hechtkopf, Schafer's sister, described how, because of Pedro and the Mexican border town motif, people often mistook the Lumbee Indians or Jews like herself for Latinos: "People will go up to them [the Lumbee] and think that they're Spanish. They will come up and think we know Spanish. They'll see dark people and think that they speak Spanish. Me, I'm dark. I'm grey-haired but I'm dark."[52] The swirling performance of identity at South of the Border can be confusing—and to some, off putting.

In 1979, Schafer dismissed complaints that came from a variety of sources—ranging from the Mexican embassy to tourists just passing through—that Pedro was "an unfair stereotype of the lazy, crafty Mexican."[53] When accused of ethnic stereotyping, Schafer admitted that he "plays on being Jewish in a small, Southern community," meaning he used his own position as a persecuted minority to deflect criticism.[54] Pedro has appeared on hundreds of Schafer designed billboards from Pennsylvania to Florida. He expands the landscape of South of the Border far beyond its three hundred acres. Rather than outsource the billboards to another business, Schafer created Ace-Hi Advertisements, which designed and produced all of the billboards for Schafer's businesses in-house. These billboards illustrate the changing nature of the Pedro stereotype, which began in the 1980s. *Roadside America* observed in 1986 that Schafer had toned down the "Pedroisms" on the billboards.[55] In a 1997 newspaper article, "Hasta La Vista, Pedro: South of the Border's Politically Incorrect Mascot Gets a Makeover, But Don't Think He's Running Scared," G. D.

Gearino described a shift from the cartoonesque (or minstrelesque) Pedro image to a more subdued silhouette: "Pedro, once shown in his swarthy, mustachioed glory, returned to the almost abstract image he enjoyed on a 1950s-era menu—a design that almost completely hides his face (although, curiously, he still seems to rest a lot)."[56] Schafer may have changed Pedro's appearance, but he was not going to be pressured into abandoning South of the Border's mascot.

Schafer defended his use of the Pedro image as a light-hearted and harmless joke. "We've had complaints for years that our advertising is insulting to the people of Mexico," Schafer admitted. "You get all that politically correct stuff. [People] don't get the joke."[57] In 1994, he boasted, "I stay politically incorrect all the time. Even people who come in bitching and complaining spend money."[58] Schafer interpreted tourist spending as a clear indication that Pedro was not an offensive stereotype—or at least not offensive enough to keep consumers from buying what South of the Border had to sell. The color of money was the deciding factor.

But by the end of the 1990s, Schafer had to admit, "We have to communicate with the present generation. These baby boomers do not have a sense of humor."[59] Political correctness, like bad taste, changes with the times. The shifting nature of what is considered politically correct may explain Schafer's reluctance to accept the criticism from consumers. When he first opened South of the Border, white supremacy and segregation were politically correct in the South. During the final years of Schafer's life (when the criticism of Pedro intensified), Pedro almost completely disappeared from the billboards. The Pedro image was replaced by a simple serape and sombrero on the corner of the billboards, which can be read as a commitment to more sensitive advertising during Schafer's later years (though Pedro returned in full effect in the years following Schafer's death).

The era of the Pedro-less billboards harkened back to the early 1950s advertising style (and billboards), before Pedro fully emerged on the scene. Gearino explains, "South of the Border's notorious and plentiful billboards, which stretch from Florida to New Jersey and are seen by millions of travelers a year, are described many ways: cultural artifact, blight on the landscape, childhood memory or amusing diversion. In the past year, they've earned a new description—politically correct."[60] With the rise in cultural sensitivity (even in the South), and with the number of Latinos in South Carolina more than tripling between 1990 and 2000, perhaps Schafer thought ethnic stereotyping might cut into his profits.[61] This process of erasing the human and leaving the material remnants of culture is similar to American culture's embrace of aspects of Mexican culture—such as food and music—while at the same time rejecting actual Mexicans with anti-immigration rhetoric. "South of the Border, denying there was pressure to alter its billboards, said any change was part of a long-term plan to dress up the business," Gearino surmised. "In other words, one man's toning-down is another man's upgrade." Public Relations Director Susanne Pelt explained that 99 percent of the advertising budget is spent on the billboards, so they must be changed often to keep tourists' attention.[62] Yet the modifications at South of the Border also reflect changing times and the fact that tourism landscapes must appeal to the conscience of consumers as well as to their pocketbooks.

Commercialization of public space is the subject of important civic debate and offers certain challenges to critics and tastemakers.[63] SOB's billboards extend the complex beyond its borders, bringing Pedro's aesthetics into the space of the traveler—even one who does not stop there. The camp aesthetic of South of the Border's billboards and built environment challenges the elitism of culturally appointed taste makers, while also promoting an ethnic stereotype that is neither transgressive nor libratory. Content and style can send contradictory messages. The billboards offered Schafer a space where he could try to convince the public that even if South of the Border was not in line with their taste, it was something to see.

It has been well over a decade since Schafer complained about "baby boomers" lacking a "sense of humor." Jesse Berger and Nate Mallard, who made the 2009 documentary *S. O. B. and the Legend of Alan Schafer* and are in their early twenties, represent a younger generation of South of the Border aficionados. I asked Berger and Mallard why they did not address the criticism of Pedro in their hour-long film. Berger explained:

> We were never interested in South of the Border as a Mexican themed place being racist . . . I don't think Schafer was out to get or slander Mexican people. I never thought that. Especially considering that there were a lot of good things he did for African Americans . . . there is a lot of value to the fact that he's a strong fighting liberal, you know, like Citizen Kane. So, that's what we thought about it. Everyone that we talked to when we were getting ready to start it was like, 'Oh, you should talk about how racist it is.' I feel like that's something that's almost at face value. But the things we were really looking at were the stories and the history of South of the Border.[64]

The young filmmakers did not find the "racist" nature of Pedro important enough to address in their documentary. Berger felt, "Either you think it's racist or it's not."[65]

Berger pointed out that "politically correct white people" were the ones upset about Pedro—more so than Mexican people, in his experience. Nate Mallard saw Pedro as representing the ironic distance and deeper meanings Schafer played with at South of the Border:

> I think that's half the fun. I feel like people at South of the Border understand that everyone feels like—especially people not from South Carolina . . . It's always like a joke. 'Oh, these people are still a little bit backwards. They think that this is funny.' That makes it funny to them [people at S.O.B]. I think South of the Border is a lot wiser to that than you'd imagine. They definitely know the brand that they're selling of this borderline inappropriateness of Pedro.[66]

For many who grew up on the humor of *The Simpsons, South Park, The Daily Show*, and [Dave] *Chappelle's Show*, South of the Border is not that shocking. The younger generation is both savvy about reading between the lines of popular culture, and less experienced with the long history of racism and ethnic stereotyping within southern culture.

At the heart of South of the Border's strange—even absurd— consumer landscape is the riddle of Pedro, an exaggerated cartoon-like representation of a Mexican man in a sombrero and serape. In exploring the strange career of Pedro, I find the import of what he represents still remains ambiguous, precisely because he can represent many things. It is clear that a Jewish liberal used this stereotypical Mexican mascot to sell an amalgamation of different "exotic" representations of identity to whites, blacks, Yankees, and anyone else who happened to be passing through. Schafer was an equal opportunity huckster, who could be easily dismissed. However, his vision, embodied in the successful roadside emporium he constructed, offers important commentary on the fluid nature of identity in a Newer South. South of the Border and the riddle of Pedro present an opportunity for discussing the complex nature of identity and representations in the twenty-first century.

Is Pedro offensive? I leave that to individual readers to decide. Will Pedro one day be history? On a 2008 trip to South of the Border, I observed a new Pedro along Highway 301. He was painted green with white shamrocks adorning his serape. Can Pedro be Irish? Can Pedro be anything?

The strange career of Pedro reflects an uncomfortable dislocation from the stable sense of identity that southern culture has held dear and, at times, defended at the peril of its own society. If properly considered, this uneasy feeling may push people to contemplate the complex clashes of culture and identity written on the tourist landscape.

South of the Border's landscape highlights the complex connections between the local and the global. Pedro proliferates throughout the many gift shops at South of the Border, but he is joined by a vast variety of consumer items from around the world, ranging from the practical to the phantasmagorical. The numerous souvenirs displayed at South of the Border represent the complex cultural and economic relationships between the South and the global souvenir trade. Schafer countered the Mexican Embassy's complaint about the stereotypical nature of Pedro by suggesting the embassy should focus instead on the "$1.5 million in merchandise he imports annually from Mexico."[67] In another interview, Schafer stated that he imported only 10 percent of his merchandise from Mexico, "because I have a tough time getting deliveries on time. So, I buy Mexican imitations in the Orient. Mexican straw hats made in Taiwan, for example; Mexican ceramics made in Hong Kong. I wish I could get it all out of Mexico."[68] Schafer's claim that he was helping Mexico by purchasing cheap souvenirs for his tourist spot is complicated by his purchase of Mexican-themed souvenirs from Taiwan and Hong Kong. The commodities for sale at South of the Border shift with the availability and price of cheap souvenirs from around the world.

When I asked Shirley Jones, who has been in charge of the gift shops at South of the Border for many years, where the business gets most of its souvenirs, she replied: "Well, our t-shirts. We print all of them. We get them from different manufacturers. We do have items from Mexico. We have a lady who lives in California and she goes into Mexico to get our Mexican items and ships them to us."[69] South of the Border's employees are leery of divulging the exact sources of their products, and Jones's explanation is far from precise. But very few of the kinds of cheap plastic items found at South of the Border are produced in the United States. Like the consumers it caters to, South of the Border has global reach.

But this is only part of the story, for Schafer continued to make money from the tensions of the insider-outsider perspective. A sign I encountered in 2008 in Mexico Shop West, the largest souvenir shop within the complex, featured an image of Pedro holding an American flag. The sign explained the origins of the cheap T-shirts found at South of the Border:

"Pedro has the best t-shirt values in America. Our million dollar print and dye plant is 'state of the art' and we buy t-shirts by the truck load direct from local factories." Schafer purchased a bankrupt textile factory, a central symbol of the New South, in order to produce his South of the Border T-shirts at low cost. This maneuver follows Schafer's do-it-yourself philosophy: "Why outsource when I can do it all right here in Dillon County?" Schafer astutely appealed to consumers' patriotism by featuring local American made items alongside souvenirs from "around the world."

In the process of blending the local and the global, South of the Border commodifies cultures and turns identities into dollars. This Mexican themed tourist spot created by a progressive Jewish man in the predominantly conservative and Protestant region of the American South, has memorialized the African American experience since the late-1950s by selling "authentic" souvenirs from Africa. In 1995, Schafer opened Pedro's Africa Shop, another ironically named attraction. A sign at the entrance of Pedro's Africa Shop welcomes visitors with these remarks:

> This shop is dedicated to the millions of Americans whose ancestors came from Africa. We have hundreds of authentic artifacts (mostly made by hand) in present day Africa. And hundreds more to remind you of the joy and sorrows of African-American history in our great country. We hope you enjoy this shop and perhaps take home a souvenir of your visit to Pedro's South of the Border.[70]

Debates on non-western art can provide a context in which to better understand the souvenir trade at South of the Border in general, and specifically Pedro's Africa Shop—especially since the artifacts are described as "authentic" and mostly "made by hand."

Lucy Lippard compares the "increased and justified mistrust" of white art consumers who seek "authentic," "typical," and "exotic" art to the mistrust of tourists. However, she continues, "[O]n the other extreme is that sector of the mainstream that considers all culturally based art debased art, non-art, folk art, crafts, etc."[71] The "connection between fine art and souvenirs" is made in a 2001 art exhibit in New Mexico, "Tourist Icons: Native American Kitsch, Camp, and Fine Art Along Route 66." Joseph Traugott, the show's curator, explains, "This particular exhibit challenges a very popular notion that all of this tourist material is unimportant, trivial, artistically inferior and that anyone who would buy some of this 'stuff' clearly had poor taste."[72] In comparison with the New Mexico exhibit, the

South of the Border souvenirs are tawdrier; they have no specific cultural group as author. The souvenirs at SOB come from everywhere. Nevertheless, the souvenirs at South of the Border still represent an aesthetic vision, one that travelers may or may not "buy." This is one of the reasons South of the Border's consumer landscape is always changing and offers such diverse products. In exploring the social lives of things, it is important to remember, as Nicholas Thomas writes, "[O]bjects are not what they were made to be but what they have become."[73] A close reading of Pedro's Africa Shop is useful in tracing the movement of meaning in South of the Border's consumer landscape.

In 1995, Pedro's Africa Shop, located in the shadow of the tremendous Sombrero Tower, was painted black and yellow, and adorned with American flags. This strange amalgamation of local, national, and global iconography reflects the spatial dislocation a tourist might experience at South of the Border.

In 2000, I found a hand-written note taped to an "authentic" African artifact, labeled "Coloninisation [sic] Figure," in the Africa Shop. The note read, "This carving represents a French colonial figure. When colonialists first came to Africa from Europe many young girls would keep dolls such as this so that their own children might be as prosperous as the new visitors."[74] It is morally suspect to sell supposedly "authentic" African handcrafts without any acknowledgment of the complex history of colonization. Such an act is even more problematic in the South, with its legacy of slavery—especially when suggesting Africans admired European power and when representing colonizers as "new visitors." Additionally, the "authentic" nature ascribed to the imagery and objects in Pedro's Africa Shop stands in sharp contrast to Schafer's claims that the image of Pedro was simply a humorous and playful joke.

Encounters like this one with the African colonization figure at South of the Border emphasize the difficulties of cross-cultural understanding and the problems of commodifying cultures and identities, both tensions inherent in global tourism. Clearly, the tourist trade at South of the Border expands southern culture beyond images of southern belles and plantation homes, but it also commodifies and simplifies other cultures.

In its fourteen years as a freestanding souvenir store (1995–2009), Pedro's Africa Shop most clearly represented Schafer's (sometimes misguided) attempt to appeal to African American consumers in a respectful way. Schafer's political power and business success were tied to the local black community, which makes up almost half the population of Dillon

County. Schafer had close and friendly relationships with local African Americans; however, the Africa Shop still had an uncomfortable and out of place feel within the faux-Mexican border town theme of a tourist complex located in the American South. Potential visitors may have expected to find lawn jockeys and African American stereotypes, such as Mammy and Uncle Mose, in the shop. Instead, the commodities for sale at Pedro's Africa Shop represented an attempt to respectfully (and profitably) present African and African American cultures within a bombastic and gaudy tourist attraction.

By 2008, the Africa Shop's original yellow and black façade had been updated with a fresh paint job that incorporated the black, red, and green colors of the Black Liberation Flag.[75] These colors were incorporated into the flags of many postcolonial, independent African nations and used by the black power movement in the United States. The shop's exterior mingled representations of Africa, the United States, and South Carolina. Zebra and giraffe statues still welcomed visitors. Flying atop the shop were eight American flags and a single South Carolina state flag.

The original 1995 sign dedicating the shop to the "millions of Americans whose ancestors came from Africa" still greeted shoppers. By 2008 there were three main types of objects sold in Pedro's Africa Shop. The first and most prevalent consisted of "authentic" African crafts, including: fertility icons; Chiwaras "good harvest" statues from Mali; rounded, beaded masks from Gabon; Dan Masks from the Ivory Coast; and Nigerian wear. These artifacts were often accompanied with hand written notes explaining their significance. Gone were the colonization figures I found in 2000. The more recent notes attempted to educate the potential consumer about the origins and purposes of the artifacts. For example, the note that accompanied the wise man or woman figures explained: "Age makes a person experienced. An old person is considered wise and his council [sic] is sought. The old people used to settle disputes and look for ways to bring peace among antagonising [sic] factions or people. An old person is also respected by the younger generation in Africa." Despite their spelling issues, these notes attempted to communicate positive information and, in a small way, educate consumers about African culture.

The second type of object for sale in the Africa Shop was the contemporary figurine, including various everyday representations of black people. A series of black men in suits posed with various instruments referencing the important contributions of African Americans to American music. A series of black domestic scenes were reminiscent of the sentimental images of the German Hummel figurines. Representations of black women in fashionable Victorian dresses and black baby dolls were also included. These figurines attempted to present more contemporary images of blackness. And the presence of such commodities showed that, contrary to Schafer's claims, he *did* pay attention to the color of his consumers' skin and not just the color of their money. These objects, placed alongside the African folk art, attempted to present overlapping aspects of African Americans' past and present. The modern figurines avoided the controversial stereotypes often found in black collectables.[76] The only figurine that employed obvious stereotypes was one of the Hummel-style figurines, which depicted a young black boy eating a slice of watermelon.

In 2008, Pedro's Africa Shop attempted to present positive and respectful commodities that the management of SOB thought African Americans would purchase. A special section called "Christian Inspirations" featured black angels, black preachers, and other Christian iconography. There is a certain class distinction between the two types of objects discussed so far: folk arts versus sentimentalized figurines.[77] The African masks and traditional handicrafts appeal to a more discriminating and high-class consumer, as is apparent in both the placement of such decorative African folk art in high-end stores (including chains like Pottery Barn) and in the display of similar artifacts in museums and art galleries. The sentimental figurines featuring contemporary African Americans signify a more popular and pedestrian aesthetic. The presentation of a range of objects seemed designed to appeal to a diversity of consumer tastes and personal preferences, showing that class, as well as race, informs consumer purchases.

Mexican-themed souvenirs, such as Pedro figurines and sombrero ashtrays, constituted a third class of product sold in Pedro's Africa Shop—though these were few in number and dispersed throughout the shop. While there was a separate section for "Christian Inspiration" and an "Elephant Hut," which sold various elephant figurines, most of the items were indiscriminately blended together on the store's shelves and in bins. There were also objects that integrated traditional African folk art with more modern motifs, such as an artifact depicting a black wooden figure with a grass shirt and straw hair riding a motorcycle. This artifact may have been chosen to appeal to the thousands of African American bikers who travel through South of the Border on their way to the annual black motorcycle festival at Atlantic Beach, South Carolina. This integration of a traditional artifact with a motorcycle blurs the distinction between folk and popular culture. Furthermore, this item was displayed between Pedro snow globes and a figurine of a black man wearing a suit and playing a guitar. South of the Border is about conjunction rather than distinction. The culturally clamorous variety of objects was not organized by place or price.

This integration of Africa, Mexico, and the American South was also apparent in the selection of apparel for sale in the shop. There were T-shirts that depicted the continent of Africa or images of African women above the words "South of the Border." The latter shirt was displayed on a white mannequin with deep red lips. The signifiers of place and identity were free floating in these clothing items. The T-shirts referenced the continent of Africa and South of the Border, with the latter's connections to both Mexico and South Carolina. In the shop, these T-shirts, presumably produced at the local plant Schafer purchased, were mixed in with traditional dresses made in Africa. Bins of American flags also signified that while this was the Africa Shop, its patrons were assumed to be proud flag-waving Americans.

To better understand Pedro's Africa Shop, I compared it with my 2008 observations of Mexico Shop West, the largest gift shop at South of the Border. The building, which is at least five times the size of Pedro's Africa Shop, was broken down into four main sections. The main shopping area featured a plethora of general souvenirs, toys, and "exotic" objects, such as Asian figurines, Hawaiian grass skirts and leis, and a small selection of the same African artifacts featured in the Africa Shop. There was a section of Christian-themed items, similar to the ones for sale in Pedro's Africa Shop; however, these items—angels, preachers, and Jesus figures— were now racially integrated. Shoppers could purchase a variety of items, including the random and the strange. In the back of the store The Dirty Old Man Shop (closed in 2010) contained soft-core pornography, sex toys, lingerie, and similar items. While these adult themed items were separated from the rest of the shop's goods, South of the Border also sold some sexually explicit items, such as sexually explicit golf towels, in the general bins in the Mexico Shop. One golf towel was adorned with an image of a cat in a martini glass and the line: "Happiness is a tight pussy."

I found a "Horny Hillbilly" in a bin with tambourines, huge pencils, and other toys and souvenirs. The presence of this figurine, in addition to other items such as "Silly Hillbilly Teeth," demonstrated that South of the Border also sold commodified images of whiteness. However, the whiteness these objects sell is coded with class. The "Horny Hillbilly," which is influenced by region as well as class, is a small rubber rendition of a bearded mountain man inside a box, decorated with the Confederate flag and the words

"The South Will Rise Again." Upon opening the box, the joke becomes clear: The horny hillbilly has an abnormally large, erect penis. Historian Patrick Huber analyzes this specific souvenir and argues that it represents "a primitive white hypermasculinity" that is also found in stereotypes of the post-Reconstruction "black brute." Huber points out that the use of Confederate imagery and Lost Cause verbiage on the box represents a certain "historical amnesia about the mountain South found in regional tourism" because, for the most part, southern Appalachia stayed out of the Civil War or fought with the Union.[78] This displaced Confederate symbolism on the Horny Hillbilly box is the only image of the Confederate flag I found within the entire complex during my trips to South of the Border from the 1990s on. This souvenir actually mocks the idea that the South (as in the Old South/Lost Cause) will rise again, instead of arguing for it.

The days of Confederateland, USA are long gone and while Confederate or Lost Cause iconography is absent from South of the Border's more recent landscape, other flags abound. Atop Pedro's Concrete Bazaar, which is an indoor flea market stocked primarily with lawn ornaments, flags of South Carolina, North Carolina, and Mexico wave in the breeze. American flags fill bins in all the souvenir stores. The South Carolina state flag still flies outside of the motor inn. While the Confederate flag flies on hallowed ground at the statehouse in Columbia, it is now absent from the landscape of entertainment and consumer culture at South of the Border.

Set off from the main emporium of consumer goods in Mexico Shop West is the Little Mexico Shop, which contains an amalgamation of Mexican crafts, clothing items, and more general merchandise, such as the ubiquitous sombrero ashtray. Like Pedro's Africa Shop, this store primarily sells folk art and traditional attire (though evoking Mexico rather than Africa). The final shop in the Mexico Shop West complex, "Hats From Around the World," sells a variety of hats. While some hats, mostly sombreros, evoke foreign places, the shop primarily sells gag hats that are shaped like hot dogs, beer mugs, pink flamingos, and a host of other cartoonish objects. The "around the world" designation refers more to the places across the globe where these items are made than to traditional representations of global folk cultures like those found in Pedro's Africa Shop or the Little Mexico Shop.

When I returned to South of the Border in the summer of 2009, I was surprised to find that Pedro's Africa Shop was gone. The building once painted in the colors of African liberation was red, white, and blue. The giraffes and zebra statues still stood guard outside, but the building had been absorbed by the adjacent fireworks store. Pedro's Africa Shop and all of its wares had been moved across the highway into a new souvenir shop, Pedro's Imports From Around the World. Its large sign included a globe at its center. The word *Pedro's* appeared in small type, leaving room for the large white type spelling out "imports." A yellow ribbon below the globe proclaimed: "from around the world." Below were smaller oval signs: "Africa" in purple, "Asia" in orange, "Mexico" in red, "Europe" in green, and, at the bottom "U.S.A." in blue. Plastic pink flamingos and a palmetto tree stood to the side. Inside, the contents from the old Africa shop, including the original welcome sign from 1995, were jumbled in with various objects "from around the world."

Pedro's Africa Shop, like Confederateland, USA, is now a part of South of the Border's history, rather than part of its landscape. The South of the Border landscape reflects generational shifts in southern culture, as well as shifting patterns of production and consumption. Like southern identity in a Newer South, the souvenir trade at South of the Border incorporates and commodifies a diversity of identities "from around the world." The increase in global trade of cheap souvenirs continues to influence the expansion of South of the Border's line of wares. Times change, consumers change, and the landscape of South of the Border changes, while still retaining its overall camp aesthetic and carnivalesque feel.

In my analysis of camp and kitsch, I argued that the aesthetic statement at South of the Border is camp because it offers an exaggerated and humorous critique of notions of what is tasteful, what is accepted, what is normal. This aesthetic statement derived from Schafer's love for the outlandish, the ornate, and the local. On the other hand, the souvenirs for sale at South of the Border are kitsch because they are mass-produced, sentimental objects, often sanitized and lacking any deeper meaning. While the kitsch status of SOB's vast array of souvenirs is undeniable, the commodities that fill the bins of souvenir shops at South of the Border possess the potential to transcend kitsch and become camp once they are purchased, imbued with meaning, and loved. This process, at least, is the lure of the souvenir.

Schafer's sister, Evelyn Hechtkopf, works in one of the large gift shops at South of the Border, Mexico Shop East. She explained that her brother often changed the items offered at South of the Border, saying that he could read trends in general society and offer consumer items that fit the current mood. He would stock more expensive items at certain times, until he noticed a shift and started to offer more silly stuff. An avid traveler herself, Hechtkopf enjoys talking to the tourists that pass through South of the Border. She told me that people come in and ask for an item they remembered from twenty years ago. While some see the cheap souvenirs as trash, these material objects can carry great significance.

In the summer of 2009, Hechtkopf told me about one especially memorable experience in Mexico Shop East. "One of my favorite stories was a couple years ago," Hechtkopf explained:

> A young girl and she had her boyfriend with her and they were going to University of Rochester. She was having a ball. It was a quiet day. She was buying all these little things and having a wonderful time, laughing. And he was saying to her, "What are you doing?" She said, "I just got to have this thing." She'd buy a key chain or something. She came up to me and she said, "I am just enjoying myself. I don't want to go." He said to her, "Why are you doing this?" She said, "I came here every year with my parents from Florida and we would stop to eat. And my mother was into educational toys, and she wouldn't ever let me buy anything here. And I'm gonna buy everything I can. Because I wanted it and she wouldn't let me have anything that was fun." I love that story. She had a bag full of key chains and Pedros. I wonder if her mother ever found out? She said she was having the time of her life.[79]

Not every purchase of a cheap souvenir at South of the Border transforms kitsch into camp, but there is always the potential for this transformation to take place. For over five decades, the roadside land of neon has united thousands of visitors with something that they love—however strange, silly, or fleeting that something might be.

The souvenirs at South of the Border are mass produced items from around the world. Yet the roadside attraction is a unique, unfranchised entity, which has been located in the same spot for over sixty years. Since the 1970s, the first sight of South Carolina for travelers heading south on 95 was a brightly colored sombrero looming in the distance. The sight of that sombrero, the hundreds of billboards, and the neon wonderland that is South of the Border have come to be recognizable symbols of the "other" Carolina.

South of the Border is a family business, and after Alan Schafer's death in 2001, the business remained in the Schafer family. Schafer's wife Patricia died in 2009. Alan's son Richard Schafer and Richard's son Ryan Schafer, along with other members of the "Schafer family," currently run South of the Border. The South of the Border family also includes many local employees who have worked at the complex for generations. Shirley Jones, who began there in 1965, explained the various roles she has taken on over the years. "When I first started to work here, I was in the original gift shop across the road. I've done a little bit of all of it," Jones explained. "I've worked as a sales clerk. I've worked as secretary. I've worked as a manager. I've worked as a general manager of all the gift shops. We did traveling going to sales, buying. Mr. Schafer, his wife, and I. And now I'm back to managing four shops now." Another loyal South of the Border employee is public relations manager Susanne Pelt, who optimizes South of the Border's hospitality. Pelt has been at South of the Border for over twenty-five years. According to Pelt, Alan Schafer not only employed a diverse work force, he also promoted women to positions of power within South of the Border. Pelt began working at South of the Border in 1984 as a temporary secretary for Richard Schafer, and now is the head of public relations and personnel for the entire complex. She told me that there are few jobs in Dillon County where a woman with a high school education can advance as she has at South of the Border.[80]

In the 1991 Napoli film on South of the Border, an unnamed African American employee describes her life-long relationship with South of the Border:

> I grew up around here. My mom worked here for forty years. So, when we were growing up it was like you worked at South of the Border in the summer. I started out as a bus girl cleaning tables when I was in ninth grade and then moved up to waitressing. I went off to college and came back every summer and worked here. I got a job teaching and came back in the summer and worked here. So, I've been around here all my life practically. It's a real nice place. Nice people.

She explained that anytime she planned to come back, she would just call Mr. Schafer, and he would set up reservations at South of the Border for her and her family. Generations of people from local communities have worked at South of the Border. Jones felt Schafer had such a good relationship with the surrounding community in part because he hired locally: "A lot of the kids worked here, sixteen years old and up during the summer months. Majority of them worked here until they graduated from college."[81] Schafer was generally seen as a fair employer who took care of the people who worked for him.

Like the Sombrero Tower, the employees at South of the Border welcomed tourists to South Carolina. I asked Jesse Berger and Nate Mallard, who made the 2009 documentary on South of the Border, if they thought the roadside attraction represented southern identity. Mallard, who is from Rock Hill, South Carolina, saw the employees as the "welcoming committee for the South." He explained:

> Everyone there is super friendly. Everyone who we talked to, when
> we asked them what their favorite part of South of the Border is . . .
> they always say meeting people and getting to talk to all these differ-
> ent people. So it is, like, strange in the South that they want to meet
> these people. They [tourists] come through and the people [South of
> the Border employees] are like, 'Welcome to our great state.' Because
> everyone in Dillon seems to love Dillon.

Berger, who is from Indianapolis, felt that the only thing that made South of the Border southern was the location and the people: "That's what makes it such a unique place. I mean all the tourist places in South Carolina are historic. They have to do with the Civil War and southern heritage, and South of the Border is just this abnormality out there. And Schafer's decision not to franchise it, but it could have been just as successful anywhere in the United States because it has nothing to do with the South. But anyone driving through will stop there because it is so unique, so weird."[82] Berger's view that southern tourism is about history—and especially about the Civil War—reflects the dominant model of southern tourism, which South of the Border challenges. Or, it could be said that South of the Border adds another layer to what southern tourism can be.

Berger focuses on the fact that South of the Border was never franchised. Schafer received numerous offers to buy or franchise South of the Border, but he was proud that it remained a local business that benefited the local community through its successes. In Schafer's "You Can't Eat Mud!" political ads of the 1960s, he touted South of the Border as a "homegrown industry, with no outside capital." And in 1964, he explained, "Just this January large and profitable holdings in Florida were sold so that the proceeds could be put to work in Dillon County creating jobs and helping the entire local economy." Mark Cottingham, who owned a business in Dillon, said that Schafer "was big on keeping things local" and would try to buy whatever supplies he could from homegrown businesses. Hechtkopf explained: "Many people wanted to get a franchise. He was really Mr. South Carolina. He didn't like to leave. He didn't like to travel. He loved it. He loved his state. He loved giving charity to his state and to the schools."[83]

Schafer also saved a South Carolina icon—Blenheim Ginger Ale—when he bought the local bottling plant and rights in 1993.

Like the Sombrero Tower at South of the Border, Belnheim Ginger Ale is a local icon. In the late-1800s, Dr. C. R. May invented Blenheim Ginger Ale by combining the famed spring water of Blenheim, South Carolina, with Jamaican ginger to make a concoction to address his patients' stomach problems. Patients liked the taste, and the drink became a popular treat served at soda fountains in local pharmacies. In 1903, Dr. May and A. J. Matheson opened the Blenheim Bottling Company to produce the spicy concoction. Fitting in with Schafer's and South of the Border's renegade image, Blenheim's kick is only for the brave. Southern food writer John T. Edge compared the soda's taste to a "slap in the face from a spurned lover." In 1998, William Grimes wrote of the ginger ale, "The first swallow brings on a four-sneeze fit. The second one clears out the sinuses and leaves the tongue and throat throbbing with prickly heat." When Schafer bought the company, he moved soda production to a new bottling facility he built at South of the Border and turned the old bottling plant into a bottlers' museum. He also expanded his soda marketing to a global scale. In the 1980s, the spicy ginger ale was featured on a national broadcast with Charles Kuralt as well as in *Playboy* magazine, but Schafer began a national advertising campaign in high-end publications like the *New Yorker*, which contributed to the soda's cultural cachet as a hip regional soda. Journalist Paul Lukas quieted fears that "kitschy" South of the Border "might cheapen Blenheim's heritage." Lukas explained, "They've [the Schafer family] maintained the brand's gorgeous bottle design and its spicy flavor, which have earned Blenheim a certain highbrow cachet among soda epicures."[84] In postmodern fashion, Schafer blurred the line between high and low culture, as well as those separating local, national, and international markets.

Schafer's purchase of South Carolina's regional soda and the fact that he relocated the bottling plant to South of the Border—where he heavily marketed the soda—shows that he was attempting to turn his empire into a multifaceted regional icon. Schafer's love of the local helped to elevate South of the Border to the status of a South Carolina icon. It also set South of the Border outside the corporate model of tourism development. Blenheim Ginger Ale has the same relation to Coke that South of the Border has to Disney World.

In 1991, Schafer discussed a buyout offer for South of the Border: "We had an offer about a year and a half ago from some Japanese people who wanted to buy it. Wouldn't that be a hell of a combo—Japanese, Mexican,

Confederate, South of the Border. It wouldn't be South of the Border. It'd lose a lot in the translation."[85] Schafer argues that South of the Border would not work without a local (perhaps even a Schafer) at the helm. It is troubling that into the 1990s Schafer used "Confederate" as a substitute for southern. Schafer was an archetype of the insider/outsider perspective on southern identity, but he was also a product of his generation, in which Old South and Confederate rhetoric were firmly embedded, making it was difficult to move fully beyond such defining aspects of southern identity.

Neon sombreros do not traditionally represent South Carolina, but over the years they have come to represent the Palmetto state. The unnamed employee from the documentary, who had worked at South of the Border since ninth grade, was asked in 1991 if she thought Dillon County's premiere tourist destination was weird. She responded:

> To us it's not weird. It's just something that we grew up with. Mr. Schafer's the kind of person that any time he thought something odd would look good at South of the Border, he brought it and it's here. So, it's not weird to us. It's sort of normal. When we walk by and see something, we don't think it's weird. We just think, oh Mr. Schafer found something new . . . It's part of the local scenery.

South of the Border has been part of the local scenery for sixty years, but new generations of southerners are now in control of the discourse surrounding the roadside tourist attraction. The "Pedroisms" of the past are replaced by a new digital presence.

In 2009, after Alan Schafer's grandson Ryan became directly involved with the management of South of the Border, promotion of the complex entered the digital era. Inkhaus, a "boutique website and graphic design studio" located in Myrtle Beach, South Carolina, designed South of the Border's first serious web presence, which can be viewed at http://www.thesouthoftheborder.com/.[86] Inkhaus claims, "We're inspired by imagination and innovation, combining creativity with technology to deliver high impact materials through various networks and media outlets."[87] Inkhaus focuses heavily on delivering a high quality product to its customers. The web designers claim to have used the South of the Border's aesthetic and "campy, fun atmosphere" as inspiration for the new website's festive design, claiming their goal was to give "visitors to the site a sense of the *vibe* of the venue—colorful, fun and hospitable to all."[88] The new (in 2009) South of the Border website is impressive, featuring high quality graphics, a regularly updated blog, historical images, and documents about South of the Border and the Schafer family. The "Links of Interest" on the South of the Border homepage lead to a site for Ryan Schafer's Border Motorsports, "a full-service car audio/video and bolt-on performance products salon located in Dillon, South Carolina." Ryan Schafer grew up racing motorcycles and is a NSPL (National Sound Pressure League) world champion.[89]

Inkhaus also brought the same media savvy to the Blenheim Ginger Ale website. Both South of the Border and Blenheim have well-maintained Facebook pages, Twitter accounts, and images posted on Flickr. As the third generation of the Schafer family takes the helm at South of the Border, the landscape expands into the digital realm, where it continues to be refashioned and, through social networking sites, further connected to today's consumers—especially the media savvy youth demographic. Yet a sense of the past and continuity with it can be found in historical pages on both the web and social networking sites—as well as in the built environment of South of the Border. The spirit of Alan Schafer remains.

Today you need not actually travel the road to South of the Border to enter its landscape. South of the Border's landscape expands through the digital refashioning of blogs and tweets as it moves further into the Newer South. From the influence of the next generation of Schafers on the marketing of South of the Border, to the film by Berger and Mallard, to the art of Rubin Ortiz Torres, to the numerous YouTube videos devoted to South of the Border road trips, and photos or travel narratives posted online, South of the Border continues to change while staying grounded in the same spot along the roadside in rural Dillon County. If you visit South of the Border, walk into the Sombrero Room and take a look around. That is where it all started—the original spot where the cinderblock beer depot stood in 1949. It was never torn down; it was just expanded. Like identity in the Newer South, South of the Border has grown to facilitate all those people buzzing by and passing through.

PLACE TWO

ATLANTIC BEACH

Chapter Four

SOUTH CAROLINA'S BLACK PEARL

Unity and Desegregation's Diaspora at Atlantic Beach, 1934–2009

Like the Sombrero Tower that rises in the distance as travelers approach South of the Border, towers loom in the distance outside the borders of Atlantic Beach, South Carolina. These towers embody the power of the booming tourism industry along the Grand Strand. The shadows of the high-rise resorts evoke a degree of trepidation in many of the town's residents and business owners—especially those who remember the golden era when Atlantic Beach was *the* spot for black leisure culture along the South Carolina coast. Atlantic Beach business owner Thaxton Dixon discussed the high-rises that bookend the town: "I told one of the city councilmen, you all keep on and don't start building something, it'll be 12 o'clock before we see the sun shine. All them tall buildings over there, we won't be able to see the sun shine till 12 o'clock."[1] Such anxiety derives from the fact that those towers of corporate tourism development threaten to overshadow the rich heritage and cultural traditions of the Black Pearl of the Grand Strand region.

Atlantic Beach is an example of the ways African Americans in the South persevered and built physical as well as psychological communities during the era of segregation. Atlantic Beach as it is today testifies to the resulting challenges of maintaining that sense of place and community even as desegregation offered wider access and mobility.[2] The Black Pearl is also characterized by what the *New York Times* in 1994 described as a "striking undercurrent of nostalgia among many blacks for the small black business, the black community school, the unified black community with lawyers and gravediggers living side by side that was lost when the South was forced to integrate."[3] Atlantic Beach is one of the last surviving beachfront communities on the East Coast with a sustained history of black ownership and self-governance dating from its inception. The town is a small parcel of land just under one hundred acres, situated in the larger Grand Strand region, which spans more than sixty coastal miles. As the

Grand Strand developed as a tourist destination for whites, Atlantic Beach began to develop its own distinct identity within the larger tourist economy. Atlantic Beach's ability to exist in the midst of a white vacation area and record only one incident of harassment (by the Ku Klux Klan in 1950) during the turbulent decades of the 1950s and 1960s makes it an important place to study.[4] Recovering the town's past (the Atlantic Beach Historical Society began this process in 2001) is an act of collective memory essential to the future of Atlantic Beach and significant to the identity of the tourism industry in South Carolina.[5]

Even as Ryan Schafer soups up cars at Border Motorsports, young people flood the Atlantic Beach area every May on souped-up Japanese speed bikes and add another layer to the landscape of the tourist town. The emerging ethos of Atlantic Beach, including the young motorcycle enthusiasts, is a continuation of the historical traditions of African American leisure. The same insider/outsider perspective that inhabits a neon tourist empire set in the midst of a rural county, characterizes Atlantic Beach, a place with its own cultural agency and distinct identity set within the context of the larger built environment of the Grand Strand.

Black-owned since 1934, when businessman George W. Tyson (1890–1967) purchased the land, Atlantic Beach was designed to be a "haven for blacks" on the Grand Strand.[6] The circumstances of the sale contradict a local rumor that a white farmer by the name of Spivey gave Tyson the land to develop a place for black servants, because Spivey's maids hung around on their days off annoying the white family with their loud and unruly behavior.[7] This myth reflects a philosophy of white supremacy and paternalism and reinforces a stereotype of uncouth and uncivilized African American workers. As Mark M. Smith writes in *How Race is Made: Slavery, Segregation, and the Senses*, the "soundscape sculpted southern race relation" and "whites frequently heard blackness as emotional and bruisingly loud."[8] Yet the actual business transaction, in contrast to the story of "loud and unruly behavior," shows that Tyson saw the potential in black land ownership and the need for a black resort on the Grand Strand.

Atlantic Beach started small. Earlene Woods, who was born in Horry County and owned businesses in Atlantic Beach from the 1950s into the twenty-first century, was interviewed in 2002 as part of the Atlantic Beach Oral History Project. She recalled coming to Atlantic Beach with her grandfather by wagon, before the Intracoastal Waterway cut off inland communities' direct routes to the sea. She remembers:

We came over to do our fishing and whatever on those oxen carts. At that time, there wasn't any light at all. So we had little candles and little lanterns on posts sticking up near the end of the road so people would know where to turn. Lanterns sticking all in the buildings, that's what I remember. I was a little girl then, this was in the 1930s before they had hotels here. We also had an Army Camp. Whites were on 37th Avenue, Blacks were on what is now 31st Avenue (then know as Carolina Avenue) . . . That hill where they had to dig out to make the camp, the dirt is still there. I remember well. The hotels came in the forties and fifties.[9]

During World War II, Atlantic Beach served as home for black soldiers who were commissioned to build the Myrtle Beach Air Force Base. In the postwar period, Atlantic Beach began to develop as a modern tourist destination, with motels, restaurants, amusement parks, and patios where men and women danced the night away.

Tyson could not handle the land venture on his own, and the Atlantic Beach Company, a group of black professionals, took up his mortgage in March of 1943 and continued to develop the area and sell small (50 x 150 feet) individual lots. The Atlantic Beach Company was composed of prominent African Americans from the Carolinas—doctors, lawyers, and educators—with the president of Fayetteville State University (in North Carolina), James Ward Seabrook, Ph.D. (1886–1974), at the helm. In a 1995 interview for the Horry County Oral History Project, Dr. Leroy Upperman (1913–96), the last surviving member of the Atlantic Beach Company and a prominent physician in Wilmington, North Carolina, explained that the "general philosophy" of the Atlantic Beach Company was "to take the land and develop it and make it into a first-class beach, rather than a haphazard thing."[10] A thriving recreational beach for all African Americans completely controlled by wealthy blacks was quite an accomplishment along the Grand Strand of 1940s South Carolina.

Upperman pointed out that it was "not out of altruism, but as a business venture" that the company sought to develop Atlantic Beach for African Americans. William P. Johnson, Sr., who was born in 1910 and lived in Atlantic Beach beginning in the 1940s, felt that it "wasn't just about money."[11] Michael Kelly, son of the late Dr. Peter Kelly, who was the treasurer of the company, agreed that it was a business venture, but one that possessed a "spiritual vision." Kelly explained, "These men saved the land so that Negroes would have a beach to go to. They went through the struggle because they bought the land with money out of their pockets. They had no help from banks or governments."[12] Kelly added, "They maintained the beach for the general black public and never restricted it to land owners. And the underlying reason for this was so African-Americans could have a place of their own."[13] Atlantic Beach is a symbol of local independent ownership and possesses an independent entrepreneurial spirit. The heyday of the Black Pearl, which gave the small area its lasting sense of place and pride, began during the years of the Atlantic Beach Company (1943–56) and lasted well into the 1960s.[14]

Upperman felt that Atlantic Beach was meant to be a haven for *all* African Americans. "So his [Tyson's] idea was to develop a black beach which would serve the needs of black people. This meant not only the domestics, but they wanted places where school teachers or others could come to the beach and have a home and enjoy the beach in that way."[15] Thursday was "Maid's Day" at Atlantic Beach, and employees would get off early for the festivities. Journalist William Moredock recalled:

> When my family vacationed here [Myrtle Beach] in 1959, our mother talked our maid into coming along, promising her a day in Atlantic Beach. Taking her there and picking her up on that July day was an adventure and—for my mother—a thoroughly unnerving experience. Driving through the little town, we were completely cut off from "our" world, completely surrounded by "the other." We had never seen so many black people—hundreds of them on the streets, in the hotels, a thousand or more on the little beachfront. Everywhere, music poured from clubs and houses as people danced and celebrated.[16]

Carrie Rucker explained, "We didn't celebrate the Fourth of July. We celebrated the sixth of July because Blacks had to work for White people (on that day). We celebrated the sixth of July because that was the day we had off. That was Black people's holiday because of the lack of recreational beaches open to African Americans."[17]

Atlantic Beach welcomed a diverse mixture of African Americans; however, as the local tourism industry began to thrive in the 1950s, the surrounding white community sought to contain black leisure culture within small pockets. The public beach along the Grand Strand was primarily a whites only landscape. Black women could only use the beach when taking care of white children. Ocean Boulevard in Myrtle Beach, the primary

Beach Scene at Atlantic Beach, SC, circa 1945. Courtesy of the South Caroliniana Library, University of South Carolina, Columbia.

location of shops and amusements along the coast, also barred African Americans.[18] Along the Grand Strand, racial barriers were physical as well as social. Ocean Boulevard was built so as to stop abruptly at the Atlantic Beach border and begin again on the other side of the town, and fences and brush separated the boundaries of the black community from the surrounding white beaches. These were political boundaries constructed from outside in the white communities rather than social boundaries created from inside Atlantic Beach.[19] Even the natural landscape was segregated when white property owners ran ropes into the ocean and placed "whites only" signs on the beach. This barrier was referred to as "The Colored Wall."

Russell Skeeters clarified, "It wasn't really a wall, it was a fence which was put on the south end and the north end of Atlantic Beach." He explained the origins of the fence: "It was put there in segregation times to keep the Blacks from entering into North Myrtle Beach, which was then Windy Hill and Crescent Beach. In fact, I can remember when they had signs on the oceanfront stating, 'This is the end of Atlantic Beach, Colored cannot go beyond this sign' on both ends." Alice Graham laughed as she contemplated the absurdity, "I cannot understand how they thought if we were in water confined to one spot that they wouldn't be contaminated by our blackness just because they put up a rope. It's water and it's flowing.

It makes no sense." When asked about "The Colored Wall," Carrie Rucker defiantly stated, "It didn't make me no never mind at the time." She also explained Atlantic Beach's relations with the surrounding white community: "We got along fine. They ran their businesses and we ran ours." Earlene Woods elaborated:

> Blacks knew where to go. There was so much going on in other areas, lynching and all that, so people were very careful. If they said, "don't cross that line," we didn't cross it. So the only contact we had with them was the business they had with us. The milk truck, any kind of food we needed. Bread trucks, we didn't have to go to the store. They were nice to us, "yes ma'am" this and "grandma," "auntie" that. We ate it up.[20]

The ropes and the road set up physical barriers symbolic of separation; however, Atlantic Beach flourished within the larger Grand Strand tourism economy.

Earlene Woods described the attraction of Atlantic Beach: "Anyone in North Carolina, Virginia, all over the states was here in Atlantic Beach because they were free to do what they wanted to do and eat where they pleased and be served by waitresses and treated like human beings."[21] A merchant during the golden era, Willie L. Isom, explained, "We had all the places wide open. Quite naturally our people couldn't go anywhere but right here, so you can imagine how clustered Atlantic Beach was at the time. People would dance in the street and you can see the dust flying."[22] Stanley Coleman recalled how white people would bring their cooks to the beach with them: "They had a separate room in their garage for the cooks. But at night . . . Atlantic Beach was in order and sometime their boyfriends from Atlantic Beach would come get them and take them up to Atlantic Beach and then bring them back when it was over that night."[23] Atlantic Beach was a safe and open place for blacks during its heyday. "You could come relax, come in, the ocean, the dunes were there, you could get a blanket and sleep all night," Earlene Woods explained. "You didn't need to rent a room, and the rooms were filled. Every little corner was someplace to sleep." Carrie Rucker echoes this sentiment: "These places used to stay open all night long. You could sleep on the beach and get up and start dancing."[24] Atlantic Beach provided a space that was outside the culture of white supremacy—and apart from whites in general. Early business owner Leugenia Walker Marshall explained, "Peoples passed, pullin'

Atlantic Beach's "famous beachfront hotel," circa 1940. Courtesy of the Avery Research Center for African American History and Culture, Charleston, South Carolina.

in here. No you can't stop here, this is a black beach, for black people. 'We seed the sign.' Wasn't no signs, wasn't no whites. Didn't need that. We just havin' a big time."[25] Atlantic Beach represents what George Lipsitz refers to as the "Black spatial imagery" in *How Racism Takes Place*. He describes the "ways in which Black people turned segregation into congregation during the Jim Crow era."[26]

Important early businesses at Atlantic Beach, like the Cotton Club, had bar piccolos (jukeboxes), as well as space for live music and, of course, dancing. Patios with partially exposed dance floors for dancing in the ocean breeze were common structures at Atlantic Beach.[27] In her discussion of the Cotton Club, Earlene Woods recalled, "They had a cement floor out there and let me tell you, that cement floor ate up many soles of shoes."[28] Other prominent patio clubs include The Patio, Punk's Patio (owned by "Punk" Daniels), Mr. Millard Rucker's Patio and Baby Grand Club, Delton Gore's Patio, and the Big Apple. Many of the early clubs had rooms for rent upstairs, but there were also numerous hotels in Atlantic Beach, with Hotel Gordon, owned by Dr. Robert Keith Gordon, the vice president and treasurer of the Atlantic Beach Company, the most elaborate and high end. Upperman remembered the Hotel Gordon, owned by his friend and colleague: "That was the only decent motel or business there— when I say decent, the others would be second and third and fourth rate compared to that."[29] Most oral histories mention the Hotel Gordon, and a post card from the period shows the impressive white art deco structure, lined with balconies, standing three stories high and perched on the edge of the beach. The copy on the postcard advertises the amenities, which were quite extensive for the time period.[30] The more modest Hotel Marshall was very popular and sturdy, surviving numerous hurricanes and serving as a makeshift church until an official one was completed in 1947.[31] In 1960, Mable Daniels Powell, "the first black female entrepreneur on the Grand Stand," built and ran the Holiday Motel, with forty-six rooms, ocean front balconies, and a dining room that sat fifty people.[32] There were numerous sandwich stands, such as Etrulia and Albert Dozier's Rabbit Box, and snacks and souvenirs were sold at temporary stands or on the street, sometimes by children.

Atlantic Beach was an independent and self-sustaining community, as well as a tourist destination for African Americans. "We had whatever we needed here," explained Earlene Woods. She elaborated:

We had a credit union, a funeral home that Mr. Rucker had. We had bathhouses all along when the water came. When the water came we finally has shower houses. Any kind of business you could think of. It was beautiful. It hurts to think of what was and what is no more. We had two filling stations, the Gores had one and Dr. Kelly had one. Mrs. Lula Webber had a liquor store and all kinds of food. In those days they called it the Beach Club where Black entertainers performed.[33]

Charles Williams grew up in Walterboro, an inland town in the Lowcountry, and remembered numerous "undeveloped spits of sand where blacks could enter the ocean" during the period of segregation. But Atlantic Beach was on another level; it was a recreational tourist destination. "You came to Atlantic Beach because it had all this stuff [Ferris wheels, merry-go-rounds, hotels, restaurants, bathhouses]. Black beaches in the lower part of the state didn't even have picnic tables. You had to travel with a potty and your own roll of toilet paper. You came to Atlantic Beach, you didn't have to do that."[34] Alice Graham, who with her husband owned numerous snack stands during the 1960s, immediately loved Atlantic Beach. "The first time I visited Atlantic Beach, I knew I had found home," Graham felt. "I had never seen that many Black people in one place. I knew I was home at last. I didn't know how or where or when, but I knew I was going to live here among these people."[35] Even after tourist season ended, things were going on at Atlantic Beach. The October fish fry brought the community and visitors together to fish, eat, and socialize. Seine fishing—using large nets to catch many fish at once—was an important communal activity.

The Atlantic Beach community weathered good and bad times throughout its heyday. In 1954, Hurricane Hazel, which destroyed much of the built environment along the Grand Strand, proved a major setback to the fledgling leisure industry. In Atlantic Beach, the illustrious Hotel Gordon and other key business were destroyed by the storm. Most people did not have insurance, which was common during this period. Earlene Woods lost the business her husband, a brick mason, had built by hand. "When the hurricane came and washed everything away, that was because if you didn't have any insurance and didn't save any money, what you going to do?" asked Woods. "All you could do is pay your taxes and try to keep the dirt, so that's what we did."[36] Like the rest of the Grand Strand, Atlantic Beach eventually recovered from the devastating hurricane, in large part because of the resiliency of its property owners and the continued influx of tourist dollars. Etrulia Dozier discussed the positive side of the destruction: "Before Hurricane Hazel, it wasn't the best situation with the buildings. When Hurricane Hazel came through, she just wiped out the beach as such. I noticed that during the replacement, there are some buildings now at Atlantic Beach that are a great improvement over earlier years."[37]

The halcyon years at Atlantic Beach coincided with the emergence of rhythm n' blues, rock n' roll, and beach music. These new musical genres were cultural expressions that possessed the potential to transcend social and physical barriers like the ones containing Atlantic Beach. Atlantic Beach hosted black entertainers such as Ray Charles (who wrote about Atlantic Beach in his autobiography), Bo Didley, B. B. King, Little Richard, James Brown, Martha and the Vandellas, Chubby Checker, Count Basie, Billie Holiday, the Tams, and the Drifters. These artists performed in but could not stay in the whites-only hotels of neighboring oceanfront communities.[38] Earlene Woods saw the entertainers as valued guests. "It didn't make any difference [that Atlantic Beach was the only option for Black entertainers], they were glad to get off and come here and entertain us for free," Woods professed. "Every night, every weekend . . . We knew they were going to come. We would feed them and they would stay here all night. . . . It's something to remember and I thank God for the portion that I remember."[39] Billy Scott, an R&B Hall of Fame member and founder of the Carolina Beach Music Awards Show, recalled being told about Atlantic Beach when his band could not find a place to stay on the Grand Strand:

"Then we would get there [Atlantic Beach] and get the red carpet treatment. We were home. The Skeeters, Earlene Woods, The Gores—all of
them, would just open the doors, no matter how late at night. Give us
clean sheets, towels, food."[40]

Beach music has deep roots in South Carolina, and the shag, a dance
accompanying beach music, is the official state dance. While the shag
has roots in African American culture, as is often the case in American popular music, whites have appropriated both the dance and beach
music. Today, the Ocean Drive section of North Myrtle Beach is full of
commercialized nostalgia for South Carolina's state dance. Middle-aged
white southerners still frequent Fat Harold's Beach Club, Duck's, or the
OD Pavilion Social and Shag Club to dance and to buy beach music or
memorabilia. *Shag: The Movie* (1989, directed by Zelda Barron) tells the
story of four white southern women who take a trip to Myrtle Beach following their 1963 high school graduation. The first image of the film is a
full screen shot of the word "Shag" filled in with the Confederate flag, and
the only black people who appear in the film are the musicians who play
during the dance sequences. Because the built environment of Atlantic
Beach had changed so little since the 1960s, the final scene of *Shag* was
filmed at the Atlantic Beach Pavilion, "one of the last of the old style pavil-
ions." Unfortunately, Atlantic Beach's pavilion burned down a few years
after being used in the film.[41]

Leisure culture was strictly segregated during the rise of beach music
on the Grand Strand, but the curiosity of a younger generation of southerners cued many to cross the racial lines to listen to music and dance.
Russell Skeeters (born 1940), who is a part of a later generation of Atlantic
Beach business owners, remembers when the color line finally began to
bend: "When we had Bo Diddley, James Brown, and Hank Ballard and the
Midnighters . . . when these entertainers performed on Myrtle Beach, the
White girls would come here to see them. They didn't care about segregation. I had an integrated business down here on Highway 17, called the Salt
and Pepper Club, and I had more White clientele than Blacks."[42] Yet, the
potential for racial integration through music and other forms of leisure
culture was often squandered, as Jim Crow segregation set up barriers to
interracial interaction during the 1950s.[43]

During the summer of 1945, as World War II came to an end, "the lure
of black music began to take hold among white dancers" in South Carolina. White teenagers who wanted to listen and dance to the new music
crossed the color line to visit Charlie's Place in Myrtle Beach. One of those

white teenagers, Harry Driver, claimed, "We had integration twenty-five years before Martin Luther King, Jr. came on the scene. We were totally integrated because the blacks and the whites had nothing in our minds that made us think we were different. We loved music, we loved dancing, and that was the common bond between us." However, that "common bond" was a serious social taboo, and the local whites in power—mostly from an earlier generation—saw it as a threat.[44]

Hostility towards integrated socialization was illustrated by an attack during the summer of 1950 on Whispering Pines nightclub, also called Charlie's Place, after the owner Charlie Fitzgerald, a prosperous black businessman.[45] Located just inland and a few miles south of Atlantic Beach in the predominantly black district of Myrtle Beach often referred to as "the Hill," Charlie's Place was a club that featured big rhythm and blues artists of the 1940s and 1950s.

The 1948 Supreme Court decision that gave African Americans the right to vote in South Carolina's primaries (it was the catalyst for Alan Schafer's involvement in Dillon County politics) drew out the staunch segregationists in Horry County, as it did in neighboring Dillon County. The Ku Klux Klan experienced a revival in the area and, during the summer of 1950, took notice of Charlie's Place. On Saturday, August 26, 1950, the Klan organized a police-escorted motorcade of over twenty cars that paraded through Myrtle Beach's main drag and then drove by Charlie's Whispering Pines nightclub. In addition to providing a space for interracial dancing, Fitzgerald evoked the ire of local whites because he owned numerous successful businesses in the area—including a motel, a barbershop, a beauty shop, and a cab company. Moreover, he and his wife Sarah were among the few African Americans in Myrtle Beach who registered to vote in 1948, when the South Carolina primaries were legally opened to all races.[46] Later that evening, the Klan returned to Charlie's Place, and Fitzgerald was forced into the trunk of a car while the Klan shot up his club and beat numerous patrons. Fitzgerald was kidnapped, beaten, stabbed, and left for dead with both of his ears severed.[47]

In a strange turn of events, even with hundreds of shots fired into Fitzgerald's club, the only individual killed at Charlie's Place that night was James D. Johnston, a Klan member, who was shot in the back during the commotion. Johnston was discovered to be wearing a police uniform beneath his Klan robe. Johnston, an officer from neighboring Conway, had recently been elected as a local magistrate. It appeared that another Klan member may have accidentally shot Johnston, but no one was sure.

No one was charged with Johnston's shooting, the attack on the club, or that on Fitzgerald. And yet, Myrtle Beach Sheriff C. Ernest Sasser arrested Fitzgerald and took him out of town to a jail in Columbia, South Carolina. Sheriff Sasser was seen as a fair-minded friend to the black community, and it is possible he took Fitzgerald out of town to protect him from the Klan. The violent attack on the club and its successful owner deterred interracial cavorting on the Grand Strand, and another potential revolution was lost.[48]

The Klan also paraded through Atlantic Beach on the same day as the attack. There was no violence; however, Emma Lee Vereen recalled, "Atlantic Beach men were armed and ready to defend themselves."[49] Atlantic Beach residents called police officers to their town the following day, and the local paper reported that a "contingent of merchants met with the sheriff and other law enforcement officers." The paper reported the merchants' response to the Klan activity:

> It is our desire and wish to give you our full cooperation in preserving law and order at this beach. There are about 10,000 colored people here now and you don't see not even one drunk or disorderly. We feel like we have better order than the white beaches. We don't feel like the Klan has the right to move in on us by parading . . . We are 100 percent southern Negroes and we have our own beach and in Conway, Myrtle Beach and other places, we try to live separately, not having any desire to mix churches, schools, or anything else. We only have ninety days to make and pay our rent here but with the Klan coming [we might] just as well fold up. When you visit the white beaches, you don't see any colored unless they are employed.[50]

This sly public statement by Atlantic Beach merchants faced with violence and intimidation from the Klan illustrates the skills needed to sustain black leisure space in the South. The "slightest semblance of unruliness" could saddle black leisure space with an unappealing reputation and sharply decrease profits.[51] The economic argument that local merchants had a mere ninety days to lure visitors and sustain their businesses appealed to the business sense of local whites who found themselves in the same situation. Atlantic Beach merchants skillfully presented racial violence and intimidation as being bad for business—for themselves and for the larger Grand Strand tourist economy. The black delegation showed it knew how to navigate the black codes enforced by white southern society when it characterized the ten thousand African Americans present at Atlantic Beach as "southern Negroes." It was the Klan that broke the code of segregation by entering the Atlantic Beach community, and it was Atlantic Beach merchants who restored order. The success of Atlantic Beach, coupled with cracks in the façade of southern white supremacy made by national legislation, threatened individuals invested in white supremacy and white control over black space.

Sheriff Sasser vowed to end further Klan harassment on the Grand Strand and publicly condemned the violence and intimidation. The paper reported after the incident: "Many colored waitresses and maids, fearful of a return visit of the Klan, left town Sunday and Monday, and this week a number of hotel operators have reported they were without domestic help of any kind."[52] Though framed as a sign of fear, the actions of the domestics can also be read as a form of protest that, like Schafer's two-dollar-bill campaign in 1948, showed the economic importance of their work to the larger economy. Henry Driver reported that he could not return to Charlie's Place to dance. "They would hate me because I was white even though I had nothing to do with it," he felt.[53] In 1951, a year after the attack at Charlie's Place, Thaxton Dixon (who later owned cottages and a motel at Atlantic Beach) first visited the area and stayed at Fitzgerald's hotel on "the Hill" in Myrtle Beach. He recalled the tensions that still lingered. "[S]omebody came out there and hollered, 'Fitzgerald's back in town. Ku Klux Klan will be back here tonight.'" Dixon remembered, "My wife sat on her suitcase all night long. Wouldn't even go to sleep. I 'member that just as good as it were yesterday. But I went on to sleep cause I was on vacation. Had me a couple of beers and says ain't no need in me worrying about it."[54]

The segregated landscape of leisure on the Grand Strand was reunified through violent means. Perhaps buoyed by the success of their own leisure and commerce activities, merchants in Atlantic Beach and black workers in the white tourism industry made their voices heard, both by standing their ground in Atlantic Beach and by leaving Myrtle Beach. The Ku Klux Klan's intimidation demonstrates that Atlantic Beach's role as a "haven for blacks" was necessary and yet tenuous. African Americans could enjoy the beach and entertainment on the Grand Strand, but they could do so only in segregated locations.

The power of land ownership and the unity of the community are recurrent themes during Atlantic Beach's golden era. When asked about the future of Atlantic Beach in 2002, Etrulia Pressley Dozier eloquently expressed the economic and social importance of black land ownership:

I hope that we have developed ourselves by realizing how important property ownership is, and what great lengths some of the former people who have owned property there have gone to create a place that is interesting to go and also educational and all of the good words that you would find descriptive of a town. Atlantic Beach is one of a kind, and when you think of how much you lose when you lose your heritage and you lose ownership of a place that has meant so much to so many people through the years . . . I hope we will all be forgiven for all those things that we didn't know to do. But with the people who are still at Atlantic Beach taking a great interest, I hope that their minds would focus in on the heritage and the legacy of a small, but interesting and a very precious piece of the history of Black folks who have lived in this area, who have owned property in Atlantic Beach.[55]

Thaxton Dixon, who, beginning in the 1960s, operated numerous cottages and a motel in Atlantic Beach, had difficulty getting a loan to buy his motel: "But this man [a banker in Myrtle Beach] that told me he had the money but didn't have it for you all's beach." Dixon explained these racist economic practices came from "one of the biggest banks in South Carolina." He eventually did receive a loan from the Small Business Administration (SBA) in Columbia, South Carolina, and ran a successful business with his wife Ernestine, who managed the motel on weekends. "And then we had a code if I made a thousand dollars, I would tell her . . . what was the word I used? I made a ball, I made a ball today. I hit a ball or something. I made a thousand. Then I'd call her again and say Ernestine I hit another ball today. And she'd know what I meant you know . . . a thousand dollars."[56] Atlantic Beach was both a social and an economic success.

Property ownership, achieved despite economic injustice and racial segregation, created an important sense of unity for the Atlantic Beach community. Janie Islom stated, "Whenever we needed anything or needed to do anything, we all joined together and worked together." Commenting on the influential individuals who peopled Atlantic Beach in early days, Earlene Woods said, "One thing, they were together. When one was in trouble, all were in trouble. We got together and bailed each other out. There was unity. You see that town hall? We built that together in unity. We in unity built the fire and police department. The cars weren't new, but we still had them. That unity is still in my heart." Russell Skeeters felt that unity was at the heart of Atlantic Beach's heyday: "Before integration Atlantic Beach was together. We had our town hall, police department, volunteer fire department, garbage collecting, etc. All these people did these things without grants. These people were the backbone of Atlantic Beach. They did not wait for a handout from the Federal Government. When they needed money, they held events to raise it."[57]

Having weathered the Klan in 1950 and a major hurricane in 1954, Atlantic Beach grew into a strong and resilient community. In 1966, Atlantic Beach was incorporated as a municipality of Horry County. This designation meant that the town's government now had the ability to control development, and could maintain its autonomy apart from the predominantly white beach communities in the area. Just two years later, in 1968, when the surrounding towns of Cherry Grove, Crescent Beach, Windy Hill, and Ocean Drive consolidated into North Myrtle Beach, Atlantic Beach opted to maintain its independence as a small black beach under black control.

As desegregation accelerated in South Carolina during the 1970s, Atlantic Beach, like other black communities and businesses, experienced an economic downturn. The town's now defunct website explained:

In the 1970s desegregation would offer new opportunities for Black tourists, vacationers and businesses. It was positive times for Black folks. They could now experience some of the freedoms they had never experienced before. They began to explore other beaches along the southeast coast. This, coupled with merchants unprepared to trade in a free market economy would have devastating effects on the Black Pearl.[58]

Neither a hurricane nor Klan intimidation could undermine Atlantic Beach. Instead, desegregation removed the luster from the Black Pearl and foreshadowed the dissolution of unity at Atlantic Beach.

Earlene Woods lived through the 1954 hurricane that destroyed much of the built environment of Atlantic Beach: "Integration was worse. Because the hurricane took the businesses, but integration took the people." Without the tourists, the black beach community would not have the economic base it needed to survive. Russell Skeeters felt, "Integration killed the business almost eighty percent, when Blacks found out they could go anywhere they wanted, and no longer had to come to this area like they used to . . . a devastating blow to the Black community." William P. Johnson, Sr., who has owned land in Atlantic Beach since the 1940s, discussed the effects of desegregation on Atlantic Beach. "Colored people started going to the

White beaches instead of the Colored ones," Johnson explained. "The Black businessmen didn't put enough money in it to make it attractive to Black people. They mortgaged much of it to White people and now about one-third of Atlantic Beach is owned by Whites."[59] After desegregation, the social fiber and the built environment of Atlantic Beach began to decay.

Etrulia Dozier lamented what was lost: "Black folks have sold property in Atlantic Beach and certainly that's an economic situation. But Horry County and South Carolina had lost some of its legacy . . . Black folks have lost some of their legacy."[60] This is a loss that affects far more than just those who lived, worked, and played in the Black Pearl during its golden era. Atlantic Beach's place in southern history and culture—one that includes both positive and negative aspects—reaches far beyond the borders of the small four-block community.

Earlene Woods explained that the current generation does not understand the legacy of Atlantic Beach:

> This generation don't know anything about the history of Atlantic Beach. They could care less. All they know about is going to Myrtle Beach where the high lights and the flags are. They (Black and White youngsters) came up together with the integration, from school, they're together and they marry each other. The White folks get upset, but it's here to stay. What can you do? No one's going back to where they came from. You can believe that.[61]

The perils of progress and of forgetting the past haunt Atlantic Beach and the entire Grand Strand. While Woods is correct that "no one's going back to where they came from," few young people really do understand the vast structural inequalities embedded in the southern past. Therefore they do not understand where they have come from. The general public needs to understand Atlantic Beach's past in order to envision the future of southern leisure space.

Complicated tensions deriving from the push for progress and the pull of holding onto an important legacy permeates both real landscapes—like Atlantic Beach and American Beach, Florida—and imagined mediascapes, such as Toni Morrison's Up Beach and John Sayles's Lincoln Beach. The emotional impact of actual places and their histories has influenced exceptional creative work examining the multifaceted emotions related to historically black spaces and to desegregation. In celebrating the achievements of the civil rights movement, we cannot overlook the traumatic loss of many once tight-knit African American communities—the very places that enabled such triumphs. Atlantic Beach represents the bittersweet memories of places fading from the landscape, as well as from contemporary consciousness.[62]

In Toni Morrison's 2003 novel, *Love*, Up Beach is the fictional location of a black resort built by Bill Cosey. The novel blends images of the resort's present decayed state with flashbacks to its flourishing past. L, the first person narrator, ties together the past/present narrative and places the reader inside and outside the thriving tourist landscape. May, Cosey's daughter-in-law, who became mentally unstable after the family's resort business failed, blames the physical and emotional destruction on freedom. Morrison writes:

> She tried hard to keep the place going when her father-in-law lost interest, and was convinced that civil rights destroyed her family and its business. By which she meant colored people were more interested in blowing up cities than dancing by the seashore . . . Fact is, folks who bragged about Cosey vacations in the forties boasted in the sixties about Hyatts, Hiltons, cruises to the Bahamas and Ocho Rios.[63]

The past glory of a beachfront community offers a fitting setting for the emotional struggles of Morrison's female protagonists. Of Up Beach Morrison writes, "The withdrawal of that class of tourist was hard on everyone, like a receding wave that left shells and kept script, scattered and unreadable, behind."[64] Human progress, like the rhythms of nature, can be an uncontrollable force that is at once freeing and tragic. Morrison's work addresses the complexity of love for the past, and the people and places that inhabit our daily lives and our memories. While the past haunts the present, it is important to remember Earline Woods's pronouncement, "No one's going back to where they came from." The goal is not to go back, but to remember—a kind of mental tourism.

John Sayles's 2002 film, *Sunshine State*, is set in the fictional Florida beachside community of Plantation Island, a place that must deal with its complex past as threats of corporate development loom. Dr. Lloyd (Bill Cobbs) attempts to galvanize the residents of the historically black community of Lincoln Beach to cultivate a pride of place and fight developers from the high-end Exley Plantation, who seek to mine the area for quick profits, while destroying the community's sense of place and heritage. Sayles was inspired to make the film when he returned to a Florida completely refashioned by corporate tourism. "The small-town Florida that I remembered was gone. It just wasn't there anymore," Sayles recounted. "This tacky kind of mom-and-pop tourism, where at least the locals owned the hotel and the restaurant, had been swept away by this wave of what seemed like corporate tourism. You couldn't go two miles without seeing a Wings [a chain of beachwear stores] or a this-and-that doughnuts, one right after the other. It was an endless loop."[65] As in Morrison's novel, a poignant and stylized nostalgia haunts Sayles's film.

As the past and the present blend together, an insider/outsider perspective becomes apparent in Sayles's most interesting main female characters. Desiree (Angela Bassett), who returns home to visit her mother for the first time after a self-imposed twenty-five-year exile, and Marly (Edie Falco), who wishes to move outside the confines and responsibilities of home and family, share little screen time, but both characters represent the at once rooted and mobile aspects of place and identity. Marly reluctantly runs her father's motel and restaurant in Delrona Beach, while dreaming of the outside world. En route to her childhood home, Desiree stops in Marly's restaurant to use the restroom. On pulling up to the old mom-and-pop style business, Desiree's northern anesthesiologist husband (James McDaniel) sheepishly asks, "Black people go here?" This question expresses the continued tensions surrounding segregated space in the twenty-first century South, demonstrating how the past lives on in the present.[66]

The film also presents generational shifts in perception. Desiree's mother, Eunice Stokes (Mary Alice), who has "never been north of Washington, D.C.," expresses dismay that her daughter has left her southern roots: "Girl caught the first thing smoking and never looked back." Desiree flatly responds, "I took the bus momma, not the train." Eunice replies, "It's just an expression." In explaining the meaning of Lincoln Beach, which, like Atlantic Beach, was founded in 1934, Eunice tells Desiree's husband, "In so many ways we were on the outside looking in. But this was *ours*." An insider/outsider perspective is essential to understanding the importance of both real and imagined places affected by a complex history of segregation and commercialized leisure culture. To see both sides—the desire to leave and to return home again, the desire to develop and preserve—you have to be both a native and an exile.

Morrison and Sayles draw from the harsh realities of actual black beachfront communities in the South. The irony is that the triumph of the civil rights movement, which opened public spaces to all races, also led to the destruction of black communities that sustained African Americans during times of racial segregation. Russ Rymer and Marsha Dean Phelts both tell the true story of American Beach, Florida, a black beachside resort founded in 1935 by the wealthy African American businessman Abraham Lincoln Lewis. Just north of Jacksonville, American Beach is located on Amelia Island—which also provides the scenery for Sayles's fictionalized film. Both Rymer and Phelts trace the emergence and success of the black resort and economic and social deterioration in the period following desegregation.

Rymer forms a bond with the fascinating MaVynee Betsch, great-granddaughter of American Beach's founder, A.L. Lewis. Betsch was a well-educated and polished opera singer in her youth and spent a decade performing in Europe before she returned to American Beach, gave up all her money, and took on the role of local preservationist and colorful character. Because of her non-traditional lifestyle, Betsch was referred to as the "Beach Lady." She had seven-foot-long dreadlocks and preferred to sleep outside and keep things natural. Her rebelliousness against the greed of American consumer culture made her a memorable symbol for the preservation of the history and environment of American Beach. She represents the rebellion from within the world of privilege and the ability to cross boundaries in the long journey towards identity formation.

Betsch's work was an inspiration for the preservation movement at Atlantic Beach. A picture of her is featured in the 2009 Images of America series on Atlantic Beach produced by Arcadia Publishing. Author Sherry Suttles of the Atlantic Beach Historical Society mentions Betsch in her acknowledgements: "I extend my greatest thanks posthumously to . . . the Beach Lady, who showed me the value of keeping prime oceanfront undeveloped, if need be, to keep a majority of it for African American posterity."[67] Rymer writes, "For MaVynee, the vista of American Beach presents not only the landscape of achievement against great odds but the landscape of defeat at the hour of triumph."[68] MaVynee Betsch fought the rich and powerful Amelia Island Plantation developers, led by Charles Fraser (who had previously developed Sea Pines Plantation in Hilton Head, South Carolina), as they encroached upon the culture, history, and natural landscapes she loved. Rymer describes Betsch's philosophy on the refashioning of southern space following a new model of corporate tourism: "The privilege of living in 'Plantations,' playing golf on 'links,' and shopping in 'chains' sounds suspiciously like slavery to her."[69] Progress associated with the corporate model of tourism development can evoke the problems of the past; however, there is another way to move forward.

The other way is through coexistence of development and preservation in the same space. Betsch, who died in 2005 at the age of seventy, began the fight for this kind of symbiosis. Local historian and librarian and life-long resident of American Beach Marsha Dean Phelts continues the fight.[70] Like Betsch, Phelts was invited to take part in the push for preservation at Atlantic Beach and attended a "Preserving Memories" conference held at Atlantic Beach's Hotel Marshall in 2007.[71]

Like American Beach, Atlantic Beach's social and economic downturn following desegregation has led to recent calls for revitalization and pres-ervation. Today, the town vacillates between hopes for redevelopment respectful of the community's distinct sense of place, and the threat of thoughtless development resulting in quick profits and historical amnesia. In 1997, a journalist for the *Atlanta Journal and Constitution* described the detrimental effects on the built environment of the town: "Atlantic Beach looks more like war-torn Beirut than an ocean sanctuary once known as the Black Pearl." Journalist William Moredock lamented that Atlantic Beach now "looks like something out of the third world." Local business owner Thaxton Dixon expresses a similar perspective: "And right now the way it looks you could go a block and a half that way and come back to Atlantic Beach it look liked another country. Those three blocks and a half to your left, Windy Hill go over there look at all them beautiful buildings, high rises. Look like you come back over here in a different world." In the late-1980s, Upperman, a founding member of the Atlantic Beach Com-pany, visited Atlantic Beach. "It looked like hell," Upperman claimed in dismay. "I passed right by it and had to turn around and ask a man of color where was Atlantic Beach."[72]

Before incorporation in 1966, Atlantic Beach had no local property taxes to assist with basic social services and lacked a governing structure. However, the community flourished owing to the hard work, social unity, and the ingenuity of its residents and business owners. Lawyer Franklin Roosevelt DeWitt (1936–2008), a Horry County local who worked under Robert Kennedy, served as the town's lawyer during the incorporation process.[73] Because Atlantic Beach did not incorporate until 1966, there is no viable census data dating from before 1970. The first mayor of Atlantic Beach, Emery Gore (1966–9), worked with other prominent community members (Daniel Gore, John Simmons, Millard Rucker, and Lee Grant Gore) to form the Atlantic Beach Urban Renewal Agency in 1967. The mis-sion of the agency was to "do all acts necessary towards the planning and betterment of the town from the health, education, and general welfare of the inhabitants and free holders thereof." This was the first step towards developing a general plan, so that the town could modernize and move forward. However, to raise funds during the tenure of the next mayor, Millard Rucker (1969–76), the water rights at Atlantic Beach were sold to North Myrtle Beach.[74] The land and political structure of Atlantic Beach were independent; however, its infrastructure and services were becoming intertwined with the surrounding white beach communities.

Using the 1970 census data as well as its own "windshield survey," the Waccamaw Regional Planning and Development Council prepared a report, "Atlantic Beach Land Use Plan and Housing Element," for the newly formed Atlantic Beach Planning Committee. The report was published in June of 1979 and analyzes the physical and social demographics of the town, while making suggestions for revitalization and reorganization. Because of economic stagnation and apprehension concerning outside developers, there have been only minor demographic and physical changes in the town since the 1970s, when desegregation's diaspora ended Atlantic Beach's heyday. Most of the changes in Atlantic Beach have involved tearing down condemned structures, which has left the town's coastline barren.[75]

For historical context, I compared the data in the 1979 report to information in the Comprehensive Plan for Atlantic Beach, 2001.[76] The impetus for the 2001 comprehensive plan was the South Carolina Local Government Comprehensive Planning Enabling Act of 1994. Both reports offer a picture of the town's physical and organizational landscape and a vision for potential development within the community over time. Upperman pointed out that in the days of the Atlantic Beach Company there was no zoning, "no organization where you had to have business and residential." He went on to explain, "But most of the zoning was natural down Atlantic Street and you'd take sometimes almost half an hour to get down because congestion. The highway was not too well developed at all."[77] The 1979 report points out that a lack of planning and zoning had contributed to the town's problems: "In Atlantic Beach, single family dwellings are plagued by an intermixture of incompatible land uses. Multi-family residential, commercial, and industrial land uses are intermixed with single family residential uses, resulting in excess traffic, excess noise, and increased danger of fire during tourist season."[78] Another issue arising from the lack of proper zoning is adult entertainment: "Atlantic Beach has found itself in legal battles that forced it to open its doors to questionable business because of the lack of consistency between the business license ordinance and the zoning ordinance."[79] The "questionable businesses" currently include the Crazy Horse, a strip club, Excitement Video, an adult movie retailer, and 4:20, a drug paraphernalia and general merchandise store, all located on Highway 17. The Waccamaw Regional Planning Commission strongly suggested instituting proper planning and zoning and utilizing federal and state programs as solutions to land use problems. Atlantic Beach did not adopt zoning ordinances until 1985, and in the 2001 comprehensive plan these are discussed as "inadequate as a guide for a proper balance of land uses." Even today, zoning problems continue to hamper the town, preventing it from moving forward with development projects.

In 1970, there were 215 year-round residents in Atlantic Beach. The population peaked in 1990 with 446, due mostly to the construction of public housing units in the town during the 1980s. The sale of the town's water rights in the 1970s and the rise of public housing in the 1980s are both believed to have led to later problems at Atlantic Beach. While the 1979 report projected 580 permanent residents by 2000, the number actually dropped to 351. As with most resort areas, the Atlantic Beach population swells during the summer months. In 1970, the town was 98 percent black. In 2000, Atlantic Beach's population was still predominately (82 percent) black, but it had diversified to include white residents (10 percent) and other races and ethnicities (8 percent), predominantly Latinos. In 2010 the total population dropped to 334. The racial and ethnic demographics of Atlantic Beach continued to change, with black residents constituting barely a majority (54 percent) of its population in 2010. The white population nearly tripled, to 29 percent. The Latino population also showed strong growth, becoming 16 percent of the population.[80] In 2002, Earlene Woods was dismayed when none of her hotel rooms were filled on the Fourth of July. She told the story of her last-minute salvation: "I looked around and saw these cars coming, the back of that truck was filled with people, they were Mexicans and took every room I had, I said, 'Thank you, Lord.'"[81] Atlantic Beach businesses may struggle as the town changes; however, many continue to survive into the twenty-first century.

The specific details of Atlantic Beach's economy are not included in the 2001 report. Instead, the report focuses on the larger regional economy: "That the local economy is not confined to the Town limits, but is shaped to a large extent by what is happening in the county, region, and state, requires us to look beyond the town when assessing economic conditions, constraints, and capabilities."[82] The economic integration into the larger Grand Strand region shows that in the twenty-first century, the town no longer viewed its identity as completely independent from surrounding communities. While recognizing some economic improvement overall, the 2001 plan noted the striking lack of development: "The Town of Atlantic Beach has not fully participated in the thriving tourist-based economy of the Grand Strand, and this is reflected in the generally thin physical development seen within the town limits." This lack of development cannot be fully blamed on the town's size or on its autonomous status:

> Many landowners and residents believe Atlantic Beach has suffered economically when all around it development has flourished and land prices have soared due to the [local] government's lack of consistency in planning, its failure to gain the confidence of the landowners, the overall perception that there are issues of integrity surrounding previously submitted development plans, and ultimately, those plans have failed to capture the goals and desires of a majority of the landowners and residents.[83]

Residents feel disconnected from their own governing body and distrustful of outside developers.

The rift between the town's government and its residents and landowners was indicative of internal strife in the community, as opposed to the model of unity that prevailed during the 1950s and 1960s, when the boundaries of the town, in physical and social terms, were stark. The report indicated that there was potential for refashioning the fading landscape. But over twenty years very little had changed in the town's level of development: Whereas 40 percent of the land in Atlantic Beach remained undeveloped in 2001, in 1979 43 percent of the area had been undeveloped. Meanwhile, the surrounding communities experienced marked growth and development. This discrepancy is striking to anyone driving through the region. Atlantic Beach has a different aesthetic—one of retro decay—than many of the surrounding communities. But the 1970s saw some positive developments in Atlantic Beach. In 1971, ground was broken for the town hall. A community center, for which Senator Strom Thurmond was instrumental in obtaining grant money, was built in 1977.[84]

A comparison of the 1979 and the 2001 reports on the town also shows little improvement in the built environment of Atlantic Beach. The "windshield survey" conducted by the Waccamaw Regional Planning and Development Council in the summer of 1978 found that out of the 201 residential structures in Atlantic Beach, sixty-seven (25 percent) were deteriorating ("needs more repair than would be provided in the course of regular main-tenance") and nine were dilapidated ("determined to be unsafe or inad-equate shelter and in its present condition endangers the health, safety, or well-being of the occupants"). Out of the sixty-seven seasonal houses, fifteen were deteriorating and one was dilapidated.[85] Furthermore, Atlan-tic Beach housing was inadequate for low-to-moderate income families, and motel rooms were often used as residences for this segment of the population. This dearth has not been ameliorated by the recommendation of a federal study published in 2009 by the United States Department of Housing and Urban Development (HUD) that all of the public-housing units in Atlantic Beach be closed. Such an eventuality could potentially destroy a strong voting bloc in the town, and HUD's recommendation has incited fears that the town's impending population drop could have dev-astating effects if a new public-private partnership or development deal is not reached in the near future.[86]

While the 1979 report pointed out the need for extensive improve-ments in the built environment, it also suggested that new housing needed to be "implemented with neighborhood conservation in mind." The section on neighborhood preservation pointed out that, "Neighbor-hoods often tend to be communities within themselves, reflecting the characteristics of their residents."[87] While in a state of deterioration, the Atlantic Beach community still contains the physical reminders of a golden era. Many of those who remember the town's more prosperous past have passed away or moved on, to be replaced by a new generation without any connection to Atlantic Beach's rich history. Many lack the context to see that a black beach formed during segregation has positive attributes worth preserving.

The 2001 report lists owner-occupied houses at 33 percent and renter occupancy at 66 percent and observes, "The transient population has had a devastating effect on every aspect of the community. It is most evident in the apathy and disinterest in the community's long-term goals. Attendance at town meetings and functions is low." However, the report also states that the value of property in the town was increasing, because Atlantic Beach offered "some of the last undeveloped oceanfront property on the Strand."[88] The potential of this undeveloped property and the possibility of heritage tourism related to the area's distinct history and culture offer the best hope for the future of the town of Atlantic Beach. This promise has yet to be realized, owing to constant economic and social struggles in the town's recent history.

As the 2001 comprehensive plan for Atlantic Beach pointed out, "There is much about the history that is incomplete. A history project to recapture the oral history of the beach should begin immediately."[89] The history and culture of Atlantic Beach is best told from the perspective of its residents and those who remember its past, in conjunction with those who are invested in its future. An investment in preservation began in Atlantic Beach in the twenty-first century. Sherry Suttles, founding president of the Atlantic Beach Historical Society and former town council member, moved to Atlantic Beach from Charlotte, North Carolina, in 2000. Suttles relates, "I fell in love with the place. It's such a rare find. There's no place where African-American people owned and controlled their own territory like that. It was so exciting to see something like that and to try and preserve that history."[90]

The Atlantic Beach Historical Society (ABHS) was incorporated in 2001.[91] The organization's mission statement is: "To preserve the history of the Coastal Carolinas African American Heritage through oral histories and memorabilia, year-round family events, and personal and real property." The historical society has accomplished many of its goals in beginning to preserve the history and memories of Atlantic Beach. The Atlantic Beach Oral History Project, which began in 2002, was a vital undertaking. In 2003, the ABHS helped put together a successful photography exhibit focused on the town at the Horry County Museum. The organization erected the first historical marker on the Grand Strand at Atlantic Beach in 2005. In 2007, the organization hosted the "Preserving Memories" conference at the Hotel Marshal, which was attended by coordinators for the South Carolina Department of Archives and History (SCDAH). An international dance exhibit sponsored by the historical society followed the conference. To celebrate the seventy-fifth anniversary of the town in 2009, Suttles produced a book of Atlantic Beach pictures and history for Arcadia Publishing's "Images of America" series.[92] The historical society brings together past and present residents with "outsiders who care" to preserve the important history of the Black Pearl.[93] As impending development looms, the work of the historical society becomes even more important.

Further public knowledge about the rich history of Atlantic Beach will help to stimulate efforts to establish a sustainable future. Projects often begin but do not survive in Atlantic Beach. The town's bare and undeveloped coastline, a relic of another time along the Grand Strand—dating from before corporate tourism development and the upsurge of the highrise—represents a lack of development, but also a great deal of potential.

The vacant canvas of the Atlantic Beach coastline can be refashioned as a distinctive landscape, adding a new layer of depth and complexity to the region. African and Caribbean culture would diversify the touriscape of the Grand Strand.

The balance of preservation and development has been a hotly debated topic at Atlantic Beach. It is an important issue that reaches far beyond the boundaries of the small four-block town, because all South Carolinians have some stake in the history and heritage of Atlantic Beach. The real challenge is for stakeholders to engage the past while moving towards the future. An insider/outsider perspective can offer tools for envisioning a future for Atlantic Beach, one that sees the connections between the past and the future of the town. Many plans for the development of Atlantic Beach have been discussed throughout the years; however, nothing substantial had materialized by 2009, the seventy-fifth anniversary of the town's founding. The Atlantic Beach of today is a town left behind by time and by the prosperity the tourism industry brought to the Grand Strand. However, as a mostly undeveloped landscape with remnants of a golden past, Atlantic Beach still possesses the potential to again be a black pearl within the Grand Strand.

The difficult nature of developing Atlantic Beach derives from the various interpretations of what is valuable about the town. Money and history blur together in discussions of Atlantic Beach's future. Property owner Flora Jones told a local journalist in 1987, "This Atlantic Beach was a God-given piece of land for poor, poor black people, and God is not gonna let this land be misused. At some point, something is going to happen to make this place worthwhile. Just not these high-rise buildings." Michael Kelly, son of the original secretary for the Atlantic Beach Company, said that some see the 1980s Atlantic Beach as a "gold mine" but that, in his opinion, it is not. "It's a place that has a golden spirit, but it is in trouble, and that is not what my father and the other men of the company wanted to happen." Providing another perspective on the town's future economic possibilities, Joe Montgomery, mayor of Atlantic Beach in the 1980s, stated, "This is a gold mine. But we want to maintain our identity, and we want a certain amount of control. We want to learn from mistakes that were made in other places, like Hilton Head."[94]

The story of Hilton Head, South Carolina, is indeed a cautionary tale for Atlantic Beach. Following emancipation, the Gullah people inhabited and owned property on Hilton Head Island. Because of geographic isolation, the rich language and culture of the Gullah was preserved, until a bridge was built that brought developers and tourists. The island now provides luxury accommodations for primarily white and wealthy newcomers. Sea Pines Plantation at Hilton Head, built by the same development firm Betsch fought against at American Beach, includes golf courses and luxury tourist accommodations that lack a relationship with the island's distinctive African American history. Gated communities even block access to old African American burial grounds.[95]

History and economics overlap in the development (or lack thereof) of Atlantic Beach. Atlantic Beach's incorporation in 1966 and its 1968 decision to remain separate from North Myrtle Beach have allowed the town, unlike Hilton Head Island, to maintain self-determination.[96] The choice to remain autonomous has also made it more difficult to develop and to reap the economic rewards of tourism needed to sustain the town. David Essex, of the Waccamaw Regional Planning and Development Council, points out that the town's basic layout is another obstacle to development: "[P]roperty in Atlantic Beach is so subdivided, numerous property owners must agree to sell." The lack of large undivided tracts means "developers have to work harder to get the land, which can have both positive and negative consequences."[97]

An increase in crime has provided another hurdle for development at Atlantic Beach. A wrongful-death lawsuit filed against the town in 1984, when an Atlantic Beach police officer shot a man at a local bar, almost bankrupted Atlantic Beach by the end of the 1980s. "In 1983 and 84 when the policeman shot a guy over here at this same building and they sued the town, the town didn't have any insurance," Earlene Woods explained. "$144,000. Who paid it out? Who did it? We did. Franklin DeWitt (a local civil rights lawyer) was our attorney. He took all those names and those people came up with $144,000. I never got my money back, but I had 10% interest in it. Those were good days, we was on unity then. We were a family."[98] This unfortunate event left Atlantic Beach without its own police force for some time, which allowed crime (primarily prostitution and drug sales) to gain a foothold in the town. The geographic and social isolation of Atlantic Beach preserved its distinct heritage but also allowed criminal activity to go unchecked.[99]

Following the 1984 lawsuit, North Myrtle Beach real estate agent and mayor, Dick Hester, organized a multi-million dollar hotel development deal for Atlantic Beach. African American investors from Tennessee supposedly backed the deal, which included a high-rise hotel along the oceanfront. The Atlantic Beach town council restricted development in the town to three stories, thereby killing Hester's development plan. Local stake-holders feared the development would erase the distinct built environ-ment and disrupt the history of black control in the town. Hester stated, "Naturally, they don't want to lose their heritage as being a black beach. But you can see everyday happenings cutting into that, and of them los-ing control as we progress in time." During the 1980s, North Myrtle Beach first began a push to open Ocean Boulevard through Atlantic Beach, but residents felt that it would "destroy the peacefulness of some sections of Atlantic Beach."[100] Road patterns reflect the containment of Atlantic Beach during segregation. But many in the town felt that since they did not put up the barriers, they were not responsible for taking them down. What began as a political boundary originating outside the town became a social boundary expressing the town's distinctiveness within the larger Grand Strand region.

In the late-1980s, a development deal based in the town's history and democratic philosophy almost became a reality. In 1987, the town of Atlan-tic Beach engaged in talks with the Columbia, South Carolina, real estate development firm Keenan Company in hopes of devising a master plan for developing Atlantic Beach with a Caribbean theme and largely local control. Keenan Company was working with another architecture firm in Charlotte, North Carolina, where Harvey Gantt was employed. Gantt, who was from Charleston, South Carolina, and summered at Atlantic Beach with his parents from the 1950s on, was in 1963 the first African American to attend Clemson College (now University) in South Carolina, desegre-gating the state's educational system.[101] Gantt explained the Keenan Plan for Atlantic Beach: "We want it to be an entertainment center for the entire Grand Strand, but also act as a kind of museum of what it was like at one time in our history." Gantt added, "It will never be a totally black town any-more." The Keenan Plan included a park and boardwalk along the ocean-front, hotels along the second row, and a Caribbean-style open-air market on 30th Avenue. By selling or leasing their land, residents could join a non-profit corporation that would oversee development. The governor's office had recently awarded the town a planning grant for $250,000, rais-ing hopes further. Business owner Thelton Gore, who supported the plan, compared it to "sitting at a card table. We either got to get in the game or we're going out backwards. It's time for a change." Longtime business owner Earlene Woods supported the plan, as did the then mayor of Atlan-tic Beach, Joe Montgomery. Montgomery felt, "Redo the town, but redo it under black control. And redo it so that the poor will be as welcome as the rich." Gantt shared Montgomery's democratic view. "There's a certain historical aspect of Atlantic Beach that should never be lost," Gantt felt. "We want to build bathhouses, so that for those who can't afford hotels, motels, there will always be an Atlantic Beach where they'll be able to go to the beach."[102] The Kennan plan was eventually rejected by the town because of a clause stating that residents who refused to sell or lease their land could have their property taken through eminent domain, a controversial policy that allows for the seizure of private property for public projects. Eminent domain has been used to displace minorities when their property got in the way of large-scale development or public works. A good plan was abandoned because of an essential flaw that threatened the rights of property owners. This impasse reflects the town's enduring focus on unity and the basic democratic philosophy of Atlantic Beach's founding. Now, though, class tensions were beginning to divide the town's approach to development. This division was between "poorer year-round residents who want jobs and commercial activities and the descendants of middle-class doctors, lawyers and teachers who established the community." The latter group is made up primarily of "property owners, many of whom live out of state" and want "continued black control of the town and a substantial financial benefit for black landowners or residents."[103]

The 1990s saw more development proposals but little action. In 1991, Atlantic Beach received a state grant to pay the South Carolina Downtown Development Association to brainstorm development ideas. The association came up with a plan, "Atlantic Beach Vision 2002," which the town rejected. In 1994, Atlantic Beach landowner David B. Richardson, of the Florida development company D.B. Richardson & Associates, created the Atlantic Beach Community Development Corporation and received $800,000 in federal grants between 1994 and 2001, when the development corporation disbanded without tangible progress.[104] For a period in the late 1990s, Atlantic Beach was barred from receiving federal money because it had previously misspent grants.[105] In 1997, the town hired Omega International to devise a development plan with funding from wealthy blacks in mind: "The vision is to create a Caribbean-style village with a boardwalk, some shops, perhaps a hotel and convention center and a few condominiums. The land will be leased to developers, not sold, town leaders made clear. Too many blacks have lost their oceanfront land, they say. Townspeople hope to create a haven for families."[106] The town council rejected this plan, as well, because of mistrust of outside developers. The past unity at Atlantic Beach further disintegrated, as some property owners saw development as the hope for the future and others feared it would erase the historical legacy of the town. As the land at Atlantic Beach appreciated in value, the populace was less united.

In 1997, Emory Campbell, executive director of the Penn Center on Beaufort County's St. Helena Island, spoke to Atlantic Beach's town council during a retreat. The Penn Center was the first school for emancipated slaves and, one hundred years later, it was also a site for civil rights activity. Martin Luther King, Jr. often spent time there. Campbell told Atlantic Beach officials, "If you lose your land, you lose your freedom . . . I say to you Atlantic Beach, if you develop, do it yourself. A black-owned resort is unheard of in this state, or anywhere, so keep your land." Campbell explained, "One of the things we do at the Penn Center is look at how to help black people hold on to their land in this onslaught of developers taking over. This is happening so much that where freedom began for us 135 years ago, we're about to be enslaved again, and this time it is not plantation but condos and exclusive resorts that are shutting us down."[107] The goal of unity remained, but the ability to trade in the free market intensified the individualistic and selfish attitudes that can accompany short-sighted capitalist ventures.

The shift from community unity to personal economic gain is reflected in the comments of Atlantic Beach business owner Thaxton Dixon:

> See all the resources today, that's what I can't understand about Atlantic Beach. See all the resources we get is from the white man. You follow what I'm saying. But yet and still we want to stay here by ourselves. With nothing. Don't want to stretch out our arms. You follow what I'm saying. People marched. People got killed. Trying to get us in the shape we are in today. But yet and still there's a lot of well-educated people, can't see it. 'Long as I'm doing alright, I don't care nothing 'bout the rest.' That's the way it seems to me.[108]

Remembering the older entrepreneurial spirit, whereby successes and profits were something to be shared with the community and were tied to the spiritual qualities of place, is necessary for successful economic development at Atlantic Beach. Yet today's potential investors are often outside corporations without a stake in the land's heritage or cultural significance.

As development plans continuously stalled, decay continued at Atlantic Beach. Journalist Lyn Riddle described the Atlantic Beach of the late-1990s:

Fifty percent of the land within the town limits is undeveloped, a staggering statistic considering virtually all other parcels along the Grand Strand, from the oceanfront inland, bear the weight of hotels, beach houses, restaurants and amusement parks. One oceanfront block here has no buildings; the next is full of ravaged ones—empty, decaying. One structure sits at the edge of the dunes, its concrete walls all that remain—no insides, no roof.[109]

The town has no high-rises, no condos, and no hotels. The town's small mom-and-pop motels cannot compete with the modern tourist facilities elsewhere along the Grand Strand. Many of the old motels serve the poor and transient rather than tourists.

Even with the increase in crime, development letdowns, and the decay of the built environment, there were still people who believed in the spirit of Atlantic Beach in the 1990s. Al Scott, who grew up locally and frequented Atlantic Beach in its golden era, brought his three kids back to live in Atlantic Beach in the late-1980s and served as the town clerk in the 1990s. "He said he left a life of integrated suburbia in New Jersey," wrote local journalist Sammy Fretwell, "because he wanted his children to know who they were and where they came from."[110] Sadly, in 1998, Scott was murdered while working in the motel he owned in Atlantic Beach, and he became an unfortunate casualty of rising crime in the region. Hope, like money, often seems to evaporate in Atlantic Beach. In 1999, after town officials spent almost $30,000 on palmetto trees as part of a beautification project, most of the trees died.[111]

Atlantic Beach stakeholders still persevered into the twenty-first century. In 1999, John Skeeters, Benedict Shogaolu, executive director for Coastal Rapid Public Transit Authority (CRPTA), and Joe Garrell created Black Pearl Land Company LLC, which developed a $300 million master plan. The 2001 comprehensive plan for the town of Atlantic Beach included another redevelopment blueprint. The redevelopment plan's expressed goal was to add resort facilities and services, while sustaining the heritage and identity of the town and avoiding controversial tactics such as eminent domain.[112]

The plan divided Atlantic Beach into four study areas. The beachfront district would include "high-rise condos, shops, and restaurants. The business district would have a central plaza for gathering and recreational activities. Adjacent to the plaza would be a one-thousand-seat performance theater, along with more shops and hotels. In keeping with the town's heritage and identity, the theater would offer an alternative to the larger venues in Myrtle Beach by featuring "small concerts that recall the musical performances of the past." In addition, the shops and restaurants were "envisioned to offer food and goods that are unique to certain cultures, including the African-American and Native American cultures." The plan envisioned the Highway 17 commercial district as presenting a "unique image," including a "new open space or 'town green'" that would distinguish Atlantic Beach's piece of the commercial strip: "The open space serves as the foreground to the new visitor's center and a place to display public art that is in keeping with the town's history or theme, thereby reinforcing the desired image." The final district presented, a residential area northwest of Highway 17, was designed to add to the community center currently located in this part of town. The plan also added a government office building and park. The First Baptist Church of Atlantic Beach would relocate from its spot on 30th Avenue in the central business district to this residential area, where it could "be better integrated into the neighborhood and become a focal point of this portion of the town." The redevelopment plan concluded, "The mix of uses, building orientations, open spaces, and pedestrian walkways all contribute to the 'village' environment envisioned for Atlantic Beach."[113] The "Atlantic Beach Landowners Association Wish List from Survey Data" is also included in the 2001 comprehensive plan. The landowner's association envisioned a "total heritage experience" for the town's future development.[114] The 2001 redevelopment plan offered a picture of what many in the town would ideally like to see realized as Atlantic Beach moves into the twenty-first century. However, this reasonable plan devised by Black Pearl Land Company never came to fruition, mainly because town management changed hands in 2001.

The controversial reign of town manager Carolyn Montgomery, from 2001 to 2004, further divided the coastal municipality. In 2002, the Tyson Beach Group—a company named after the town's founder, but owned by Gerald Montgomery, husband of Carolyn Montgomery—created the New Atlantic Beach Company LLC to develop the area. Property owners could place their property in the company for development. Many residents blamed a lack of progress in the new century on Carolyn Montgomery's management. Long-time resident Jannie Islom stated, "This town has always worked together in the past, but now [2004] we're split like never before, and it's because of her." Some claim that Montgomery had a stranglehold on the town. Complaints included claims she fired employees who disagreed with her; pushed the council to remove height restrictions (which increased the value of her and her husband's ocean-front property); placed a moratorium on new development until planning documents and new zoning laws were worked out; and tore down dilapidated (and possibly historic) structures. Montgomery had a tense relationship with the Atlantic Beach Historical Society (ABHS), as shown by a citation served on the founding president Sherry Suttles for "an alleged ordinance violation" committed by the ABHS: using the organization's name in a flyer about a holiday party without using a disclaimer that ABHS is "not an official agency of or not supported in whole or in part by the Town of Atlantic Beach." Suttles detailed the controversy in a letter to the *Sun News* in March 2005, and claimed that in 2001 "Montgomery told me that she thought it was 'two years too early' for an Historical Society (and Chamber of Commerce) and that she was going to create these functions in her capacity as town manager."[115]

In her defense, Montgomery claimed that she had balanced the town's finances and helped to rid Atlantic Beach of illegal activities, such as drugs and prostitution, that were thriving in derelict buildings. "I can understand the Grand Strand not wanting a drug-infested and prostitute-infested Atlantic Beach in its midst," Montgomery explained. "Atlantic Beach has a responsibility to clean that up."[116]

In the twenty-first century, drug dealers were being prosecuted in an attempt to clean up the town. In 2001, town councilman Vander More Gore was "charged with being the leader of a 20-year conspiracy to sell cocaine and marijuana in the town." Two of Gore's sons were also charged. Gore is currently serving a life sentence, but new drug dealers reportedly replaced him.[117]

In the March 26, 2006 edition of the *Sun News*, three front-page articles on Atlantic Beach appeared under the main headline, "Solutions in development." The articles contrast recent real estate purchases and promises of development and community improvement with problems of corruption, crime, and insufficient law enforcement in the town.[118] The articles list numerous logistical and organizational hurdles to development, such as the previously discussed small land parcel and infrastructure issues, but the "distrust of outsiders, particularly white-owned development groups" was presented as the "underlying reason" for lack of development.[119]

Despite constant setbacks and controversy, development planning has continued to move forward. In 2006 and 2007, a Miami, Florida, architecture firm, Zyscovich, developed a master plan that involved a mix of residential and commercial development "all laid out to preserve the view of the ocean down any of the town's streets." This plan is similar to previous ones and could potentially cost an estimated $400 million to implement, including over $40 million in infrastructure amenities for which the town would be responsible. On top of these issues, the major hurdle to development is rewriting the town's zoning ordinances. Hope emerged in early 2009 when, with the help of Senator Dick Elliott, the town received a state grant of $225,000 for planning. However, the money was gone in six weeks. Half of it was used to pay debts and keep the town afloat. Fourteen thousand was paid to Joe Grant, a political lobbyist long involved with the town. The town did hire planners from the Waccamaw Regional Council of Governments to rewrite the ever-important zoning ordinances, but the organization stopped work when they were no longer being paid. The town has asked Myrtle Beach and Horry County to consider finishing zoning ordinance revisions using in-house planners; however, the zoning rewrite and therefore the most recent master plan were on hold as Atlantic Beach's seventy-fifth anniversary came and went.[120] However, heirs of the town's founders still hold eleven of the beachfront lots, while only nine are in the hands of development corporations.[121]

Atlantic Beach's small population and size, combined with a fluctuation in police presence, make the crime rate in the town difficult to parse out. As in all tourist towns, transient groups in Atlantic Beach raise crime statistics during the summer months. However, it is clear that in the later decades of the twentieth century, Atlantic Beach had issues with crime. Local and state officials have recently made progress in addressing the area's crime, especially drug-related crime. In 2009, the new chief of the State Law Enforcement Division (SLED), Reggie Lloyd, met with Atlantic Beach's town manager, police chief, and members of the town council. Local officers and officials claimed that due to recent criminal prosecutions and the destruction of derelict buildings, "Atlantic Beach's drug trade had mostly subsided." Yet state and local officials were working together to prepare for the summer months, when crime spikes. "These guys are getting it done," Atlantic Beach councilman Donnell Thomas said of local law enforcement. "People that live here say, 'It's better than it was when I first came.'"[122] Due to the influx of people during the summer months, tourist towns often have a surge in crime that skews statistics, which are based on residential population figures. Southern cities and tourist areas have the highest overall crime rates, according to the FBI's uniform crime statistics. Crime rates usually group together all the communities constituting the larger Myrtle Beach area, including all surrounding beaches and suburban areas. Both the state of South Carolina and the Myrtle Beach region rank among the five areas in the United States with the highest crime rates. While property crime in Myrtle Beach outranks that in Atlantic Beach, the small town of Atlantic Beach has a higher rate of violent crime.[123] And it must be remembered that Atlantic Beach has fewer than four hundred people, while Myrtle Beach has over thirty thousand residents.

Positive developments in the twenty-first century brought some new faces to Atlantic Beach. Donnell Thompson, who played in the NFL for the Indianapolis Colts in the 1980s and ran his own construction company in North Carolina, vacationed as a child in Atlantic Beach during its golden era. When looking to return to the area, he realized that for the cost of a Myrtle Beach condo, he could build an entire beach house in Atlantic Beach: "I thought it would be a challenge, but I've been able to approach challenges head on all my life, and I thought it would be very good if I could be instrumental in the process of turning Atlantic Beach around. This place is certainly worth the chance." Thompson built the only elevated beach house in Atlantic Beach to date, and he serves on the town council.[124] White Atlantic Beach developer Amy Breuing, a registered nurse from Connecticut, found her calling restoring old buildings. Her first restored apartment building in Atlantic Beach is called The French Quarter. Breuing said, "[M]ore people need to help and the Grand Strand's perception of Atlantic Beach needs to change."[125] A more positive image—born of diverse investment, new stakeholders, and fresh perspectives on the future of the Black Pearl—began to emerge in the early years of the twenty-first century.

And yet, the nearly constant air of controversy surrounding town leadership compounded problems at Atlantic Beach. For example, in the contentious 2007 mayoral election, challenger Retha Pierce unseated the incumbent Irene Armstrong by one vote (71 to 70). Armstrong asked for a recount, but before it could get underway, in March of 2008, Armstrong and town manager Marcia Conner were indicted for alleged misconduct in office and buying votes. The charges resulted from a long-term State Law Enforcement Division (SLED) investigation into the town's finances. Following the arrests and Connor's suspension, it was discovered that the town was $600 thousand in debt. After new elections, court challenges, and a plethora of confusing and contentious maneuvers, Pierce finally took office as mayor in early 2009.[126]

Pierce had her own scandals, including a Christmas 2007 arrest for disorderly conduct after she tried to flee on foot when an officer pulled over the car she had been driving; an arrest for hit and run and driving without insurance; and an incident in which she was charged with trespassing and disorderly conduct in the Atlantic Beach town hall following an altercation with town employees in early 2009. Pierce filed a federal lawsuit claiming a "widespread conspiracy to discredit her." In May of 2009, Pierce was stripped of her duties as mayor.[127] During the summer of 2009, business owner and former town advocate, Amy Bruenig, formed a "charter club" to ask South Carolina Governor Mark Sanford (who had his own ethics problems at the time) and other state officials to revoke the town's charter. The group cited grievances about police, high property taxes, and the embarrassing acts of elected officials in letters that convey Bruenig's dismay and feelings that "Atlantic Beach is beyond repair."[128]

The twenty-first century has been a political roller coaster ride so far. Earlene Woods feels that if residents would "stop bickering like frogs and crabs" that Atlantic Beach could come together and build a positive future. Janie Islom echoes Woods's sentiment: "It could be better if all of us would get together and do whatever we need to do. There's some pulling one way and some pulling another way, and you can't work like that. You have to be together as one to make things move. Some of the local government, the council members are not together. If they're not together, we're not together. So they need to come together in order for us to get together."[129] Thaxton Dixon adds, "[W]hat good is your name up on a place and ain't got 'nough money to paint it or keep it up . . . You ain't got enough money to keep it up but you still go keep it all Black. That's what confuses me . . . Well I say what the hell you want to be Black for you poor. It's alright for history what you doing is nice [collecting oral histories], you know what I mean? But that ain't putting no money in my pocket."[130] The diverse perspectives—seeing Atlantic Beach as a profitable investment versus seeing the town as a rich symbol of culture and heritage—need to be brought together. Atlantic Beach's potential lies in seeing both views as intrinsic aspects of the landscape essential to its survival as a distinct place along the South Carolina coast.

Today, Atlantic Beach remains virtually unchanged since the 1970s. Some dilapidated buildings have been torn down, and a few palmetto trees dot the landscape. Full-scale redevelopment has yet to begin. The last bit of undeveloped oceanfront property on the Grand Strand remains empty for now. With the national housing market and the larger American economy in turmoil, 2009 was not the moment for Atlantic Beach to realize its development goals. That the town held onto its roots as a black community in the face of rampant and homogenizing development on the Grand Strand is indicative of the tenacity of some residents and local leaders. But the true test of Atlantic Beach's spirit will begin the moment development moves from planning to action.

At the end of 2010, the town of Atlantic Beach was once again discussing opening the road that has, from the start, segregated the community from the surrounding area. At the request of the Atlantic Beach Planning Commission, the Waccamaw Regional Council of Governments (WRCOG) did a survey. Sixty-two percent of "property owners" prefer opening Ocean Boulevard through Atlantic Beach, but the "actual residents" of Atlantic Beach want the road to stay closed. Robert Dolphin, who raised his family in Atlantic Beach, said, "It's not about keeping other people out, it's about keeping what we have established in the town."[131] Property owners reportedly "believe opening the road would spur development," while residents "want the Black Pearl to preserve its walkable character." The real question is, can the town get beyond these two divergent perspectives to find a new way that achieves both goals?

A balance between understanding the past and sustaining the future of Atlantic Beach is difficult to envision. This vision cannot be achieved without a stable economy and a culture that remembers the past and respects the present development of black leisure culture. During its flirtations with big-time development, Atlantic Beach has taken on a new layer of African American history owing to the annual motorcycle festival the town began hosting in 1980. While looking back on the heyday of Atlantic Beach's past and reflecting on its present state of disrepair, we need also to look forward to emerging aspects of African American leisure culture—including the black biker.

NEON MOTORCYCLES BY THE SEA

The Atlantic Beach Bikefest Controversy Refashions the Grand Strand

While the Atlantic Beach Bikefest has yet to restore the Black Pearl's past luster, it does constitute a lively event whereby the town's past overlaps with the complexities of today's black motorcycle subcultures. The motorcycle festival has garnered the town both positive and negative publicity. The few available histories of Atlantic Beach often conclude the town's story with a reference to the motorcycle festival; however, the festival is the beginning of a new story connected to the town's past. The founding of the Atlantic Beach Bikefest adds another layer to the town's history.[1] The motorcycle festival offers hope for the town both because the event permits Atlantic Beach to act as a location for the growth and diversification of African American leisure culture, and because it and brings back the lively, crowded streets, blasting music, and sidewalk vendors so fondly recollected by early inhabitants of the town. However, the controversy surrounding the festival, beginning in the late-1990s, also exemplifies a refashioned racism that plagues the Newer South.

Two motorcycle festivals are held annually in the Grand Strand region during the month of May. The Harley-Davidson motorcycle festival, which began in 1940, is predominantly white, occurs for ten days in the middle of May, and is commonly referred to as "Bike Week." The Atlantic Beach Bikefest, which began in 1980, is predominately black, takes place over the Memorial Day weekend, features Japanese speed bikes rather than Harleys, and is often referred to as "Black Bike Week." As is often the case, an event characterized by whiteness is invisible and presented as the norm, while any non-white alternative is considered secondary or "other."

The Atlantic Beach motorcycle festival was the brainchild of the Carolina Knight Riders Motorcycle Club and Atlantic Beach councilman John Skeeters. The club, which began in 1977 as the Flaming Knight Riders, received a charter in 1982 and became the Carolina Knight Riders of North Myrtle Beach Motorcycle Club. The club's purpose is to "promote the

Hotel Marshall, built in 1945, survived four hurricanes. By the time of the 2009 Bikefest it was marked by the ravages of time. Photo by author, May 2009.

social welfare of its members and to uphold the highest standards and best traditions of the community." The motorcycle club is open to anyone, but it primarily consists of adult black men who ride Harley-Davidson motorcycles (the Japanese speed bikes came later), though black women are also members of the club and hold office. When the black motorcyclists wanted to start a rally, "they had no place to go except the town of Atlantic Beach." The event began as a small festival and parade on Memorial Day weekend where revelers "ate chicken bog, danced, and vied for trophies in contests for the best looking motorcycle." In the 1980s, the Carolina Knight Riders and the town of Atlantic Beach "parted ways when their ideas didn't match," meaning that while the Carolina Knight Riders wanted a motorcycle event, the town wanted to "turn it into a social event." The dispute stems from conflicting perspectives concerning what was more central to the event: motorcycles or the town itself. Once new town leadership took over, the two groups rejoined forces, and the event began to grow.[2] The Atlantic Beach Bikefest combines the motorcycle's mobility with the festival's rooted focus on the town.

In the 1990s, the Carolina Knight Riders began to extend an invitation to other African American motorcycle clubs located outside the area. The small festival reportedly began to attract visitors in excess of thirty thousand after 1996, and by the twenty-first century these visitors numbered in the hundreds of thousands according to some.[3] The festival's growth corresponded to the growth of both black motorcycle clubs, such as the Carolina Knight Riders or Charleston's Band of Bruthaz, and large events staged specifically for African American youth, such as Freaknik/Freedomfest in Atlanta, Georgia or the Black College Reunion in Daytona, Florida. During the late-1990s, the demographics of the Atlantic Beach Bikefest also began to shift. Younger African Americans driving Japanese speed bikes and even young revelers with no bikes at all began to dominate the event. Members of the Carolina Knight Riders referred to these new tourists sans motorcycles as "tag-alongs," young people who come to town only to party during the festival. "The media lumps everyone in town that weekend into the biker category and everyone is not a biker," explained club member George Livingston. "Those kids come to party and this is just not us."[4] Livingston's observations about the media's representation of the bike festivals and the insider/outsider dynamic of tourism and motorcycle culture are astute. The locals who started the festival were older and drove more traditional Harleys, but the more rebellious younger generations choose the lighter, faster, cheaper, and brighter neon speed bikes.

For the first fifteen years, the Atlantic Beach Bikefest brought large numbers of people into the town without major incident. When the festival began to grow beyond the boundaries of the black beach, the press and local politicians in the neighboring predominately white communities began to take notice. The landscape of Atlantic Beach overflowed its own boundaries, creating an insider/outsider dialectic within the region's tourism market. This new generation of African Americans on motorcycles roared through barriers in the *de facto* segregation of the region's leisure space. Atlantic Beach Bikefest attendees effectively claimed territory and created new landscapes simply by riding their motorcycles through the Grand Strand. Like Alan Schafer and the Atlantic Beach merchants of 1950 responding to Klan intimidation, the black bikers of the twenty-first century used economic arguments and stood their ground, transforming the white beaches of the Grand Strand.

The controversy surrounding the Atlantic Beach Bikefest—a reaction against young African American bikers as an undesirable group of tourists on the Grand Strand—reflected the refashioned racism evolving in a Newer South. During May of 1996, a front-page article in the *Sun News* noted that officials from Myrtle Beach and North Myrtle Beach were "preparing for a Memorial Day weekend overflow of bikers from Atlantic

Beach." The festival's hub was located in Atlantic Beach, but attendees traveled throughout the larger Grand Strand region. The police presence in the area was increasing; however, Myrtle Beach was no longer able to send officers to North Myrtle Beach because they were needed to deal with an overflow of incidents into their own city. The article described how officials were "mobilizing police" to deal with a crowd expected to double from the fifteen thousand tourists who attended the previous year.[5]

The thousands of outsiders attracted by the festival could not be contained within the four-block community, with its meager tourist accommodations. The article described Atlantic Beach as the "tiny black beach town," which had recently "re-established its defunct police department" and had "two officers on hand to help during the festival." Tom Leath, Myrtle Beach city manager, was quoted as saying, "Up until last year, the Memorial Day bike fest didn't really impact us. Last year [1995], it did." The impact was coded as negative, and the article described "incidents on Ocean Boulevard that included bared breasts and buttocks and noise complaints." The black bikefest participants were presented as "wilder" and their motorcycles "louder" than the predominantly white riders and their Harley-Davidsons who had appeared at the motorcycle rally held the week before the Atlantic Beach festival.[6]

Mark Smith's work on the sensory aspects of race and racism and Andrew W. Kahrl's work on black steamboat excursions and resorts in the Washington, D.C., area explore the importance of moving beyond simply "seeing" race. Focusing on the late-nineteenth century, Kahrl discusses a "broader tendency to describe African American culture in aural terms and to equate the open forms of expression associated with the postemancipation generation of African Americans with barbarism." The local criticism of the Atlantic Beach Bikefest was born of this aural aspect; the quality of the "barbaric" sound has been updated through technology—the motorcycle's engine—but the response of the critics remains the same: The noise is too loud. This aural racism echoes in the same space as the false foundational myth, based on a white farmer having established Atlantic Beach to keep his noisy black maids away from the house on their days off. Similar aural prejudices haunt the claims of local white politicians, who declare that black youth party differently and make more noise than their white counterparts. Kahrl explains: "By the turn of the twentieth century, 'black noise' had become a metaphor for the nation's descent from an imagined bygone era of race relations, when blacks knew their place and were deferential to whites."[7] Through the expansion of the touriscape of Atlantic Beach into the neighboring white beach, we can see how this metaphor travels with new technologies while remaining embedded in one-hundred-year-old racist practices.

In Atlantic Beach, the festival's growth produced positive results. An article by Yolanda Jones in the local paper explained that in 1995, Atlantic Beach, "which often struggles to pay its bills," made almost $10,000 from the $150 license fees required for vendors. Jones remarked upon the publicity created around the 1996 rally when the Atlantic Beach town clerk, Earl Bellamy, went on The Doug Banks Show, a popular nationally syndicated radio program. She reported that the town planned to lure more families and children to the rally by offering watermelon eating and double-dutch jump rope contests.[8] Atlantic Beach was attempting to blend a focus on motorcycles with the atmosphere of a local festival that might appeal to a broader audience. Keeping families and children involved was a way to shield the festival from growing criticism.

In 1997, when the black motorcycle festival began to draw crowds reported to be as large as sixty thousand, the negative press intensified. North Myrtle Beach's city council discussed but did not pass a "cruising ban," the first official attempt to limit the mobility of the black bikers. Atlantic Beach officials pointed out that it was not bikers alone, but general tourist traffic that caused gridlock during the busy Memorial Day weekend.[9] Complaints about the festival caused a marked increase in the number of police present, prompting local resident Pat Bellamy to ask, "They complain that we cause traffic and this and that, but do they say that during Harley week? Can't African Americans take vacations?"[10]

Bellamy's question became even more relevant the day after the 1997 Atlantic Beach Bikefest, when an article appeared on the front page of the Sun News announcing that Mark McBride, Myrtle Beach city councilman and (soon to be) mayoral candidate, was proposing a referendum on banning bike weeks in Myrtle Beach. He proposed to allow residents to vote against either or both of the bike festivals; however, the article stated that McBride was "much more critical of the Memorial Day festival." McBride stated that race was not a motivating factor in his call for the referendum. "I don't care if it was a golden-age bus tour," McBride claimed, "[W]e wouldn't want the bus tour." McBride told the press that he had personally witnessed "public nudity, drug activity, what appeared to be a stabbing and a near riot" during the black motorcycle festival. Police denied there had been a riot and said that although an individual pulled a knife out, there had been no stabbing. McBride countered that he went into the hotel in question himself and "saw a lot of blood and a fork." The article also quotes Bradley Roberts, the front desk clerk at the historic Chesterfield Inn, located on Ocean Boulevard in Myrtle Beach: "We've had several rooms check out early, because they didn't want kids exposed to these kind of things."[11]

A *Sun News* article about McBride's proposed referendum addressed the mounting controversy: "Race, politics and youth came together with thousands of bikers last weekend, creating high tensions and a lot of talk." Jerome Smith, who traveled from Charlotte, North Carolina, was insulted by the discussion of banning the black motorcycle festival. "I saved up my money to come to Atlantic Beach for the biker fest," Smith explained. "Then we hear they want to ban us from coming and for what, because they don't want black people here? It's just plain crazy and is pure and simple racism." Myrtle Beach resident Cherry Hannah shared Smith's ire. "Don't single out the black bikers and use the white bikers as pawns," Hannah complained. "McBride expects to win this election because he has some whites on his side. But why are they so afraid of black people? Can't we come to the beach? Apparently not in Myrtle Beach." Myrtle Beach resident Frank Burgess argued for more tolerance from the city. "One thing we don't want is for this to turn into a racial issue," Burgess stated. "The problem is nobody was prepared for such a large group of black people coming into Myrtle Beach. They were scared."[12]

Burgess doesn't seem to be aware of the irony of his statement. How can the fear of black people not be seen as a racial issue? But race is not the only issue. Age, class, sexuality, and taste contribute to the problems. The Bikefest controversy was part of larger trend in southern (and American) politics in which prejudices, such as racism and homophobia, are recast as "family values." In addition to his rants against the black bike festival, McBride led a crusade against a local gay bar and the Gay and Lesbian Pride Festival held in Myrtle Beach in 1998.[13]

The election of Mark McBride in 1998 ushered in a new era in Myrtle Beach politics. The thirty-four-year-old McBride defeated Robert M. Grissom, a twelve-year incumbent in his seventies, by a meager forty-two votes. While McBride challenged the expansive real estate development of the Burroughs & Chapin Company, he was also part of a movement "toward bringing a family atmosphere back to the downtown."[14] The fact that McBride eked out a victory at the polls speaks to both the public's fears of rampant corporate tourism development and the growing success of "family values" as a significant political issue in the 1990s. In the age of Walmart, "family values" conjures up images of a simpler time when mom-and-pop businesses did not have to fight against the effects of globalization. But this same call for a simpler time often veils an attempt to roll back the victories of the civil rights movement of the 1950s and 1960s. McBride's narrow margin represented a divide in the local community's attitudes towards the controversial issues of development and preservation.

An increased police presence and the general hostility of law enforcement drew mixed reactions from local residents. Not everyone wanted to see the city turned into a hostile police state as it awaited the one hundred thousand African Americans expected to attend the 1998 Atlantic Beach Bikefest.[15] That year, police instituted the first street closures on the main drag, the Grand Strand's Ocean Boulevard, but only during the black festival. When asked why the street closures were not in effect during the previous week's Harley Davidson Festival, Myrtle Beach Police Chief Warren Gall said, "Historically the traffic situation during Harley Week has never been as bad as traffic during the [black bike festival]."[16] The town of Atlantic Beach hired the consulting firm Omega International to handle organization of the bike festival, and some events were located at the south end of Myrtle Beach in an attempt to spread out the traffic and replicate the patterns during Harley Week.[17]

After the festival, local business owners along Ocean Boulevard expressed dismay that the festival was over-policed and that the road closures hindered sales. Airbrush artist Jesse Smith said his business went way down: "I'm not registered to vote but I'm going to register tomorrow to get that mayor [McBride] out." Beachworld manager Mark Patterson thought the police presence and behavior were excessive. He saw tourists arrested for shooting water guns at one another in a playful manner: "It's 95 degrees, squirt me. I understand [police] need to maintain control but sometimes you can overdo things. It's a misuse of justice."[18] In July of 1998, Horry County suggested that Atlantic Beach misspent public money on the festival. The town's officials denied the charges, and, after a county audit, they were cleared of any misappropriation of funds in November of 1998.[19]

Under the leadership of Mayor McBride, Myrtle Beach became very pro-active in discouraging the Atlantic Beach Bikefest. In October of 1998, the Council of Myrtle Beach Organizations, or COMBO, made up of local marketing and political lobbying groups, began to plan their own Memorial Day celebration, geared towards bringing military veterans from the southeast to the Grand Strand. In the article, "Veterans to get Memorial festival: Event could impact black bikers," Ashley Ward, head of the Myrtle Beach Area Chamber of Commerce and a member of COMBO, is quoted as saying: "We get a lot of complaints that Memorial Day is a major holiday and the Grand Strand doesn't do anything to celebrate it." Ward adds that the festival's purpose is to "bring more balance to the weekend and return to the historic reasons for the weekend." Critics saw the plan as "an attempt to supplant black bikers by filling area hotel rooms with veterans and military families." But black bikers also have families and often serve in the military. Bill Gasque, a member of the Bike Week Task Force, which lobbied local municipalities to write letters to the Atlantic Beach Town Council asking what they were going to do to "make the event go smoother," is annoyed that some have turned the task force's work into a racial issue. "It's not a racial issue. It's a behavioral issue," Gasque said. "I don't care if you're black or white, if you don't behave yourself in public, it's a behavioral problem." The task force, made up of mainly white business owners from Myrtle Beach, framed the controversy as an us-versus-them issue. Task force member and owner of the Breakers Hotel, Vernon Drake, said, "It started in Atlantic Beach. It's y'all's festival." Merv McMillan, Town Manager of Atlantic Beach, saw the event as a "Grand Strand situation" and not just an Atlantic Beach issue. The town of Atlantic Beach is part of the Grand Strand. "I recommend that all the municipalities of the Grand Strand and the county get together and discuss it," suggested McMillan.[20] However, rather than open a dialogue, the Myrtle Beach City Council increased regulation and enforcement.

Myrtle Beach's focus on limiting the mobility of black bikers by closing off public streets hearkens back to the rope, fences, and road patterns that contained black revelers in Atlantic Beach during the Jim Crow era. In December 1998, the Myrtle Beach City Council and the city's police chief announced further road closures for the 1999 Atlantic Beach Bikefest. Ocean Boulevard passes through the major tourist business district along the ocean and is always packed during the summer months with young tourists "cruisin' the boulevard." Myrtle Beach is often advertised as a family beach, but since the 1960s students have made up the largest contingent of tourists visiting the area.[21] The new proposal was intended to close this main thoroughfare from 29th Avenue South to 30th Avenue North. The road closure recalls the Grand Strand during segregation, when blacks were barred from Ocean Boulevard all together. The idea for the road closure was partially attributed to consultation with Atlanta officials, who were dealing with their own controversy surrounding Freedomfest (formerly known as Freaknik), a large festival for young African Americans in downtown Atlanta. It cost almost two thousand tax dollars to send city, county, and other leaders to Atlanta to learn how officials there were dealing with Freedomfest. Myrtle Beach city manager Tom Leath said, "What Atlanta [officials] said is to make the vehicular festival a pedestrian festival." Of course, a motorcycle festival is by nature vehicular. Limiting mobility in this way seems like an attempt to eliminate the black motorcyclists from certain parts of the Grand Strand, a new tactic for segregating public space. The limitation on mobility is a limitation on freedom. Chief Gall of Myrtle Beach also suggested contacting the National Guard "to assess the situation and come up with a plan as to how it could help Myrtle Beach during the weekend." This bold proposal drew intense controversy from the start. Myrtle Beach councilwoman Judy Rodman stated, "If you make it look like we're having a war, we'll have a war."[22]

Myrtle Beach did not heed the warnings and increased their police presence, which in turn increased the tensions building along the Grand Strand. Only eighteen police officers were brought in from outside of Myrtle Beach in 1997. In 1999, that number had grown to two hundred, so that there was now one police officer for approximately every two hundred bikers, an expansion of services that cost an estimated $200,000. This excessive police presence further limited the mobility of the bikers.[23]

Mayor McBride and the Myrtle Beach City Council continued to pursue "assistance" from the South Carolina National Guard during the black motorcycle festival, despite local opposition to the plan. When the state's Democratic governor, Jim Hodges, publicly stated that he did not think sending in the Guard was a good idea, the Myrtle Beach City Council asked the mayor to meet with the governor personally. Mark Kruea, Myrtle Beach's public information officer, remarked, "The city doesn't *want* to call the Guard. We *need* additional man power" [emphasis mine].[24] Myrtle Beach resident Jim DeFeo suggested that city officials consider using trained police dogs from New Jersey during the black motorcycle festival. The city declined because police dogs brought to mind images of police abuse of civil rights activists in Birmingham, Alabama, in 1963. Governor Hodges was unwavering in his opposition to the use of the National Guard in Myrtle Beach, because he felt their presence would be "inappropriate" and would "send the wrong message to visitors."[25] The city eventually backed down on the plan to close Ocean Boulevard altogether; instead they restricted it to one-way traffic during the Bikefest.

The National Guard troops and police dogs used to quell racial unrest and civil rights protests in the 1960s were replaced in the late 1990s by more subtle tactics, such as manipulation of access to public roads, creation of a competing festival (which never took off), and an increase in hotel rates and business closures. Following the 1999 Atlantic Beach Bikefest, which occurred without any major incidents, the United States Department of Justice took notice of the situation. Ernie Stallworth, from the Justice Department's Community Relations Service, arrived in Myrtle Beach to "assess racial tensions that he said were heightened by the idea of bringing in the National Guard." Stallworth generally praised the local police's behavior; however, Mayor McBride did not agree with Stallworth's conciliatory conclusions. "Everybody has an opinion," McBride said. "I just expect more—I have higher standards. I think it's a sad commentary on societal problems that a community is expected to just accept and deal with this."[26] Myrtle Beach and Atlantic Beach officials took part in an October conference organized by the Justice Department that included officials from Atlanta, Georgia, and Daytona Beach, Florida (all the participating areas were cities that host large African American festivals).

After the Justice Department's conference, Myrtle Beach officials still would not admit that the problems associated with the large black motorcycle festival had anything to do with race. This refusal further exacerbated tensions in the area. Ozell Sutton, the Justice Department's director of the southeast region, said, "Just face the issue. The issue is race." However, Myrtle Beach city manager Tom Leath held onto his position that the problem was not race, but the fact that the groups "party differently" that led to the different treatment of white and black bikers. Leath explained, "During spring break you have a limited area of Ocean Boulevard where predominantly white kids hang out, hoot and holler. The white crowds party in smaller groups. During Memorial Day weekend, it seems to be one large party."[27] Leath and McBride were relying on casual observation for their conclusions about the different partying habits of white and black youth, and they did not consider how their own social positions affected their perception.[28]

Atlantic Beach mayor Irene Armstrong and Beverly Clark, who heads the Friendship Team welcoming committee for the Bikefest, agreed with Ozell's assessment that race played a part in the controversy. Clark said, "Caucasian residents create this fear within themselves. The problem is they're so used to being in the majority, and when they find themselves in the minority, they feel uncomfortable."[29] This assessment recalls William

Moredock's story about his mother's "thoroughly unnerving experience" taking their maid to Atlantic Beach in the 1950s. "Driving through the little town, we were completely cut off from 'our' world, completely surrounded by 'the other,'" explained Moredock. "We had never seen so many black people."[30] While the times have changed, this uncomfortable "outsider" feeling is still central to racial perceptions in the Newer South. Public space is legally desegregated, but how often do people actually leave their comfort zones to enter unfamiliar territory?

An insider/outsider perspective offers a means of critically analyzing and processing this uncomfortable feeling and then moving productively beyond it. Individuals experience a shift in consciousness when they move from being inside to being outside the majority (and vice versa) in various senses (race, sexual orientation, gender, religion, class, origin, age, etc.). This psychological discomfort must be recognized as a transitional stage—from feeling discomfort to feeling at home in a given place. The transition requires staying grounded in a place that is not comfortable and looking for ways to see connections to it.

In the twenty-first century, the Atlantic Beach Bikefest controversy changed from a local to a national issue. The NAACP had recently instituted a tourism boycott of South Carolina to protest the state's flying the Confederate flag atop the state house dome. In February of 2000, the NAACP mailed letters to numerous African American motorcycle clubs asking for their support of the boycott. An article in the *(Raleigh, North Carolina) News & Observer* stated, "Atlantic Beach residents also want the flag hauled down, but many fear the boycott will harm them, some of the very people the NAACP wants to help." While the town of Atlantic Beach adopted a resolution in support of bringing down the flag (as did the Myrtle Beach Chamber of Commerce), some critics still thought that condemnation was not enough to justify spending tourism dollars in South Carolina—even at a black motorcycle festival based in a historically black town. This issue brought up the complexity of boycotting a state with a large percentage of African Americans, because their state government supported racist symbols. Some thought "attending the Bike Festival will send a message to opponents of the event that it's not going away." Chandra Cox, financial secretary of the Carolina Knight Riders, the local motorcycle club that originally organized the event, stated, "We have people in positions in all jobs along the Grand Strand, and we don't want to jeopardize our own jobs by supporting these economic sanctions on our own places of employment." Irene Armstrong, mayor of Atlantic Beach, responded to criticism of the town continuing with the festival by posing the question: "If you know that's your lifeline, do you cut it off?"[31]

The 2000 motorcycle festival experienced a drop in attendance. Hilton Jones of Columbia, South Carolina, attended and sold T-shirts that read, "It would've been more babes & bikes if it weren't for the flag."[32] Following the 2000 festival, Stallworth, a United States Department of Justice official, stated that his department was looking into complaints of "heavy-handedness" by the police. In addition, Rev. H. H. Singleton, president of the well-organized Conway, South Carolina, branch of the NAACP, also announced that the NAACP had received complaints that it was investigating.[33] While the NAACP boycott and Confederate flag debate may have kept some Bikefest participants away, the controversies also focused greater national attention on the racial unrest occurring on the Grand Strand. The flag debate further polarized the perspective on the ground in Atlantic Beach, the Grand Strand, and South Carolina.

South Carolina lawmakers had passed a compromise in 2000 that moved the Confederate flag from atop the statehouse dome to a Confederate memorial on statehouse grounds, and began plans for an African American memorial to be erected on the grounds. While the NAACP was not satisfied and continued its tourism boycott of the state, its effects on the Atlantic Beach Bikefest specifically appeared negligible. In 2001, the bike festival was expected to draw a reported four hundred thousand attendees, and the South Carolina Human Affairs Commission attended both the Harley-Davidson Rally and the Atlantic Beach Bikefest to observe the treatment of tourists.[34] The town of Atlantic Beach was proactive in maintaining control of the event and of their town. When North Myrtle Beach tried to take over the section of Highway 17 that ran through Atlantic Beach by passing a bill in the state legislature, residents of Atlantic Beach successfully protested at the state capital. The residents were able to maintain control of the highway that ran through their town and the motorcycle festival originating within their borders.[35] While the town was successfully managing certain aspects of the festival, attendees still complained of excessive police patrolling. "The week before [during the Harley rally] there were no police. Then all of a sudden you get all these blacks together and there's fear of a riot," lamented A.C. Walker of Daytona Beach, Florida. In 2002, the town of Atlantic Beach paid the public relations firm Single Source Consulting of Chesapeake, Virginia, $64,000 to organize the Bikefest and promote the town on a national scale. Mayor Irene Armstrong stated, "We are getting national recognition and national inquiries. The returns should be far greater than the money we put out for providing services."[36] Yet Atlantic Beach would receive more extensive press from discrimination lawsuits filed in 2003, on the eve of that year's motorcycle festival.

The controversy surrounding the Atlantic Beach Bikefest moved from the street to the courtroom in May of 2003, when twenty-five plaintiffs, assisted by NAACP lawyers, filed suit against Myrtle Beach, Horry County, and a local hotel, alleging racial discrimination during the Atlantic Beach Bikefest. The city and county were accused of "overly aggressive traffic restrictions and policing," and the Yachtsman Resort Hotel was accused of "violating civil rights of bikefest attendees." Mark Kruea, spokesperson for the city of Myrtle Beach, claimed that it was "absurd to think that the city's response to these motorcycle events is in any way based on race."[37] The following day, African American plaintiffs filed discrimination complaints with the South Carolina Human Affairs Commission, accusing over twenty local businesses (mostly restaurants) of "discriminatory practices," including closing for business to avoid serving black customers and hostile treatment of blacks. Restaurant owners responded by claiming that traffic congestion caused their businesses to close during the black motorcycle festival.[38] In 2004, a class action suit was filed against four Myrtle Beach restaurants: J. Edward's Great Ribs & More, and Fleming's (both owned by J. Edward Fleming), Damon's Grill, and Greg Norman's Australian Grille (all businesses were cited in the complaint made to the South Carolina Human Affairs Commission in 2003).[39]

The instances of discrimination were framed as bad ethics and bad economics. Kweisi Mfume, president of the NAACP at the time, remarked:

> In this day and age, you would think that business owners realize that discrimination is not just illegal, but also immoral. It's bad for business and bad for America. In Myrtle Beach, these restaurants are clearly not making good business sense. They are in effect reducing profit and losing market share because of their stereotypical and prejudicial attitudes about Black people. That kind of discrimination can't hold up in a court of law.[40]

Cited as evidence in the case was a 1998 letter J. Edward Fleming wrote to the Myrtle Beach Area Chamber of Commerce. "Before I will tolerate the takeover by a group of such as what we have experienced, I will close my doors and take the loss. . . ." Fleming wrote. "Something must be done, but it is going to be difficult with this group being black as they have all the rights in America anymore." In the letter, Fleming threatened to close his restaurant in 1999 "if something isn't done to prevent such a racist group of people from disrupting our lives and business from which we are accustomed." Fleming also wrote letters to Mayor McBride, urging him to "keep pushing restrictions for the bike rally and add more law enforcement if necessary to protect the city." In a 2003 article breaking the story, Fleming is quoted professing, "I am not a racist."[41] The lawsuits reflect the rise of a refashioned racism in the Newer South.[42]

The plaintiffs argued that the suits should begin a much-needed dialogue on race relations in the area to address a "continuing legacy of a race problem the community isn't likely to discuss and even less likely to admit." Plaintiff Clint White, an avid motorcyclist who had attended the Bikefest for over a decade and also attended the Harley festival, explained that, "[T]his is one of those things you accept as an African-American," adding that while it would be easier simply not to attend the festival on the Grand Strand, the plaintiffs needed to take a stand and start an honest conversation. Atlantic Beach Mayor Irene Armstrong pointed out, "The controversy over Bikefest is part of a problem older than Atlantic Beach." The plaintiffs felt that if the "lawsuit prompts a discussion about race among business owners, officials and ordinary residents, then it will have succeeded."[43]

By the summer of 2005, it seemed as if the push for a dialogue was being realized when a two-day court appointed mediation between the NAACP and the city of Myrtle Beach took place. However, forced dialogue did not seem to bring the sides together. The day after a bike rallies forum, organized by the Myrtle Beach Chamber of Commerce, took place at the Myrtle Beach Convention Center, the *Sun News* reported, "Bike forum settles only on more talks." Area political and business leaders were included in the round table discussion, but the audience to the talks pointed out that "the conversations wouldn't be useful until everyone had a chance to speak." The format of the forum was not conducive to the submission of ideas from those inside the biker communities. Despite pleas, the "mostly biker-supportive crowd" was not allowed to address the panel. Local biker Jim Horton pointed out, "A task force is ineffective without including local residents."[44] The failure of the forum shows the difficulty of comprehensive dialogue without an insider/outsider perspective. Not all locals viewed the rallies in the same way. Different categories of identity—such as local, biker, black, and business owner—can and do overlap. All of the stakeholders—locals,

tourists, business owners, bikers, and community members of all races—
needed their perspectives to be validated and considered in order to properly resolve the Atlantic Beach Bikefest controversy.

Businesses, which depend on the good will of consumers to make a
profit and are by law held to non-discriminatory policies, began to settle
with the plaintiffs. In October of 2004, Mfume announced an "amicable
groundbreaking settlement" with the Yachtsman for $1.2 million. Just
over 50 percent of the settlement went to the named plaintiffs, and the
rest went to all hotel guests registered during the time period in question.
Additionally, the Yachtsman agreed to "offer a 10 percent coupon for the
guests' next stay at the Yachtsman; cover the plaintiffs' cost and legal fees;
apply consistent policies for all guests year-round; expand its non-discriminatory policies and training procedures; designate an ombudsman to
investigate future complaints of discrimination and allow monitoring by
the NAACP counsel." Plaintiff Michael Little thought the best part of the
settlement was that it would "encourage other local businesses to change
too."[45] In 2005, the NAACP lawyers also settled with J. Edward Fleming,
owner of two of the restaurants named in the suit. The settlement included
an undisclosed monetary sum as well as the requirement that Fleming
keep his restaurants open during the Atlantic Beach Bikefest. In 2006,
Damon's Grill also settled, with an agreement to remain open during the
black motorcycle festival and pay $125,000 to the plaintiffs.[46]

In order for the businesses sued by the Bikefest plaintiffs to make a
profit, they had to make amends. Conciliatory talks with the city of Myrtle
Beach were not as successful. The city refused to admit that the different treatment accorded the two festivals had anything to do with race and
would not change the one-way traffic pattern instituted only during the
black motorcycle festival.[47] The legal battle between the NAACP and the
city of Myrtle Beach was based in the streets—or rather an attempt to keep
black bikers off the streets through restricting traffic patterns.

Even though the case did not go to trial until 2005, in December of
2003, NAACP lawyers sought an injunction against Myrtle Beach to "stop
some of the alleged discriminatory activity"—mainly the one-way traffic pattern instituted during the black festival.[48] In a *Legal Affairs* article,
"Uneasy Riders: Myrtle Beach's Separate and Unequal Biker Rallies," Paul
Wachter discussed the inspiration for the suit in Myrtle Beach: a similar
1999 suit the NAACP won in Daytona Beach, Florida. The US district court
found that a "cumbersome traffic plan" enacted only during a black college reunion and not during similarly large events staged for white tourists

(such as the Daytona 500 and spring break) "restricted the reunion guests' right to travel." Manipulation of travel and traffic patterns was becoming a new phase in civil rights litigation in the Newer South. The design of Ocean Boulevard, which bypassed Atlantic Beach during Jim Crow, was a material representation of containment and legal segregation. The current manipulation of Ocean Boulevard in Myrtle Beach, the same strip of road that banned blacks during segregation, created a space for civil rights litigation in the twenty-first century.

During 2005, the city of Myrtle Beach and the civil rights organization were entangled in public and legal wrangling. In February of 2005, the NAACP filed an injunction in the US district court in Florence, South Carolina, to prevent the planned closure of a one-way street during the black motorcycle festival. The group wanted "similar traffic management plans" for both of the festivals, including the predominantly white Harley festival.[49] In March, the city's lawyers filed a last minute motion to block the injunction.[50] The NAACP was prepared to fight what they saw as the city's reliance on "racial stereotypes" that African Americans are more prone to "engage in illegal and anti-social behavior" in instituting its traffic patterns. The civil rights organization felt that Mayor McBride's "racial biases" and "rhetoric" were to blame for encouraging discrimination by the city and local businesses.[51] When the two sides had their day in court, NAACP lawyer Paul Hurst argued that the city's discriminatory traffic pattern was based on "subjective, vague generalizations" about African Americans, and that the "city's lack of empirical data about the number of attendees shows it made the decision based on gut feelings instead of facts." The city's lack of comprehensive hard numbers formed the cornerstone of the NAACP's case. The latter showed that the city's assumptions were not based on evidence but on subjective assumptions.[52] Van Osdell, the city's lawyer, pointed out that the NAACP's own expert witness admitted that the Bikefest attendees were "much younger" than those attending the Harley-Davidson rally.[53] But the argument that discrimination was based on age, rather than race, did not fly.

When a judge sided with the NAACP in May, ruling that Myrtle Beach would have to use the same traffic pattern for both motorcycle festivals, the city appealed and was granted a stay on the ruling. The city was therefore allowed to implement the one-way traffic pattern only during the black motorcycle festival. The NAACP struck back by organizing a rally and a news conference on the steps of Myrtle Beach's city hall. The organization announced it was launching Operation Bike Week Justice, a monitoring

program that would be in place during both the white and the black motorcycle festivals. Organizers hoped that Operation Bike Week Justice would
send a message to the city that "the eyes of the world are watching and will
be watching for the next several weeks." Leaders of local NAACP branches
were especially offended by Mayor McBride's deposition in October, in
which he claimed black tourists "want to disregard the law and sit on the
tops of their cars and smoke dope and drink and do whatever they want to
and disregard everything." Rev. Kenneth E. Floyd, president of the Conway
branch of the NAACP, stated, "This is 2005 and this kind of racism must
and will stop in Horry County." Anson Asaka, assistant general counsel for
the NAACP, argued, "[T]he city has no legitimate explanation for what
they're doing." He called the differing traffic patterns an "apartheid traffic
plan."[54] Hurst said the NAACP wanted to compromise with the city, but
that Myrtle Beach was stalwart and unmoving.[55]

Lawyers for the city of Myrtle Beach fought a public opinion battle
against the civil rights organization. Tourism officials in Myrtle Beach
framed the suits as part of an unsuccessful attempt by the NAACP to
harm tourism in the region, and Mayor McBride decried the litigation as
a "publicity stunt."[56] The court ruled against Myrtle Beach's request to see
NAACP sealed documents related to the case, which the city hoped would
"provide proof that 'profit' is an alternative basis for plaintiffs' lawsuits, not
merely to 'right' a civil injustice."[57] University of South Carolina law professor Andrew Siegel located the Myrtle Beach case in a "larger tradition of
white Southern defiance. . . . They see the NAACP as an outside group,
and outsiders portraying them as a bunch of racist rednecks, so they don't
want to back down."[58] The city remained steadfast in insisting upon the
two different traffic patterns for the two primarily segregated bike rallies
during the month of May.

In early 2006, after almost three years of legal maneuvering and intense
debate, a federal judge approved a compromise settlement between the
NAACP and the city of Myrtle Beach (the suit against the county was
dropped in 2005). The settlement "requires that the city use identical traffic patterns during certain periods of May's two motorcycle rallies." The
city of Myrtle Beach decided to use the one-way traffic pattern during
both the Harley-Davidson Rally and the Atlantic Beach Bikefest, rather
than abandon their regulation of motorcycle mobility.[59] The NAACP also
remained resolute as well, announcing that it would continue to monitor
the bike festivals and keep Operation Bike Week Justice alive. Local colum-
nist Issac A. Bailey wondered if black bikers would feel less discrimination

now that the Harley riders would also be riding one-way in Myrtle Beach. He wrote that while the successful NAACP case may be "considered progress by some . . . for me, the settlement may have been necessary to stop wasting tax payer dollars on court costs but was little more than silly."[60]

The city of Myrtle Beach refused to admit that race played any role in the unequal access to a public roadway—despite a long history of racial segregation, containment, and hostility toward both black businesses and tourists in the Grand Strand region. Left with no choice, the city limited the mobility of white bikers, too. The black bikers now had the same right to ride their bikes in Myrtle Beach as white bikers did during the Harley rally. Yet an analysis of the black biker subculture and style shows that—while they wanted the freedom of the road—the black bikers (especially those of the younger generation) were equally concerned about the freedom to pursue their own individual style—a style that contrasted with the black leather and big bikes seen during Harley week. Younger African American bikers used the sleek, globalized style of their bright neon speed bikes to claim space and exert their identities in novel ways along the Grand Strand during Memorial Day weekend.

As the Atlantic Beach Bikefest controversy illustrates, the road can represent both freedom and oppression. The motorcycle, an icon of the open road, functions as an important symbol of freedom and expression in contemporary American culture. J. B. Jackson, the father of American vernacular landscape studies, gained perspective by cruising the countryside on his motorcycle. Eddy Harris chose a motorcycle as the vehicle to discover his roots as an African American in a South of haunted dreams. The motorcycle and its resulting subcultures have an intimate and direct relationship to place and identity.

The fight to claim territory—especially Ocean Boulevard in the city of Myrtle Beach—is at the heart of the controversy surrounding the Atlantic Beach Bikefest and the negotiation of identity that Japanese speed bike riders engage in every May on the Grand Strand. While these debates fall within the realm of leisure and tourism, they also address important issues of identity and power. British scholar Dick Hebdige, who laid the groundwork for analyzing postwar youth subcultures, discusses the relationship between subcultures and space: "Each subculture represented an attempt to win 'space,' both real space—street corners, neighbourhoods, etc.—and symbolic space: areas in which new forms of identity could be developed beyond the given cultural and ideological parameters." Ken Gelder, an English professor in Australia, describes the importance of claiming territory

for subcultures as producing "subcultural geographies."[61] Young black bikers claimed space by riding different bikes, wearing different attire, and
adopting a different subcultural style in general.

This important performance was enacted in the public space of the roads
of the Grand Strand. In "Subcultures of Consumption: An Ethnography of
the New Bikers," John W. Schouten and James M. McAlexander define a
"subculture of consumption" as a "distinctive subgroup of society that self-
selects on the basis of a shared commitment to a particular product class,
brand, or consumption activity." These subcultures often possess "an iden-
tifiable, hierarchical social structure; a unique ethos, or set of shared beliefs
and values; and unique jargons, rituals, and modes of symbolic expression."
To outsiders, "including nonbikers and aspirants to the subculture, the
variety of group identities may appear virtually indistinguishable, even stereotypical."[62] This lack of understanding about the semiotics of motorcycle
subcultures may explain why there have been two different and segregated
rallies in the Grand Strand area during the month of May, and why non-
biker residents dislike neon speed bikes that flood into their town. There
has been no academic or extensive popular work addressing the subculture of predominantly young African Americans who choose to ride Japanese speed bikes. This is a fruitful area for further research, but the lack of
attention speaks to the central role that Harley-Davidson motorcycles have
played in dominant American identity construction, especially in relationship to motorcycle subcultures of the past.[63]

The significance of Harley Davidson motorcycles to American popular culture is vast. Peter Stanfield's article, "Heritage Design: the Harley-Davidson Motor Company," analyzes the design of Harleys and the
company's "dual emphasis on heritage and national identity" in explaining
why these bikes possess "a signifying role in popular culture that far out-
weighs European and Japanese competitors." The heft of Harley-Davidsons
represents the American desire to have the biggest and the best consumer
items. Stanfield argues that beginning in the 1970s, when faster and lighter
Japanese bikes emerged on the American scene, Harley-Davidson began
to promote its American heritage actively. Harley's marketing success
proved the company's ability to present their bikes as quintessentially
American without detracting from the cool cachet of "otherness." But the
Japanese speed bikes created a "new niche" in the consumer market for
motorcycles. The creation of the "lightweight sports/leisure motorcycle"
enabled Japanese companies to "differentiate their products on a design,
function and marketing front."[64] These material and social differences in

motorcycles and their resulting subcultures are important in understanding the Atlantic Beach Bikefest controversy. The issue was racial discrimination, but, if examined further, much of the furor was related to the idea of a younger generation of African Americans' attempts to claim space and exert agency through the semiotics of style.

Harley-Davidson moved from the brand of actual outlaws to a lifestyle brand that was "safely" rebellious. The Harley rally possessed a negative outlaw image in its early days in the 1950s and 1960s; popular culture representations of the time include white juvenile delinquents clad in leather jackets and biker boots. But hotels began to accept white bikers in the late 1970s in Myrtle Beach. This acceptance slowly spread to restaurants and other tourist locations. By the 1990s, "Welcome Bikers" signs could be seen throughout the Grand Strand region during the Harley-Davidson festival. The refashioning and normalization of the Harley rally coincided with a similar shift in the Harley-Davidson brand. The diversification of the brand—with Harley-Davidson cigarettes, Harley-Davidson coffee, Harley-Davidson apparel and accessories (even for pets)—brought mainstream acceptability of the renegade image. Wealthy baby boomers in the throes of mid-life crises acquired Harleys to reclaim (or at least purchase) youth and rebellion. The successful 2007 film *Wild Hogs* is a stark contrasts to the rebellious biker films of the 1950s and 1960s, such as Marlon Brando's *The Wild One* (1953), Monte Hellman's biker exploitation films like *The Wild Angels* (1966), and especially *Easy Rider* (1969).

Easy Rider was an immediate success when released in 1969. The film was the first independent movie put out by a major film company, and it led the way for the new American cinema. Today, as in 1969, *Easy Rider* is often viewed as an important stylistic representation of the 1960s counterculture.[65] In "The Road to Dystopia: Landscaping the Nation in *Easy Rider*," Barbara Klinger points to the symbolic importance of region in the film. "In the Southwest, the protagonists enjoy the freedom of the road, the hospitality of those they encounter, and the beauty and mystery of the region's wilderness," Klinger explains. "Conversely, the small-town South . . . is demonized in *Easy Rider* as the region most identified in the 1960s with militant ignorance, racism, and violence."[66] Furthermore, the film's white male protagonists are the heroes (or, anti-heroes) of the film—the ones with agency, the ones riding the bikes. African Americans are presented only in passing or as a part of the southern scenery. They utter no words. They ride no bikes. The aural effect of the other is eliminated altogether.

A couple of decades later, in Atlantic Beach, African Americans do ride bikes. The founding generation appropriated the Harleys of the "Easy Riders" of the 1960s; however, as the festival grew, neon Japanese speed bikes came to represent the dominant aesthetic of the new bike rally. The act of riding fast, bright motorcycles through a predominantly white southern landscape is an expression of the freedom to purchase, to move, and to claim territory while touting a non-traditional and globalized style. Brian Alexander's *New York Times* article, "Now Racing: Black Motorcyclists Move From Street to Track," notes that the "Harley-Davidson style cruisers" are seen as being "co-opted by middle-aged doctors and lawyers," and that the "less expensive" and "faster" street bikes present "a different version of the old outlaw biker cachet." These newer bikes also represent brand consumption as a lifestyle, the contestation of power, and the diversification of American motorcycle subcultures. Alexander writes: "From Myrtle Beach, SC to Brooklyn [NY] to Los Angeles [CA] to St. Louis [MO], motorcycling, like other motor sports long a bastion of white males, has been diversifying." While motorcycling has diversified, motorcycles have also "seeped into urban black culture."[67] The film that is representative here is 2003's *Biker Boyz*, which focuses on urban motorcycle clubs and African Americans doing street tricks on Japanese speed bikes.

This new outlaw aesthetic is described as "a kind of Quentin Tarantino sensibility with a dash of techno Ninja warrior, a pinch of globalism and hip hop defiance," though this emergent style and culture can be read as a continuation of the past rather than as a break from it. The continuity within change found in refashioned subcultures represents rebellion, but a newer rebellion located within the confines of consumer culture. American Motorcyclist Association (AMA) champion and Atlantic Beach Bikefest alum Rickey Gadson explains that, "like the early stock-car drivers who ran moonshine during the week and raced on weekends, he is a product of that outlaw culture." Furthermore, Gadson points out "what is outlaw today will garner sponsorship tomorrow."[68] The fluidity of outlaw styles and images is important in understanding motorcycle subcultures. Some may argue that when rebellion is appropriated by a dominant culture, the insurgency loses power. However, in the process, the outside is brought inside—in other words, the subculture begins to define how the dominant culture moves, rather than the other way around.

Recognizing the aesthetics and styles of biker subcultures is important to understanding the complex significance the motorcycle possesses in the American imagination. Recognizing the histories and cultures of the

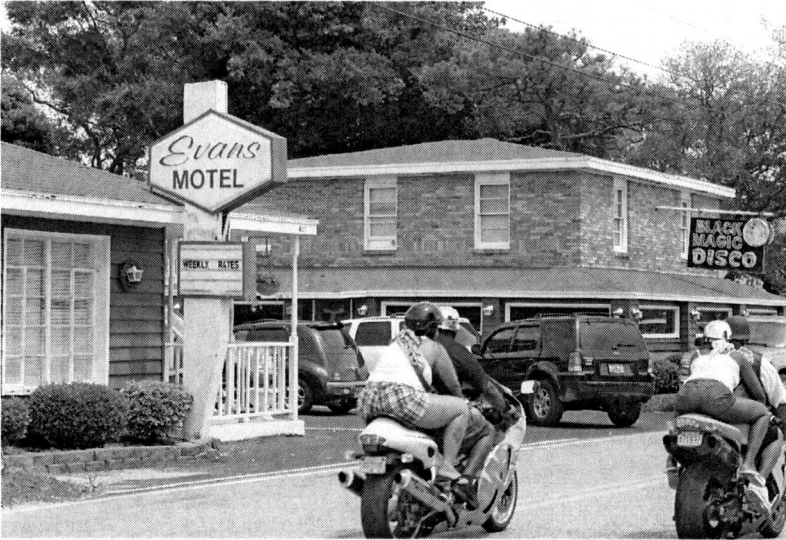

Young people on Japanese speed bikes drive by the Black Magic Disco and the Evans Motel, businesses owned by Earlene Woods, one of the original Atlantic Beach entrepreneurs. Photo by author, May 2009.

two separate and segregated motorcycle festivals in the Grand Strand is an important part of respecting difference. On the other end of the spectrum, acknowledging the things those two sets of bikers share creates common ground. "Motorcycle enthusiasts argue that a touch of danger and showing off have always been part of the sport," Alexander explains. "The fact that urban young people, many of whom are black, are riding fast bikes does not make it much different from white suburban boys souping up a Trans-Am and laying rubber on a highway."[69] The rebellious spirit of biker culture remains the same, but the signs of this rebellion are changing and expanding to incorporate different identities within the larger biker category. Black motorcycle enthusiasts do not offer a new theory of subcultures, but their actions trace the material and social effects of the expansion of subcultural style in a Newer South.

The diversification of professional motor sports—from NASCAR's Drive for Diversity program to black New Jersey native Ricky Gadson's multiple national championships in the AMA—represents this expansion. "Every year I used to go down to Myrtle Beach for bike week," Gadson explained. "It used to be more old-timers on cruiser bikes. Now it's a sport bike event. Thousands and thousands of young black folks are down there with the fanciest, trickest bikes they can find."[70] When a young future-biker posts a question on a Yahoo discussion board about Harleys versus Japanese speed bikes, he begins by stating he feels Harleys are for "old people." The respondents agree, pointing out the stylistic differences between the bikes with comments such as, "I like [the speed bikes] because they have a futuristic (Neo Japan) look."

The attendees at the Atlantic Beach Bikefest are answering Desiree's husband's question in *Sunshine State*—"Black people go here?"—with an affirmative rev of the engine. But the attendees at the Atlantic Beach Bikefest are talking about more than just race, instead embodying the more youthful, flexible, and globalized expression of identity found within the various black biker subcultures of today.[71]

Realizing that different motorcycle subcultures (defined by different motorcycles, clubs, clothes, and the like) have distinct styles and signify differences of race, class, age, gender, sexuality, and taste is an important step in understanding the controversies associated with the Atlantic Beach Bikefest and motorcycle subcultures in general. Anthony Anderson, a black biker traveling to the Atlantic Beach festivities from Chicago, felt that the controversy was not simply about race, but "more about economics and social perception." He explained: "Discrimination is based on post-9/11 attitudes and what kind of bike—American vs. foreign—a given biker rides. When I rode a [Japanese Kawasaki], I used to get hassled a lot more by police. These days, when truckers see [my] bike is a Harley, they give me the road."[72] While young people who purchase Japanese speed bikes may be influenced by economics (these bikes cost less than Harleys), their decision has become much more about identity and the semiotics of style. Christopher T. Shields, a.k.a. "Black Echo" or "the Dark One," wrote a diatribe of over seven thousand words on his site, goingfaster.com. The essay, entitled "Why Harley Davidson Isn't a Real American Motorcycle," presents the Harley as a combination wheelchair-recliner. For Shields, the higher price of a Harley-Davidson is just hype. He explains that a "top of the line Harley costs many thousands more than a comparable import motorcycle, is less dependable, doesn't enjoy the quality or workmanship, and won't even perform as well." Shields points out that while Harleys are made in Milwaukee, they contain Japanese parts, and many Japanese bikes are actually made in the United States. He writes:

> You [Harleys] don't stand for youth, you stand for old age and mediocrity. You stand for slow and weak when we want fast and powerful!

Where do we turn to? Those who can make and sell what we want! Hear this, Milwaukee. If you made a decent sport bike like the Japanese and Italians, those of us who live in America and ride CBRs and Ninjas would probably buy it, if it was just as fast, reliable, and affordable as those that Japan offers.[73]

From online diatribes to the streets of the Grand Strand, different motorcycles signify different takes on identity, place, and taste.

Knowing how to read these different subcultures descending on the oceanfront communities of the Grand Strand region is important to understanding the role of leisure culture and consumer culture as central aspects of identity in the Newer South. The freedom black bikers have to ride through the Grand Strand—even with the one-way traffic pattern on Ocean Boulevard— stands in stark contrast to the scare tactics of the 1950 Klan parade through Atlantic Beach, when African American leisure culture was confined to four oceanfront blocks.

When I attended the 2007 Atlantic Beach Bikefest, the CEO for Ruff Ryders Entertainment—a hip hop label that also includes a motorcycle club, a video production department, and a clothing line—briefly spoke to the crowd: "Is the South in the house? [cheers from crowd] Is the South in the house? [louder cheers] That's what I'm talking about because I'm from the South. Yeah, what's up? I ain't got much to say, you know, 'cause I ain't a talker I'm just about doing. Love is love. I'm from New York City, but the Earth's my turf. One. Y'all be safe."[74] In this brief statement, the CEO of Ruff Riders claims a southern identity, states that he is from New York City, and professes to be a citizen of the world The statement expresses the new mobile perspective on southern identity, which sees the regional, national, and global aspects of identity as intersecting parts of a whole. This complex (and only seemingly contradictory) statement was delivered in the heart of Atlantic Beach, from a stage constructed near the dunes, with the ocean as a backdrop. In this same place decades before, during Jim Crow, black revelers danced to rhythm and blues under the stars. Atlantic Beach's (now defunct) website claimed "that every wave that laps her [Atlantic Beach's] shore originated in Africa four days earlier."[75] The connections between the diverse and mobile aspects of identity and place represent the continuity within change that is a central aspect of southern identity in the Newer South. Change and progress do not have to erase the past. Motorcycle subcultures add new layers to the landscape of Atlantic Beach, and people need better observation skills and analytical abilities to recognize and respect these subcultures for the cultural work they do.

Differences within motorcycle subcultures also make crossover possible. On the eve of the 2007 Atlantic Beach Bikefest, Harley-Davidson announced its intention to have its first-ever presence at the black motorcycle event. Lynn Bonner, Harley-Davidson's director of market research, explained, "As a part of our ongoing initiative, we've partnered with a number of rallies that appeal to a number of different bikers. African American and Hispanics are a growing consumer market for our motorcycles and products." Keith Hyman of the National Association of Black Bikers was open-minded. "They are trying to redevelop the infrastructure of the event. They are going to bring some good things to it," Hyman felt. "I think everybody will come to appreciate that Harley isn't trying to take over the event, they are trying to bring enhancements to it."[76] Harley's American identity adds to the local flavor of Atlantic Beach and the globalism represented by the Japanese speed bikes.

This merger of brands and subcultures was framed as a "first step toward finding common ground between the demographics of the two rallies." Like Upperman's claim that Atlantic Beach was developed both as a business venture and an altruistic gesture, bike manufacturers see their participation in Bikefest as "mainly a business decision, but they do want to help the festival grow." Jonathan Formo, owner of Redline Powersports, which sells sports bikes and not Harleys, said, "It's already happening . . . we are seeing more sports bikes in the first bike week and more cruisers in the second week. And we are seeing more blacks and whites riding together." Myrtle Beach biker Vantrous Graham added, "I'd like to see it where everyone can come together. This is a good thing. It's always been that things were separated. Now everybody is coming together. This is the first step. This is going to go a long way." Atlantic Beach City Council member Sherry Suttles admitted, "If this marriage or whatever it is brings in more Harleys and more diversity, then everything is all good."[77]

Issac Bailey's column on the 2007 "bike month" characterized the celebration as the "least disruptive we've had." Bailey wrote, "We owe a lot of the success to the Harley-Davidson dealers of the Carolinas, Redline Sports and other bike manufacturers." Bailey recalls when the Harley rally was an "utter mess" and recollects the often-told story of armed standoffs between police and biker gangs in the 1970s.[78] "Things changed when the Harley dealers realized their brand was being tarnished. It was a business decision, one born of necessity. A business decision also prompted them to get involved with Bikefest this year, presumably because it could grow the number of future Harley buyers. The Grand Strand will long benefit from that business acumen." Bailey quipped, "After all, NASCAR icon Dale Earnhardt Jr. teamed up with rap mogul Jay-Z for a commercial and video. Why wouldn't Harley team up with Bikefest?"[79] However, the influx of the Harley brand into the Atlantic Beach Bikefest can also be read as an attempt to co-opt the competition. Blurring the lines between the two different festivals privileges the larger and more established Harley rally as a large conglomerate that can absorb smaller subcultures.

Not everyone was happy with the Harley-Davidson Corporation's presence in Atlantic Beach. Despite her previous positive outlook, councilwoman Suttles was "upset that there was no agreement for Harley to give the town a cut of its profits." Suttles felt "this is about business."[80] Because of past problems with outside influences, Suttles may have worried that Bikefest would lose its connection to the city of Atlantic Beach, and that the city would lose the money and the publicity that originated with the festival. The availability of other leisure opportunities for African Americans was the starting point for Atlantic Beach's original downturn. There are fears that the Atlantic Beach Bikefest could disappear into just another motorcycle festival, one without a distinct heritage grounded in the history of the Black Pearl. Or, Bikefest could simply disappear, just as Atlantic Beach tourists did after desegregation.

In September of 2008 the city of Myrtle Beach passed fifteen new ordinances and amendments that took effect in early 2009. The primary and most controversial new law was the requirement, which contradicted state law, that all individuals riding a motorcycle in city limits must wear a helmet. Mayor John Rhodes and the city council clearly and openly instituted these new laws with the express purpose of ridding the city of Myrtle Beach of all motorcycle rallies. This tactic—the attempt to legally regulate the types of tourists that visit an area—directly relates to the contested nature of a place's and a community's identity in the Newer South. Can locals control the types of tourists who visit their town? Thwarted in attempts to regulate the black motorcycle festival, the city decided to prohibit motorcycle festivals in general.[81]

Following adoption of Myrtle Beach's new ordinances, the Harley-Davidson Carolina Dealers' Association, which held the first rally in the area in 1940, moved its rally to neighboring New Bern, North Carolina, because the group did not want to get mixed up in the battle the city was

creating.[82] On its website the city of Myrtle Beach clearly stated the ratio-
nale for its antagonistic attitude towards the rallies:

> The rallies grew too large and lasted too long. The back-to-back rallies
> attracted several hundred thousand bikers and event-goers and over-
> whelmed the city for nearly three weeks. The rallies drove other visi-
> tors away. Through the years, the city tried to work with the organizers
> and attendees, but the rallies did not improve. Instead, they became
> larger, longer and louder. Myrtle Beach welcomes people who ride
> motorcycles lawfully, but the rallies have ended.[83]

Defying the new bike week ordinances was an infraction, rather than a
crime. The penalty for defiance was a one hundred dollar fine. A separate
administrative court, which some refer to as the "motorcycle court," was
created to process tickets issued for violating the new ordinances.

The new ordinances were highly controversial and produced numerous lawsuits. The city approved a $3 million property tax increase to pay
for the new anti-rally ordinances and their enforcement. The controversial
tax was expected to raise around $1 million per year over the next three
years. Mayor John Rhodes proposed using $25 thousand of the revenues
during the first year to start a Military Appreciation Days festival during
Memorial Day weekend (coinciding with the Atlantic Beach Bikefest).
This proposal was similar to the unsuccessful 1998 efforts of Council of
Myrtle Beach Organizations (COMBO) to start a competing festival to
bring military veterans to Myrtle Beach during Bikefest.[84] The bulk of the
remaining tax money was to be spent on surveillance of tourists during
the motorcycle festivals in Myrtle Beach.[85] All of this spending began in
2008, when the US economy was in the worst shape it had been in since
the Great Depression, and South Carolina's unemployment rate reached
above 12 percent. Carol and William O'Day, motel owners in the city of
Myrtle Beach, unsuccessfully filed suit to keep the ordinances from going
into effect in February of 2009, and challenged the constitutionality of the
so-called "motorcycle court." The O'Days said of their motivations, "This
is about the freedoms we have. As soon as you stop fighting for your freedoms you lose them."[86]

Myrtle Beach's harsh anti-rally stance divided the Grand Stand region,
while also unifying the different biker subcultures. Cities north and south
of Myrtle Beach still supported the rallies. North Myrtle Beach, which
surrounds Atlantic Beach, was the most hospitable of these communities.

"The bikers are just like any other tourists," said Mayor Marilyn Hatley. "We're expecting people to come and abide by the laws and enjoy themselves." Various businesses, even in the city of Myrtle Beach, displayed "Welcome Bikers" signs. The *Sun News* reported, "Riders shared information on how to ride without going into Myrtle Beach, and where to buy T-shirts to protest the new regulations, including the city's helmet ordinance." The biker subcultures were transforming into a counterculture. John Glover, president of the Carolina Knight Riders Association, pointed out that the city of Myrtle Beach never officially sponsored the bike weeks in the first place, adding, "neither rally is Myrtle Beach's to end." "Now they want to pull the plug on the bike rallies," Glover said. "I'd like everyone to know, there's more to the Grand Strand than Myrtle Beach."[87]

The *Sun* News reported that in January 2009, black and white biker groups united in a "defiant stand against what they see as a common enemy: harsh laws and negative publicity from the city of Myrtle Beach" in front of the Atlantic Beach Town Hall. The bikers "parked their Harley cruisers and Japanese sport bikes *together* under a small stand of trees" to declare that the rallies would go on. Rick Walls, a regular attendee at the Harley Rally and a member of the Patriot Guard Riders, declared: "This ain't a white issue about white rallies. This ain't a black issue about black rallies. This is a civil rights issue for both colors."[88] The push to end the bike rallies may have further united bikers of all races and made them more determined not to be run off their selected turf. Identification as a biker had the potential to transcend racial differences.

When talking to bikers about why they love riding motorcycles, the word "freedom" often comes up. Right after the new ordinances took effect, a group of around two hundred riders (some with helmets, some without) met in Murrells Inlet at The Beaver Bar to begin Myrtle Beach Freedom Ride, a non-violent protest of the new laws. The police were waiting on Ocean Boulevard in Myrtle Beach to hand out tickets. "Fast Fred" Ruddock of North Charleston heads Bikers of Lesser Tolerance, a bikers' rights collective that opposes discrimination against bikers. He later pointed out, "I wore my helmet all the way here—because it's my choice. It's the law, not the device, that we oppose." Bruce Arnold, who rode all the way up from Miami Beach, Florida, said, "To me, the helmet issue is just a surface issue. To me, it's about discrimination. It's about telling a group of Americans that they cannot be in a certain part of America."[89] This is a fascinating use of the rhetoric of civil rights to address the freedoms of motorcycle subcultures.

After Memorial Day, it was time to assess the effects of Myrtle Beach's new rules and plan for the following May.[90] Many residents felt that a tourist town should not be turning away tourists—especially during a recession. Local business owner Bruce Kligman protested, "You can't tell people not to come here when your town is based on tourism." Furthermore, the push to rid Myrtle Beach of motorcycle subcultures, which are often associated with a working-class and rebellious style, took on the patina of class bias. Myrtle Beach has never been an elite resort destination. It has always been a democratic and working-class tourist destination, full of high-rise condos, beachwear stores, and beautiful yet crowded beaches. With over one hundred golf courses and more than a dozen strip clubs, Myrtle Beach tends to attract men looking for a good time.[91] Motorcycle festivals may not fit in with the image civic boosters want to create, but it fits right in with the reality on the ground: dicey attractions hidden behind a family fun façade.

The bike week controversy in 2009 must have made ex-mayor Mark McBride nostalgic for old times. In a Myrtle Beach city council meeting, the former mayor—who vehemently attacked the Atlantic Beach Bikefest when he was in office—stated, "There has to be a compromise. I'm asking you on behalf of the small-business owners to work up a compromise for Harley Week. A five-day, city-sponsored rally. The city is big enough for everyone to have a piece of the pie."[92] McBride did not mention the Atlantic Beach Bikefest in his plea. In September of 2009, Mark McBride announced his candidacy (again in the midst of a bike week controversy) for mayor of Myrtle Beach, but after a run-off election incumbent John Rhodes retained his position as mayor.[93]

The predominantly white city of Myrtle Beach may have hoped, with its comprehensive 2009 ordinances, to move beyond the decade long (1996–2006) controversy surrounding the African American festival. By making their new laws anti-biker rather than anti-black biker, the city made itself less susceptible to lawsuits based in civil rights claims. While many bikers felt that their rights were being infringed upon, it is not illegal to discriminate against a group based on their choice of vehicle. In 2010, the South Carolina Supreme Court declared Myrtle Beach's helmet law unconstitutional because it failed to comply with state laws, but the hostility between the city and bikers remains.[94] Myrtle Beach had to refund all monies paid for tickets given to motorcyclists riding without helmets. The process of mailing the refund checks (with interest) cost the city almost $16,000.[95]

Atlantic Beach Bikefest attendees drive down 31st Avenue by the E & E Motel, named after Eloise and Emory Gore (Emory was the town's first mayor). Photo by author, May 2009.

The culture and controversy surrounding the black bikers adds another layer to Atlantic Beach's story, which has always revolved around business, profit, and the branding of culture. Atlantic Beach should be able to blend all the elements of its history, culture, and identity to create a fascinating, unique, and profitable revival—one based in both continuity and change. As the city's website proclaims, "Black entertainers once performed on the Grand Strand and stayed in Atlantic Beach because they had to, now we look forward to the day when entertainers and everyday folks will stay with us because they can. No matter who you are, feel at home in Atlantic Beach, we're just family."[96]

The tourist landscape at Atlantic Beach continues to expand in the twenty-first century with the recreational bikefest and a more heritage-based focus on African American history. Beginning in 2005, the town began hosting a Gullah/Geechee festival late in the summer season. Atlantic Beach was chosen as the site of this cultural festival because of its history as "the summer home for many blacks before integration occurred." An article on the 2007 cultural festival held at Atlantic Beach describes the booth of "Bunny" and Andrew Rodrigues: "Their booth was a magnet for those with money in hand and a mind open to learning about the Grand Strand's Gullah heritage."[97] Open minds and open wallets are necessary for the continued sustainability of this fascinating Black Pearl on the Grand Strand.

Individuals who understood both the spirit of good entertainment and good business founded Atlantic Beach. This spirit and this history live on in the local activists who work to govern and promote the town, and in the tourists who are drawn to the area. Atlantic Beach displays a hybrid culture where Africa and America come together in the Gullah people, the business owners and black performers of the town's heyday, and the young black bikers who now flood the town every May. While it is difficult for a small coastal town to maintain a sense of identity in contemporary American consumer culture, the ongoing traditions of Atlantic Beach present possibilities for its future.

CONCLUSION

Preserving the Past, Developing the Future

Both Alan Schafer's declaration that "we checked only the color of their money, not their skins," and Leroy Upperman's claim that the Atlantic Beach Company developed the black beach "not out of altruism, but as a business venture," demonstrate the role of entrepreneurship in social change. Schafer's attention to the "color of money" attempted to make his profitable tourist empire a place of social equality. This logic often excludes those without money from the expressive realm of consumer culture and tourism. However, many Americans view a vacation, no matter how meager, as a right of citizenship and a way of expressing identity.

The place studies in this book are intended to shed light on the aesthetics, politics, and histories of two idiosyncratic places as they have weathered—and in some cases brought about—vast changes in the southern landscape. I have argued that a kind of critical tourism, alert to these elements, can promote social change. But the critical tourist perspective can also aid in the preservation of the entrepreneurial visions of particular localities. But whether tourism is critical or not, it brings change and the newer the South becomes, the more attention we must pay to the preservation of the bygone built environment. Envisioning these places as touriscapes allows us to see a future where preservation and development can coexist.

The vision of a newer regional identity and the importance of developing an insider/outsider perspective on change and progress apply not just to these tourism landscapes or to the South. Today, the business of tourism reaches every corner of the globe. This book and these studies of specific sites of recreational tourism in South Carolina address the importance of envisioning the preservation of the tawdry recreations dating from the past as part of the development of the future. Preservation works when a sense of place survives and is symbolically taken up by the next generation. Development itself, as an entrepreneurial concept, requires a new and innovative refashioning to be successful; however, in a practical sense, past models of development (and the past itself) must be engaged with even as we move beyond them. It is essential to preserve unique places like South of the Border and Atlantic Beach for future generations. These tourist landscapes have surpassed the "fifty-year rule," which marks them as historic landscapes.[1]

Sustainability, in reference to cultural landscapes, is an influential concept for twenty-first century development. It is important to keep several points in mind when considering preservation of historic tourist landscapes. First, the tourist landscape must remain economically viable, which means producing a profit. These landscapes must do so, while at the same time retaining the identities and sense of place that made them distinct and historic in the first place. This principle means no corporate buyouts by big developers lacking historical perspective or a sense of place. The third aspect of sustainability concerns environmental issues (related to both the coast and the roadway in these place studies). Historic tourism landscapes must develop while also preserving the natural environment. This is tricky balance to maintain in places like South of the Border and Atlantic Beach, which were developed in an era when environmental concerns mattered little. Corporate development along the Grand Strand that seeks big profits without considering the potential for pollution, erosion, flooding, and the impact of hurricanes has led to a ravaged coast line in danger of disappearing. Today's rapidly rising gas prices and the ecological and political threats tied to American automobile culture are approaching the point of producing catastrophe. Both Atlantic Beach and South of the Border must consider environmental preservation as part of their long-term plans. It is unlikely that the desire to drive down south to the beach for a vacation will decline precipitously in the twenty-first century. But even if these tourist sites are preserved as ruins from a lost age of wastefulness, their stories matter. These tourist landscapes are distinctive because of their complex histories and their surrounding environments. Constructing a compelling public narrative is necessary to sustain historic landscapes. This is the cultural work this book has undertaken. The stories of these places must endure if we are to learn from them.

South of the Border was born of the idiosyncratic vision of one individual and is now in the hands of his immediate family. Atlantic Beach was first the spiritual and economic vision of one man, then of a company of ten individuals, and now of a group of landowners. South of the Border and Atlantic Beach have changed; however, both survive with a certain continuity of vision and an independent aesthetic intact. The dialectic of continuity within change has sustained these places, making them distinctively local and "southern."

While attempting to envision a future where recreational and heritage tourism can come together to keep these sites alive, it is helpful to view these sites as touriscapes, where the intersection and overlap of categories is central. Dolores Hayden writes in the forward to *Preserving Cultural Landscapes in America*, "Commercial speculation and exploitation lurk as enemies of the unique, the authentic, and the local."[2] In many cases—mostly those involving exploitation—what she says is true; however, commercial speculation created both South of the Border and Atlantic Beach. In a period shortly after Prohibition was lifted, Schafer entered the business of selling alcohol and later the tourist trade, as he ascended the political ladder. The African American businessmen who built Atlantic Beach did so as a business venture, but one imbued with a larger spiritual vision of providing recreation for blacks in a space that offered freedom from discrimination in addition to freedom to take part in the hospitality industry. Both of these landscapes are based in commercial speculation, and both certainly represent the unique and the local. To discount the importance of the commercial and the recreational to the historic American landscape is to miss out on the rich stories these places, and many others, possess, and to lose sight of how they have influenced later generations creating a Newer South.

I conclude by offering some brief suggestions about how the meaning of these places might be preserved and developed in new ways. The recent emergence of various organizations focusing on preserving the recent past and commercial architecture reflects the evolution of historic preservation into a field that appreciates the inventive vernacular architecture and culture that dot the American roadside.[3]

Travelers entering the Sombrero Room Restaurant at South of the Border stand in the very spot where Alan Schaffer built his original cinder-block beer depot. Because of the constant manipulation of the built environment of South of the Border, little of the original structure remains for historical designation in the traditional sense. The remaining structures at Atlantic Beach also have not survived in a form fit for traditional preservation.[4] New and innovative models for preserving these landscapes as living places must be created. That is, their preservation must make use of the same innovative spirit as their creation.

One of the problems in writing this book and researching tourist landscapes in general is lack of material about the tourists who visit and value these spaces. South of the Border has developed a Facebook page where tourists are invited to post their memories, and the Atlantic Beach Historical Society has begun to collect oral histories. But there needs to be a way to archive the stories of today's tourists, many of who are loyal repeat visitors who have a long and lasting connection to these places. A story booth, like the photo booths that are common fixtures at tourist sites, would be one way to both produce revenue and collect historical narratives.

A similar model has worked for StoryCorps, an "independent non-profit project whose mission is to honor and celebrate one another's lives through listening." In the organization's numerous StoryBooths, Story-Corps provides spaces in which to professionally record memories. Participants are given a free CD of their recording, and their stories are archived with the Library of Congress. In the entrepreneurial spirit of Alan Schafer and the Atlantic Beach Company, contemporary tourist sites could offer StoryCorps-style recording booths and charge tourists a small fee to record their stories. A CD of the recording could function as a high tech souvenir and would also be digitally archived for public use by researchers or for promotional purposes. The project could include local libraries and schools. "The Border Foundation: Pedro Helping Our Community" already "donates monies annually to both local and regional charities," and could be used to fund such a project. Many of the surviving images of tourists from the golden era of Atlantic Beach are souvenir photos taken at a street side stand.[5] Given the inexpensive nature of modern recording and the reliability of digital storage devices this endeavor could be a low investment, high return project that connects tourists to the local community.

Many tourists would certainly relish the experience in an era when it is common to digitally archive even the briefest trip or journey. In my years of research, I have found that many people have a South of the Border or Atlantic Beach story to share. Digital souvenirs could also create an archive of information on the understudied biker subcultures that visit Atlantic Beach every May. Such entrepreneurial, academic, and community-based efforts would enable the perspectives of tourists to play a larger part in the narratives of these historic tourist landscapes.

While preserving stories (especially the elusive ones of tourists just passing through) is important, there is also a vast and constantly changing recreational landscape to preserve. Since both South of the Border and Atlantic Beach lack the architectural integrity to be preserved following the traditional model, one mode of preservation suitable for these touriscapes could be something like "imagically preserved landscapes." In

"Selling Heritage Landscapes," Richard Francaviglia writes, "When used effectively, images can actually be superimposed onto the real scene, thus increasing the sense of drama about the passage of time."[6] The possibilities are limitless, given the advances in digital technology—such as augmented reality, a term for a live or indirect view of a physical, real-world environment containing elements augmented by computer-generated sensory input, such as sound or graphics that can be accessed using a smart phone or similar device. These tourist sites could continue their typical tourist trade while adding a historic aspect to the landscape, including images and other forms of material culture from the past. Past and the present could be blended together on the landscape. South of the Border has experience with quasi-historical representations such as Confederateland, USA, Pedro's Africa Shop, and the old Blenheim factory tour. Atlantic Beach has the benefit of having an historical society (ABHS) that has already begun to work with exhibits, conferences, and a historic marker.

In 2003, the ABHS outlined a feasible preservation/development proposal, the "Motel Row Project," integrating the past with a vision of the future. The plan lays out the problem at Atlantic Beach and a possible solution:

> What remains of [Atlantic Beach's] heritage is falling victim to years of neglect as bulldozers remove the last few historic buildings that still stand, a silent witness to its segregated past. . . . Atlantic Beach Historical Society, alarmed at the potential loss of Black history and culture, would like to reverse the tide of disinvestment that has been sweeping over Atlantic Beach by acquiring and renovating two of the former anchors of the local economy." The E & E Motel (named after Eloise and Emory Gore—the first mayor of the town) and the Parkview Motel, both on 31st Street, would be "renovated utilizing a 50's style nostalgic décor with one, as a tribute to their storied past, and a 21st century nouveau décor with the other as a beacon for the future.[7]

This vision is one based in both historical memory, found in the built environment, and the economic development of the future. Literature promoting the plan explains, "ABHS's Motel Row will be a living tribute to a past that is no more. More importantly, it will function as an economic engine that will assist in the renewal of the entire Atlantic Beach area and provide its citizens with an opportunity to once again share in the rising tide of tourist dollars that are flooding the entire coastal area." This project was part of a larger planning effort called "The Colored Wall: Atlantic Beach Arts Renaissance (ABaR)," which was designed to "support the process of community planning and design" through an "arts and economic development project." The ABaR was designed to "involve identifying proposed participants, formulating project goals, projecting the long-range economic impact through arts initiatives."[8] The seeds of planning for such projects are promising. Calling the arts renaissance "The Color Wall" takes a boundary constructed by the white community to segregate Atlantic Beach and turns it on its head. As a symbol of the rebirth of the distinctive heritage of the beach, the boundary is an important piece of the fabric of the Grand Strand and the process of remembering.

Atlantic Beach has floundered because the vast array of stakeholders—residents, business owners, preservationists, outside developers, and surrounding communities—are unable to agree on a vision for the town's future. Yet this difficulty has arisen from attempts to integrate the perspectives of all of these different stakeholders—insiders and outsiders alike—into a refashioned landscape. Preserving the past and developing the future of South of the Border and Atlantic Beach is important for future generations, but it is not easy work.

This book contributes to the preservation and development of these landscapes. Both South of the Border and Atlantic Beach offer fascinating stories of southern places enacting and being enacted upon by change. These tourist landscapes are by no means ideal or perfect places. They represent the legacy of controversy at the heart of southern culture. They are dirty, raunchy, tacky, and old, but they are distinct and important places where future generations can go to better understand the trials and tribulations, the change and the continuity, the inside and the outside, of what it means to be southern.

NOTES

Introduction

1. According to the 2010 United States Census, Horry County, which has a total population of 269,291, is 80 percent white, 13 percent black, 6 percent Hispanic or Latino.

2. Mechling, Jay. "An American Culture Grid with Texts." *American Studies International*, 27 (1989): 2–12.

3. Tara McPherson, "On Wal-Mart and Southern Studies," *American Literature*, Volume 78, Number 4, December 2006, 698.

4. According to Google Maps it is 604 miles (10 hours and 35 minutes) from New York City to South of the Border, and 680 miles (11 hours and 4 minutes) from South of the Border to Miami, Florida. It is 646 miles (11 hours and 38 minutes) from New York City to Atlantic Beach, South Carolina, and 729 miles (12 hours and 4 minutes) to Miami, Florida. The fastest route (taking Interstate 95) goes right past South of the Border, but you must get off the interstate and head to the coast to hit Atlantic Beach.

5. Tim Cresswell, *In Place/Out of Place: Geography, Ideology, and Transgression* (Minneapolis, MN: University of Minnesota Press, 1996), 22.

6. *Corridor of Shame: The Neglect of South Carolina's Rural Schools*, DVD, directed by Bud Ferillo and produced by Ferillo and Associates, Inc. (Columbia, SC, 2005). Ferillo's documentary dramatizes the case of *Abbeville v. State of South Carolina*, in which local residents sued the state for violating the right of its children to a public education.

7. Richard R. Hourigan explains the specific history of road construction in his dissertation, "Welcome to South Carolina: Sex, Race, and Tourism in Myrtle Beach, 1900–1975" (Tuscaloosa, AL: Department of History, University of Alabama, 2009): "The first road connecting Conway to Myrtle Beach opened in 1914, although it was not officially completed until 1921. Until it was paved in 1927, it was more of 'a cow trail.' The road went several miles south to the town of Socastee before making a ninety-degree turn towards Myrtle Beach. Highway 501, the direct route from Conway, was not completed until 1948; it would cut the journey by fourteen miles. Others came to Myrtle Beach from Charleston or Wilmington by way of the Ocean Highway (Highway 17)." Also see Durward T. Stokes, *The History of Dillon County, South Carolina* (Columbia, SC: University of South Carolina Press, 1978) and Barbara F. Stokes, *Myrtle Beach: A History, 1990–1980* (Columbia, SC: University of South Carolina Press, 2007).

8. Howard Lawrence Preston, *Dirt Roads to Dixie: Accessibility and Modernization in the South, 1885–1935* (Knoxville, TN: University of Tennessee Press, 1991), 1.

9. I do not see the twenty-first century as "postsouthern" or argue that southern identity no longer exists, or has been absorbed into or has become American culture—though these pronouncements all possess some truth. See John Edgerton, *The Americanization of Dixie: The Southernization of America* (New York, NY: Harper's Magazine Press, 1974); Martyn Bone, *A Postsouthern Sense of Place in Contemporary Fiction* (Baton Rouge, LA: Louisiana State University Press, 2005).

10. Recent work on southern tourism includes Tim Hollis, *Dixie Before Disney: 100 Years of Roadside Fun* (Jackson, MS: University of Mississippi Press, 1999); Lynn Morrow and Linda Myers-Phinney, *Shepherd of the Hills Country: Tourism Transforms the Ozarks, 1880s–1930s* (Fayetteville, AR: University of Arkansas Press, 1999; Harvey K. Newman, *Southern Hospitality: Tourism and the Growth of Atlanta* (Tuscaloosa, AL: University of Alabama Press, 1999); Richard Starnes, ed., *Southern Journeys: Tourism, History & Culture in the Modern South* (Tuscaloosa, AL: University of Alabama Press, 2003); Alecia P. Long, *The Great Southern Babylon: Sex, Race, And Respectability in New Orleans, 1865–1920* (Baton Rouge, LA: Louisiana State University Press, 2005); Richard Starnes, *Creating the Land of the Sky: Tourism and Society in Western North Carolina* (Tuscaloosa, AL: University of Alabama Press, 2005); Anthony Stanonis, *Creating the Big Easy: New Orleans and the Emergence of Modern Tourism, 1918–1945* (Athens, GA: University of Georgia Press, 2006); Brooks Blevins, *Tourism in the Mountain South: A Double-Edged Sword* (Knoxville, TN: University of Tennessee Press, 2007); Ann Denkler, *Sustaining Identity, Recapturing Heritage: Exploring Issues of Public History, Tourism, and Race in a Southern Town* (Lanham, MD: Lexington Books, 2007); Aaron Ketchell, *Holy Hills of the Ozarks: Religion and Tourism in Branson, Missouri* (Baltimore, MD: Johns Hopkins University Press, 2007); Anthony Stanonis, ed., *Dixie Emporium: Tourism, Foodways, and Consumer Culture in the American South* (Athens, GA: University of Georgia Press, 2008).

11. John Shelton Reed, "The South: What Is It? Where Is It?" pp. 5–28 in *My Tears Spoiled My Aim: and Other Reflections on Southern Culture* (Orlando, FL: Harcourt, Inc., 1993), 7; originally published in Paul Escott and David Goldfield, eds. *The South for New Southerners* (Cambridge, MA: Harvard University Press, 1991).

12. Scott Romine, *The Real South: Southern Narrative in the Age of Cultural Reproduction* (Baton Rouge, LA: Louisiana State University Press, 2008), 16.

13. Jean Baudrillard, *America*, trans. Chris Turner, (London, England: Verso, 1989).

14. Warren Belasco's 1979 social history of early American travel argued that in the beginning, "hitting the road" engaged those central American values of independence and self-reliance; however, as a growing consumer society evolved, the roadside became a tame and commercialized landscape. In 2002, David Laderman examined how the road movie's "overt concern with rebellion against traditional social norms is consistently undermined, diluted or at least haunted by the very conservative cultural codes the genre so desperately takes flight from." In 2006, Cotton Seilers

directly challenged the "idealized conception" of the road and argued, "[T]he space of the American road, like the contours of citizenship, was established under specific regimes of racialized inequality and limited access whose codes it reproduces." Warren Belasco, "Commercialized Nostalgia," in David L. Lewis and Laurence Goldstein, eds. *The Automobile and American Culture* (Ann Arbor, MI: University of Michigan Press, 1980), and *Americans on the Road: From Autocamp to Motel, 1910–1945* (Baltimore, MD: Johns Hopkins University Press, 1979). David Laderman, *Driving Visions: Exploring the Road Movie* (Austin, TX: University of Texas Press, 2002). Cotton Seiler, "So That We as a Race Might Have Something Authentic to Travel By": African American Automobility and Cold-War Liberalism," *American Quarterly* 58.4 (December 2006), 1091–117, and *A Culture of Drivers: A Cultural History of Automobility in America* (Chicago, IL: University of Chicago Press, 2008).

15. Recent discussions of social entrepreneurship as a generational movement include Ian Sparina's article, "For This Generation, Vocations of Service: Recent College Grads Forgo Traditional Careers, Money to Start Nonprofits Focused on Outreach," *Washington Post*, October 14, 2008. Sparina writes, "Social entrepreneurship, the movement in which people launch nonprofit or business ventures to address systematic problems in impoverished areas, emerged nearly three decades ago and is growing in appeal among young adults who want to help vulnerable people." In addition, a section in the *New York Times* from March 8, 2008, profiling the "faces of social entrepreneurship," quotes Kyle Taylor, a twenty-three-year-old advocate for the social entrepreneurship movement: "Our generation is replacing signs and protests with individual actions. This is our civil rights movement and what will define our generation."

16. Preston, *Dirt Roads to Dixie*, 6.

17. Sandoval defines "U.S. third world feminism" as a "central locus of possibility, an insurgent social movement that shattered the construction of any one ideology as the single correct site where truth can be represented." Chela Sandoval, *Methodology of the Oppressed* (Minneapolis, MN: University of Minnesota Press, 2000), 59.

18. Sandoval, *Methodology of the Oppressed*, 58–59.

19. Sandoval, *Methodology of the Oppressed*, 61. Sandoval writes, "African-American feminist theorist Patricia Hill Collins describes the skills developed by U.S. feminists of color who, through exclusion from male-controlled race liberation movements and from white-controlled female liberation movements, were forces to internalize an 'outsider/within' identity that guides movement of being *according to an ethical commitment* to equalize power between social constituencies" (61).

20. "Steps Forward And Steps Back," *New York Times*, July 31, 1994; James C. Cobb, *Away Down South: A History of Southern Identity* (New York, NY: Oxford University Press, 2005), 276.

21. Sandoval, *Methodology of the Oppressed*, 141.

22. For Sandoval this trajectory involves a productive pain similar to Robert Young's "aesthetics of crisis." Like Sandoval, Robert Young mines the big figures of

his field of African American literary/cultural theory, specifically Henry Louis Gates, Jr. and Cornel West, to move beyond them in creating something new. He pulls from Richard Wright's *Black Boy* (1945) to show how the "difference of race disrupts the operations of dominant ideology." Young explains: "With the 'aesthetics of crisis,' daily life is reconceptualized not only as the site for oppression and exploitation but also, dialectically, the foundation for transformation. It is this utopian dimension that provides a theoretical-political space for reconstructing contemporary African-American literary/cultural theory. In foregrounding the political economy of race, materialist knowledges reclaim the transformative possibilities of theory." Robert Young, The Linguistic Turn, Materialism and Race," *Callaloo*, Vol. 24, No. 1 (Winter, 2001), 343.

23. Carol Vogel, "The Inside Story On Outsiderness: Glenn Ligon's Gritty Conceptualism Makes Art Out of Others' Words," *New York Times*, February 27, 2011.

24. Pierre Bourdieu, *Distinction: The Social Critique of the Judgement of Taste*, trans. Richard Nice, (Cambridge, MA: Harvard University Press, 1984; originally published 1979), 1.

25. Sally Price, *Primitive Art in Civilized Places*, second edition (Chicago, IL: University of Chicago Press, 2001; originally published 1989), 20, 130.

26. Preston, *Dirt Roads to Dixie*, 128.

27. Lucy Lippard, "Foreword" in Dean MacCannell, *The Tourist: A New Theory of the Leisure Class* (Berkeley, CA: University of California Press, 1976, 1999), ix–x.

28. The interdisciplinary field of place studies is emerging in university centers, programs, and projects throughout the United States. For example, The Iowa Project on Place Studies "fosters teaching and research in the concept of place, the interconnections between places across the globe, and local, state, and regional studies." According to their website, "Place studies" is an "emerging interdisciplinary area recognizing the centrality of natural, built, social, and cultural environments in the formation of individual, group, and communal identity, as well as the ways in which human beings interact with the world. Although 'place' is grounded in local geography, it is also the ground from which humans connect with virtually everything else. Understanding one's place, then, involves understanding global ecosystems and economics just as much as the local landscape, community history, and regional arts." [http://www.uiowa.edu/~ipops/] Place studies at New York University consist of an "online magazine, discussion forum, and research source for the study of place. It's about how we experience places, how they influence us, and how literary and artistic works shape our perception of places." [http://placestudies.com/content/about-place-studies] Place Studies at the University of Nebraska, Lincoln, is housed in the English Department and believes "in the 21st Century the most important task of literature, and of literary studies, is to enable humans to re-imagine our place in an increasingly threatened and deteriorating natural environment." [http://english .unl.edu/placestudies/index.html] In addition, Arizona State University's Institute for Humanities Research has a focus on Place Studies [http://ihr.asu.edu/place/resources],

and Kansas State University's Environment Behavior and Place Studies (EBPS) "focuses on the behavioral and experiential aspects of person-environment relationships and their implications for environmental design and research. The program examines varying philosophic and methodological approaches to issues in environment behavior and place experience." [http://www.capd.ksu.edu/arch/academic-programs/post-pro fessional-degree-program/environment-behavior-and-place-studies-emphasis] At my own university, the University of Maryland Baltimore County (UMBC), I direct the Orser Center for the Study of Place, Community, and Culture, which "creates a space for innovative collaborations between scholars, students, and community organizations at UMBC. The Center's goal is the study and preservation of places, communities, and cultures through scholarly research, teaching, and public programming." [http://amstcommunitystudies.org/] This is a sample and not an exhaustive list of emerging programs in Place Studies in the United States.

29. Rev. Walter W. Skeat, *An Etymological Dictionary of the English Language* (Oxford, England: Clarendon Press, 1879, 1953), 656, 673.

30. Sandoval, *Methodology of the Oppressed*, 30.

31. *American Heritage Dictionary of the English Language* (Boston, MA: Houghton Mifflin Company, 1992), 1011.

32. John Brinckerhoff Jackson, *Discovering Vernacular Landscape* (New Haven, CT: Yale University Press, 1984), 7–8. Jackson paid a great deal of attention to the landscapes of mobility, mainly roadside architecture, and regional distinctiveness in his work. See *A Sense of Place, a Sense of Time* (New Haven, CT: Yale University Press, 1994) and *Landscape in Sight: Looking at America* (New Haven, CT: Yale University Press, 1997). The basic analysis of the relationship between artifacts and humans is expanded to include nature in Jeremy Korr's 1997 article, "A Proposed Model for Cultural Landscape Study" (*Material Culture*, Fall, 1997).

33. John Brinckerhoff Jackson, "The Word Itself," from *Discovering the Vernacular Landscape* (New Haven, CT: University Press, 1984), 3–8.

34. Arjun Appadurai, "Commodities and the Politics of Value," Introductory Essay, *The Social Life of Things: Commodities in Cultural Perspective*, Arjun Appadurai, ed., (Cambridge, England: Cambridge University Press, 3–63).

35. Lewis, "Axioms for Reading the Landscape."

36. Yi-Fu Tuan, *Place and Space: The Perspective of Experience* (Minneapolis, MN: University of Minnesota Press, 1977), 3–7.

37. SHA talk 2010

38. Russ Castronovo and Susan Gillman, *States of Emergency: Object of American Studies* (Chapel Hill, NC: University of North Carolina Press, 2009), 7. The editors offer further elaboration on the potential for such a method in their introduction: "Such spatiotemporal paradigms would go a long way towards counteracting the tendency within conventional area studies, not only the older, pre-cultural studies variety but also the 'new American studies,' to privilege either space or time but never both at once."

39. James C. Cobb, *Away Down South: A History of Southern Identity* (New York, NY: Oxford University Press, 2005), 6–7. Emphasis in original.

40. Romine, *The Real South*, 2.

41. In the realm of popular culture, I reference the Drive-By Truckers album, *Southern Rock Opera* (Lost Highway, 2001); the Ebony Hillbillies (see *Garden & Gun*, February/March 2011); and films by Ray McKinnon, which include *The Accountant* (dir. Ray McKinnon) Ginny Mule Productions, 2001, *Chrystal* (dir. Ray McKinnon) Chrystal Productions, 2004, and *Randy and the Mob* (dir. Ray McKinnon) Capricorn Pictures, 2007. For an excellent analysis of the Drive-By Trucker's 2011 album and general cultural significance, see Bryant Simon, "'We're Almost There': The Drive-By Truckers' Art of Place," *Southern Spaces* [http://southernspaces.org], March 28, 2011. Simon begins: "The Drive-By Truckers have always done their best and most arresting work about place. They clearly think that where you come from matters, though this is not for them about a spot on a map or a street address. It is about the songs, tastes, truths, lies, and burdens we inherit from our parents and where we come from that makes us who we are."

42. Rebecca Bridges Watts, *Contemporary Southern Identities: Community Through Controversy* (Jackson, MS: University Press of Mississippi, 2008), 6, 9, 12–13. Tara McPherson, *Reconstructing Dixie: Race, Gender, and Nostalgia in the Imagined South* (Durham, NC: Duke University Press, 2003). In this book, McPherson challenges the "lenticular logic of racial visibility," which she describes as a "monocultural logic, a schema by which histories or images that are actually copresent get presented (structurally, ideologically) so that only one of the images can be seen at a time," 7, 96–101. McPherson, *Reconstructing Dixie*, 8.

43. Lizabeth Cohen, *A Consumer's Republic: The Politics of Mass Consumption in Postwar America* (New York, NY: Knopf, 2003).

44. Addressing "global-local linkages" Wayne Gabardi writes, "This condition of globalization . . . represents a shift from a more territorialized learning process bound up with the nation-state society to one more fluid and translocal. Culture has become a much more mobile, human software employed to mix elements from diverse contexts." (Wayne Gabardi, *Negotiating Postmodernism* (Minneapolis, MN: University of Minnesota Press, 2000), 33. Also see James Watson, *Golden Arches East: McDonald's in East Asia*, second edition (Palo Alto, CA: Stanford University Press, 2006). Recent work about the global and transnational in southern studies include: David L. Carlton and Peter A. Coclanis, *The South, the Nation, and the World: Perspectives on Southern Economic Development* (Charlottesville, VA: University of Virginia Press, 2003); Jon Smith and Deborah Cohn, eds., *Look Away! The U.S. South in New World Studies* (Durham, NC: Duke University Press, 2004); James Cobb and William Stueck, eds., *Globalization and the American South* (Athens, GA: University of Georgia Press, 2005); James L. Peacock, Harry L. Watson, and Carrie R. Matthews, eds., *The American South in a Global World* (Chapel Hill, NC: University of North Carolina Press, 2005).

45. James Peacock, *Grounded Globalism: How the U.S. South Embraces the World* (Athens, GA: University of Georgia Press, 2007), xi.

46. Barbara Ellen Smith writes: "These struggles [over globalization in the South] do not simply defend a static geographic place, fixed in time and space; they create place by invoking selective constructs of what a specific place represents. The place that is both defended and created is rarely the region, for what is at stake is far more specific, concrete, and personal: the ten blocks of a neighborhood, a small watershed or hollow, a rural community." "Place and Past in the Global South," *American Literature*, Volume 78, Number 4, December 2006, 693.

47. Works that deals with the mobility of southern culture in literary studies include: Houston A. Baker's *Turning South Again: Rethinking Modernism/Rereading Booker T.* (Durham, NC: Duke University Press, 2001), and Suzanne W. Jones and Sharon Monteith, *South to a New Place: Region, Literature, Culture* (Baton Rouge, LA: Louisiana State University Press, 2002).

Chapter One

1. The South Carolina Department of Parks, Recreation, and Tourism (SCPRT) describes tourism as "South Carolina's number one industry." "The Economic Contribution of Tourism in South Carolina-2008 Tourism Satellite Account Results" (Spring 2010) states that spending on travel or on behalf of tourism reached $18.4 billion in 2008, which represents a 7.1 percent increase over 2007. Tourism supported nearly one in ten South Carolina jobs. The fiscal impact was $1.2 billion in state and local taxes (http://www.scprt.com/our-partners/tourismstatistics/researchreports .aspx). Michael MacNulty, Executive Chairman, Tourism Development International, "Tourism Is Now South Carolina's Largest Export," *South Carolina Business*, February 1, 2008.

2. In 2010, SCPRT changed the official motto for South Carolina's tourism industry from "Smiling Faces. Beautiful Places." to the more generic slogan "South Carolina: Made for Vacation."

3. Stephanie Yuhl, *A Golden Haze of Memory: The Making of Historic Charleston* (Chapel Hill, NC: University of North Carolina Press, 2005).

4. Preston, *Dirt Roads to Dixie*, 128.

5. Preston, *Dirt Roads to Dixie*, 161.

6. Preston, *Dirt Roads to Dixie*, 109–16.

7. Preston, *Dirt Roads to Dixie*, 42–48, 130–32; John Hammond More, *The South Carolina Highway Department, 1917–1987* (Columbia, SC: USC press, 1987); Advertisement, *Holiday*, November 1946.

8. Edgar, *South Carolina*, 491.

9. Preston, "Chapter 2: The Promise of Accessibility," in *Dirt Roads to Dixie*, 39–68; *Looking Beyond the Highway: Dixie Roads and Culture*, Claudette Stager and Martha

Carver, eds. (Knoxville, TN: University of Tennessee Press, 2006). The Dixie Highway
was partially the project of Carl Fisher, who was building a resort in Miami, and the
Capital Highway was greatly supported by Leonard Tufts, whose family built Pinehurst
golf resort in North Carolina. Road construction was closely tied to big business
interests.

10. Later in the twentieth century, political issues around road construction
included ecological damage and sprawl. There is a down side to the money roads can
bring to communities.

11. The Carolinas Inc. advertisement *(Kingstree, South Carolina) County Record*,
May 2, 1935.

12. This is still an important issue for tourism boosters in the twenty-first century,
and 2010 census data seems to support tourism's role in bringing new residents to
South Carolina. For example, Horry County, the most popular country in the state for
tourism and the location of the Grand Strand, had a 37 percent permanent population
growth from 2000 to 2010. Responding to the census figures, Brad Dean, current
president and CEO of the Myrtle Beach Area Chamber of Commerce, said: "For many
people, the same reasons they come down for vacation are the same reasons they
come down to buy property." WMBF news, "Census number point to connection
between tourism, permanent moves," March 27, 2011, http://www.wmbf.com; Jake
Spring, "Horry County growth rises 37 percent in 2010 Census," *Sun News*, March 24,
2011.

13. The Carolinas Inc. advertisement, *(Kingstree, South Carolina) County
Record*, May 2, 1935; Richard D. Starnes, "Creating a 'Variety Vacationland': Tourism
Development in North Carolina, 1930–1990," in *Southern Journeys: Tourism, History,
& Culture in the Modern South* (Tuscaloosa, AL: University of Alabama Press, 2003),
140–2.

14. Nancy Rhyne, *The Grand Strand: An Uncommon Guide to Myrtle Beach And
Its Surroundings* (Charlotte, NC: East Woods Press, 1981), 42; Richard R. Hourigan,
"Welcome to South Carolina: Sex, Race, and Tourism in Myrtle Beach, 1900–1975,"
Dissertation, Department of History, University of Alabama, 2009, 28–35.

15. Edgar, *South Carolina: A History*, 493.

16. Lizabeth Cohen, *A Consumers' Republic: The Politics of Mass Consumption in
Postwar America* (New York, NY: Vintage, 2003).

17. For a discussion of the influential postwar development in South Carolina
within the context of industrial recruiting, see Mark Maunula, *Guten Tag Y'all:
Globalization and the South Carolina Piedmont, 1950–2000* (Athens, GA: University
of Georgia Press, 2009), especially chapter two, "Origins of the Latest South," 33–56.
Maunula points out that from the 1950s until 1975, the "South would be the fastest-
growing region in the United States." Furthermore, "Within the Old Confederacy,
South Carolina would consistently remain the second fastest-growing state, behind
only the emerging retirement haven of southern Florida." (39). South Carolina is
constantly competing with the tourism market in Florida, while also being greatly

influenced and changed by the traffic heading to the Florida beaches. South of the
Border and the Grand Strand (where Atlantic Beach is located) would not have
experienced such rapid development without the existence of a bustling tourism
market in Florida.

18. Betty I. MacNabb, "South Carolinians Roll Out the Carpet for Nation's Free-
Spending Tourists," *Columbia Record*, November 6, 1952; South Carolina State
Chamber of Commerce, *Dollars in Flight: A Manual Showing Why and How South
Carolina Should Promote Tourist Trade* (Columbia, SC: January, 1951), Tourism in
South Carolina, Vertical Files Collection, South Caroliniana Library, University of
South Carolina.

19. In her front-page article, MacNabb notes that South Carolina ranked last
in the southern states and near the bottom nationally in obtaining tourist dollars.
The breakdown for the $67 million tourists spent in South Carolina is: retail stores
$16,750,000; restaurants $14,740,00; lodging $11,390,000; gas, oil, etc. $8,040,000;
transportation $4,690,000; and miscellaneous $6,360,00. MacNabb, "South
Carolinians Roll Out the Carpet for Nation's Free-Spending Tourists." *Dollars in
Flight* pointed out that South Carolina spent only $3,000 annually on tourism—only
Alabama spent less. South Carolina State Chamber of Commerce, *Dollars in Flight*.

20. "Tourist Advertising Program Almost Too Successful in SC," (*Columbia, South
Carolina*) *State*, March 15, 1955, Tourism in South Carolina, Vertical Files Collection,
South Caroliniana Library, University of South Carolina.

21. Edward B. Borden, "Tourism: A Top SC Industry," *Sandlapper* May 1968: 57–61,
Tourism in South Carolina, Vertical Files Collection, South Caroliniana Library,
University of South Carolina.

22. McNair moved from lieutenant governor to the position of governor after the
death of United States Senator Olin Johnson. The current governor, Donald Russell,
wanted to assume Johnson's senate seat and worked out a deal with McNair: McNair
could be governor if he appointed Russell to the senate seat as soon as he took over the
office. Edgar, *South Carolina*, 542–4; Hourigan, Chapter 5: "Selling South Carolina," in
Welcome to South Carolina, 130–61.

23. Dwight Holder, the head of McNair's inaugural committee, was appointed
chairman of the SCPRT and worked to create six commissioners from each
congressional district in the state. Fred Brickman, current director of the Ocean Hiway
Association and former Myrtle Beach Chamber of Commerce president, was first
asked to be executive director, but ended up serving as the assistant executive director.
However, as assistant director, he worked with the governor to find the right executive
director. Hourigan, *Welcome to South Carolina*, 145-146.

24. Edward B. Borden, "Tourism: A Top SC Industry," *Sandlapper*, May 1968
(57–61).

25. For a discussion of how the residents of the South Carolina Piedmont were
expected to promote the positive aspects of their community, see Mark Maunula,
Guten Tag Y'all: Globalization and the South Carolina Piedmont, 1950–2000 (Athens,

GA: University of Georgia Press, 2009), especially chapter three, "The Roots of International Recruiting," 57–75.

26. MacNabb, "South Carolinians Roll Out the Carpet for Nation's Free-Spending Tourists."

27. Barbara McAden, "Now Travelers in S.C. Will Feel Like Guests" and "Welcome Center Manager Is Experienced Greeter Already," *State*, February 22, 1968. The welcome centers were also a part of $13 million proposal to upgrade the state's tourism and recreational facilities, which SCPRT developed in its first year of operation. Edward B. Borden, "Tourism: A Top SC Industry," May 1968, 57–61, Tourism in South Carolina, Vertical Files Collection, South Caroliniana Library, University of South Carolina.

28. See John Urry, *The Tourist Gaze* (London, England: Sage, 2002, 1990). In addition, Hourigan's *Welcome to South Carolina* discusses a travel promotional booklet, *Peninsula Pete Guides You Along the Ocean Highway By Way of Del-Mar-Va Peninsula: Fast-Safe-All Weather Route From Northern Pines to Southern Palms* (Wilmington, DE: Ocean Hiway Association, 1942) that only shows African Americans as local color rather than as tourists. Hourigan writes: "Of the fifty-eight illustrations, only five pictured African-Americans all in the role of servant. None of the images showed blacks engaged in any leisurely activity," 49. For a more recent focus on issues of race and tourism promotion, see Amy Elias, "Postmodern Southern Vacations: Vacation Advertising, Globalization, and Southern Regionalism," in *South to a New Place: Region, Literature, and Culture* (Baton Rouge, LA: Louisiana State University Press, 2002). Elias offers an analysis of the continuation of racist tourist advertising by corporate tourist businesses in *Southern Living* magazine.

29. "In terms of development efforts, a comparatively peaceful desegregation process allowed South Carolina to preserve its image as a promising place to do business, and the end of segregation drew new types of business, investment, and tourism to the state as it shed its reputation as a repository for the gothic, the benighted, and the backwards." Lacy K. Ford Jr. and R. Phillip Stone, "Economic Development and Globalization in South Carolina," *Southern Cultures* (Spring 2007), 18–50. This article is an excellent overview of South Carolina's manufacturing industry in the context of the rise of globalization, though the previous quote from pages 28–29 is the only mention of tourism in the entire article. The article's lack of attention to the economic impact of tourism demonstrates the need for an economic perspective that includes the growing service industry, especially tourism. However, the article's basic argument that South Carolina needs to invest in education and innovation to move beyond its history of low wages, low tax economics, and "smokestack chasing," is a solid one. While tourism is a central industry in South Carolina, it suffers from the same low wage problems (and short periods of seasonal employment) detrimental to the state's poor standing in national economic development.

30. Governor McNair, who formed SCPRT in 1967, attempted to stop the violence and "worked diligently to restore trust and goodwill" in South Carolina after the

Orangeburg Massacre. Orangeburg was along the busy tourist highway 301. Politicians and boosters alike saw racial unrest and violence as bad for the state's wellbeing, image, and ability to recruit industry (tourism included). See Edgar, *South Carolina*, 542–4, and Jack Bass and Jack Nelson, *The Orangeburg Massacre*, (Macon, GA: Mercer University Press, 1996, 1984).

31. Charles Joyner, "Foreword" to Catherine H. Lewis, *Horry County, South Carolina, 1730–1993* (Columbia, SC: University of South Carolina Press, 1998), xi.

32. "Advertising Study–effectiveness of SCPRT's 1972–1973 advertising campaign," compiled by South Carolina Division of Tourism, Columbia, SC, 1973, Tourism in South Carolina, Vertical Files Collection, South Caroliniana Library, University of South Carolina.

33. George S. Bliss, "Charleston South Carolina Garden Tour: A Notebook of a trip to Charleston and other points, 1941," South Carolina Historical Society, Charleston, South Carolina.

34. "History of Brookgreen Gardens," http://www.brookgreen.org/history_of_brookgreen.cfm.

35. Richard M. Coté, "In My Own Words," Amazon.com profile.

36. Richard N. Coté, *Redneck Riviera* (Mt. Pleasant, SC: Corinthian Books, 2001).

37. The "redneck Riviera" moniker is not handled uncritically by academics, who still must acknowledge this influential cultural distinction. In his master's thesis in geography, "Using GIS to Analyze Leisure Business Districts in the Myrtle Beach Area of South Carolina" (University of South Carolina, 1995), Jack Hall Maquire explains: "Many persons within the state of South Carolina derisively refer to the Myrtle Beach area as a 'redneck Riviera.' Visitor data refute this label, but how this diverse area is marketed internationally is a serious and timely issue. Litchfield, Pawley's Island, and DeBordieu are certainly not 'redneck' areas and the same is true for several other portions of the Grand Strand. The Myrtle Beach area's image in the regional, national, and international arenas is an important marketing and planning consideration" (62).

38. Hourigan, "Welcome to South Carolina," 9.

39. The study also found the average expenditure per party to be $251.31; length of stay was 4 to 8 nights during April to August; 28 percent were first-time visitors, and 72 percent returning; the primary method of travel was the automobile; major destinations were the Grand Strand (54 percent), Charleston (18 percent), and Hilton Head (6 percent). This was the first time Hilton Head ranked as an important destination. South Carolina Division of Tourism in Columbia, "Success of 1972–1973 Campaign." Tourism in South Carolina Vertical Files Collection, South Caroliniana Library, University of South Carolina.

40. John A. Pearce II, Bruce Schmidt, and Fred R. Davis, "The Problems of Small Business in SC Travel and Tourism Industry" in "S.C. Development and Tourism Issue" *Business and Economic Review* Volume XXVI, no. 5, April 1980, 18–23, Tourism in South Carolina Vertical Files Collection, South Carolina Library, University of South Carolina.

41. Douglass Mauldin, "S.C. Tourism Office Gets National Praise," *State*, July 29, 1977, Tourism in South Carolina Vertical Files Collection, South Caroliniana Library, University of South Carolina.

42. John A. Pearce II, Bruce Schmidt, and Fred R. Davis, "The Problems of Small Business in SC Travel and Tourism Industry," in "S.C. Development and Tourism Issue," *Business and Economic Review*, Volume XXVI, no. 5, April 1980, 18–23, Tourism in South Carolina Vertical Files Collection, South Caroliniana Library, University of South Carolina.

43. This rise in South Carolina's tourism market despite national economic downturns is touted in the South Carolina press with articles such as: Katherine King, "Despite Recession, S.C. Vacation Spots do Well," *State*, July 20, 1980; Fred Monk, "Tourism credited for state unemployment drop," *Columbia Record*, June 3, 1980; Jim Tharpe, "1981 becoming 'gold rush' for state tourism," *Greenville News*, June 11, 1981; "Don't tell the rest of the economy, but the tourism economy in SC is booming," and "Tourism efforts are paying off," *Greenville News*, June 13, 1981, Tourism in South Carolina Vertical Files Collection, South Caroliniana Library, University of South Carolina.

44. Arch G. Woodside, Ellen M. Moore, and Michael J. Etzel, "Vacational Travel Behavior and Perceived Benefits of Home State Residents," in "S.C. Development and Tourism Issue," *Business and Economic Review*, Volume XXVI, no. 5, April 1980, Tourism in South Carolina Vertical Files Collection, South Caroliniana Library, University of South Carolina. John A. Pearce II, Bruce Schmidt, and Fred R. Davis, "The Problems of Small Business in SC Travel and Tourism Industry," in "S.C. Development and Tourism Issue," *Business and Economic Review*, Volume XXVI, no. 5, April 1980. Tourism in South Carolina Vertical Files Collection, South Caroliniana Library, University of South Carolina.

45. William Stracener, "Tourism Spending In 1980 Highest in State's History," *Columbia Record*, March 1, 1981; according to SCPRT, 38.1 million tourists spent $2.19 billion in 1980, Tourism in South Carolina Vertical Files Collection, South Caroliniana Library, University of South Carolina.

46. "Sleeping Tax: Useful Tool for Tourism," *State*, February 2, 1984; SCPRT Press Release, August 1, 1985; Accommodations Tax Revenue Distribution Full Fiscal Year, 2009–10, SCPRT, Tourism in South Carolina Vertical Files Collection, South Caroliniana Library, University of South Carolina. SCPRT Press Release, March 9, 1986, Tourism in South Carolina Vertical Files Collection, South Caroliniana Library, University of South Carolina.

47. SCPRT Press Release, March 9, 1986, Tourism in South Carolina Vertical Files Collection, South Caroliniana Library, University of South Carolina.

48. SCPRT Press Release, May 17, 1985, Tourism in South Carolina Vertical Files Collection, South Caroliniana Library, University of South Carolina.

49. "State to change focus of tourism advertising," *Columbia Record*, September 16, 1982, Tourism in South Carolina Vertical Files Collection, South Caroliniana Library, University of South Carolina.

50. Margaret Corvini, "Aggressive tourism ads ready to go: S.C. wants to attract some Florida-based vacationers," *State*, October 30, 1985; Beverly E. Shelley, "Myrtle Beach tops survey of state tourism attractions," *State*, February 20, 1989. Shelley points out that 54 percent of South Carolina's tourists are still passing through on the way to Florida. Tourism in South Carolina Vertical Files Collection, South Caroliniana Library, University of South Carolina.

51. These are the same international markets the Piedmont of South Carolina was wooing in hope of bringing global industries (such as automobiles and textiles) to the state. See Mark Maunula, *Guten Tag Y'all: Globalization and the South Carolina Piedmont, 1950–2000* (Athens, GA: University of Georgia Press, 2009).

52. SCPRT Press Release, May 20, 1987, states European visitors to SC in 1986 spent an unprecedented $8.6 million in the state, a whopping 30.54 percent increase over 1985 and a return of $86.55 for every promotional dollar in attracting the new visitors. William J. Sigmon, Sr., "The Lure of the Palmetto State: Cooperative Efforts to Keep Tourism Going," *South Carolina Business*, 1990, Tourism in South Carolina, Vertical Files Collection, South Caroliniana Library, University of South Carolina.

53. Karen Hayden, "Canadian-American Days," *Coast*, March 19–25, 1978, South Carolina Historical Society, Charleston, South Carolina. Hayden explains that in April of 1961 the Can-Am Days festival began with a meager nine planned events with fewer than 500 participants and "mushroomed into a program of over a hundred events involving 60,000 people" by the late 1970s.

54. "Canadians visit beach, but prices curb spending," *Columbia Record*, March 27, 1982, Tourism in South Carolina, Vertical Files Collection, South Caroliniana Library, University of South Carolina.

55. SCPRT, "International Visitation to South Carolina," December 2010, http://www.scprt.com/files/Research/InternationalVisitationtoSouthCarolina2009.pdf. Data on Canadian visitors to South Carolina comes from Statistics Canada's International Travel Survey. The International Travel Survey is a mail survey of travelers to and from Canada that is balanced with Canada's E-311 customs data. Data on the volume of overseas visitors to South Carolina comes from the United States Department of Homeland Security, Office of Immigration Statistics' I-94 form, which all international travel parties arriving in the United States by airplane must fill out.

56. SCPRT Press Release, October 7, 1991,

57. Edgar, *South Carolina*, 580–1; SCPRT Press Release, September 29, 1989, Tourism in South Carolina, Vertical Files Collection, South Caroliniana Library, University of South Carolina; Associated Press, "Large waves of tourists hitting S.C. beaches despite Hugo," *State*, June 27, 1990.

58. Jack Hall Maquire, "Using GIS to Analyze Leisure Business Districts in the Myrtle Beach Area of South Carolina," Masters thesis, Geography (University of South Carolina, 1995), 33.

59. SCPRT Press Release, September 5, 1991, Tourism in South Carolina, Vertical Files Collection, South Caroliniana Library, University of South Carolina.

60. William J. Sigmon, Sr., "The Lure of the Palmetto state: Cooperative Efforts to Keep Tourism Going," *South Carolina Business*, 1990, Tourism in South Carolina, Vertical Files Collection, South Caroliniana Library, University of South Carolina.

61. Erin MacLellan, "Drawing a Crowd: Tourism and Economic Development Are Profitable Partners," *South Carolina Business*, 1994, Tourism in South Carolina, Vertical Files Collection, South Caroliniana Library, University of South Carolina.

62. SCPRT and the South Carolina State Museum, *To Walk the Whole Journey: African American Cultural Resources in South Carolina: A Directory* (Charleston, SC: South Carolina Historical Society, 1992).

63. Dewanna Lofton, "S.C. heritage: State seeks black tourist," *State*, March 12, 1996, Tourism in South Carolina, Vertical Files Collection, South Caroliniana Library, University of South Carolina.

64. Eddy L. Harris, *South of Haunted Dreams* (New York, NY: Henry Holt and Company, 1993), 36.

65. Psyche A, Williams-Forson, *Building Houses Out of Chicken Legs: Black Women, Food, & Power* (Chapel Hill, NC: University of North Carolina Press, 2006), 114.

66. SCPRT Market Research Office, "Report on African-American Travel & Tourism in South Carolina," October 1997, State Documents, Coastal Carolina University, Conway, South Carolina.

67. South Carolina National Heritage Corridor, "Brochure on African American Heritage," 2005, State Documents, Coastal Carolina University, Conway, South Carolina.

68. Congressman James E. Clyburn, News Release, 12 July 2004; Meghan Hogan, "National Park Services Releases Gullah-Geechee Study," January 25, 2006. http://www.nationaltrust.org/magazine/archives/arc_news_2006/012506.htm.

69. I heard Michael Allen speak as part of an excellent panel, "Public History Round Table: The Gullah/Geechee Heritage Corridor," at the Organization of American Historians (OAH) Conference on April 9, 2010 in Washington, D.C.; *Coastal Heritage*, Volume 24, Number 2, Fall 2009; Prentiss Findlay, "African Passages shows relics of brutal time," *(Charleston, South Carolina) Post and Courier*, February 27, 2009; Jessica Johnson, "Slave trade story made real in Sullivan's exhibit," *(Charleston, South Carolina) Post and Courier*, March 12, 2009. A pdf of the brochure for the "African Passages" exhibit can be downloaded from the NPS website: www.nps .gov/fosu/planyourvisit/upload/African_Passages.pdf.

70. John M. Coski, *The Confederate Battle Flag* (Cambridge, MA: Harvard University Press, 2005); Rebecca Bridges Watts, "Stories of War: The Confederate Flag in South Carolina," *Contemporary Southern Identity* (Jackson, MS: University Press of Mississippi, 2007), 87–116.

71. Ben Chapman, "South Carolina Loses $100 Million In Boycott," *Successful Meetings*, September 2000, Vol. 49 Issue 9, 21. Melissa Blanton, "NAACP boycott still at work here: State loses tournament in Myrtle Beach, among other events" *Journal*

Watchdog, July 30, 2009, http://www.journalwatchdog.com; Schuyler Kropf, "Worry sparked over NAACP boycott," *Sun News*, November 2, 2010.

Chapter Two

1. In 1930, the racial demographics of Dillon County were 51 percent white and 46 percent black, and in 2010 the census showed 48 percent white and 46 black. Over those 80 years, the difference between the white and black populations varied from 2 to 10 percent, with whites always slightly higher. The Latino population is small but has grown from 0.3 percent in 1990 to 1.8 percent in 2000 and 2.5 percent in 2010. U. S. Census Bureau, 1930 to 2010.

2. The white population was 47 percent in 1930 and steadily decreased to 29 percent in 2010. The black population also decreased over the twentieth century, from 34 percent in 1930 to 24 percent in 2010. The American Indian population had the opposite experience, growing from 22 percent in 1940 (listed as "other races") to its current status as the majority population in the county, with 38 percent. Robeson has historically had a large percentage of North Carolina's American Indian population (which declined from 69 percent in 1940 to 42 percent in 2010). U. S. Census Bureau, 1930 to 2010.

3. Robeson County is the poorest county in North Carolina. Robeson County is also much more populous (134,168 in 2010) than Dillon County (32,062). U. S. Census, 2010.

4. Anna Griffin, "South of the Border Turning 50," Sun News, March 19, 2000.

5. Brett Bursey, "Meet Alan Schafer, Grandmaster of Tack," *Point*, October 1993.

6. Maxa, "South of the Border;" Joan Mower, "Schafer unhappy with Carter," *Columbia Record*, August 11, 1980; Lawrence Toppman, "You're a Beeg Wiener at Pedro's, You Never Sausage a Place," *Toronto Star*, January 27, 1990.

7. Laura Koser's thesis, "Planned by Pedro," discusses South of Border within the context of American roadside culture.

8. Institute of Southern Jewish Studies, "Dillon/Latta, South Carolina" in the *Encyclopedia of Southern Jewish Communities*, College of Charleston. http://www .msje.org/history/archive/sc/Dillon_lata.html. Durward T. Stokes, *The History of Dillon County, South Carolina* (Columbia, SC: University of South Carolina Press, 1978), 123.

9. Stokes, *History of Dillon County*, 127–28.

10. Herbert Ravenel Sass, ed., *The Story of the South Carolina Low Country* (West Columbia, SC: J. F. Hyer Publishing Co., 1956), 410; Maxa, "South of the Border Down Carolina Way," 16; "The Schafer Company Traces Its Roots to 1870," *Dillon Herald*, February 4, 2010.

11. Bursey, "Meet Alan Schafer."

12. Edgar, *South Carolina*, 485, 489.

13. Stokes, *History of Dillon County*, 360.

14. Dillon County, South Carolina, http://www.dilloncounty.org/index.php?c=
lifestyle.

15. The family had a difficult time selling the general store during the Depression.
They were paid with a "farm property nearby and six bales of cotton," which they used
as collateral on a second truck to haul beer south from Baltimore. Sass, *The Story of
the South Carolina Low Country*, 410; "The Schafer Company Traces Its Roots to 1870,"
Dillon Herald, February 4, 2010.

16. "74 Liquor Stills Destroyed in '59," *Dillon Herald*, February 5, 1960. Nineteen
fifty-nine was not an abnormal year. The paper reports regular busts of bootleggers in
the area throughout the decade.

17. Ad, *Dillon Herald*, June 6, 1954.

18. "Alan Schafer Story," *Dillon Herald*.

19. Stokes, *History of Dillon County*, 123, 376.

20. Institute of Southern Jewish Studies, "Dillon/Latta, South Carolina," in the
Encyclopedia of Southern Jewish Communities, College of Charleston, http://www
.msje.org/history/archive/sc/Dillon_lata.html.

21. Maxa, "South of the Border Down Carolina Way."

22. Sass, *South Carolina Low Country*, 411.

23. Edgar, *South Carolina*, 513.

24. Pete Daniel, *Lost Revolutions: The South in the 1950s* (Chapel Hill, NC:
University of North Carolina Press, 2000), 9. For more on the effects of World War II
on southern culture see: Pete Daniel, "Going among Strangers: Southern Reactions to
World War II," *Journal of American History* (December 1990), 888–91; Neil McMillen,
ed., *Remaking Dixie: The Impact of World War II on the American South*, (Jackson,
MS: University of Mississippi Press, 1990); Charles Chamberlain, *Victory at Home:
Manpower and Race in the American South during World War II*, (Athens, GA:
University of Georgia Press, 2003). See Edgar, *South Carolina*, "All in One Lifetime,"
512–52, for a discussion of the changes in South Carolina after World War II.

25. The Supreme Court ruled in 1944 that blacks could not be denied the right to
vote in Texas Democratic primaries. South Carolina acted swiftly to make primaries
"private affairs" beyond the reach of federal laws. In 1948, Judge J. Waties Waring
finally opened the primaries to black voters. Waring felt, "It is time for South Carolina
to rejoin the Union." See Edgar, *South Carolina*, 515–16, 519.

26. The same year, in response to President Harry Truman's decision to integrate
the US military, a group of southern Democrats, including South Carolina politician
Strom Thurmond, formulated the States' Rights Democratic Party (the Dixiecrats)
platform, with Thurmond serving as the party's eventual presidential candidate.
Thurmond's opposition to African American civil rights won him every county in
South Carolina, except for Anderson and Spartanburg in the Upcountry. Edgar, *South
Carolina*, 520–21.

27. Maxa, "South of the Border Down Carolina Way."

28. During the vote buying scandal of 1980, Schafer called the opponent of the candidate he supported the "darling of the local press and the lily whites." He also used phrases such as "the rednecks" to discuss his political foes. Schafer, "The Alan Schafer Story."

29. Schafer, "Alan Schafer Story."

30. Schafer, "The Alan Schafer Story," *Dillon Herald*.

31. For more on the diversity of white southern reactions to civil rights see Jason Sokol, *There Goes My Everything: White Southerners in the Age of Civil Rights, 1945–1975* (New York, NY: Vintage, 2006).

32. This was brought to my attention in Laura Koser's masters thesis, "Planned By Pedro: South of the Border, 1950–2001," 10. "Will Flood County With $2.00 Bills," *Dillon Herald*, August 26, 1948. "Schafer $2 Bills in Circulation," *Dillon Herald*, September 2, 1948.

33. Maxa, "South of the Border Down Carolina Way."

34. In *Blacks in the Jewish Mind*, Seth Forman points out that although the 1915 lynching of Jewish businessman Leo Frank in Atlanta is well known, "[T]hese kinds of actions were tempered by countervailing Southern ideas concerning the equality of all white men, the overriding concern with the subordination of Blacks, and the usefulness of the Jewish presence as merchants and artisans." Seth Forman, *Blacks in the Jewish Mind: A Crisis of Liberalism* (New York, NY: New York University Press, 1998), 34–35.

35. The Scottish Chief, "Lumberton Bans the Amber Brew," *Dillon Herald*, February 10, 1960. "The dry forces clobbered the wets by a 380-vote margin in a Saturday beer referendum in Lumberton. . . . Lumberton will continue the war of prohibition, which began February 10, 1948 when Robeson County abolished beer and wine by an overwhelming majority." Dillon County had more lax regulations on the sale of beer and wine that adhered to state (rather than local) law.

36. Lisa Napoli (director), *Southern Lens: South of the Border*; Videography: Tim Taylor; Production Assistance: Preston Wiles; Editing: Elaine Cooper, South Carolina Educational Television (SCETV), 1991. Napoli recently uploaded her film to YouTube: http://www.youtube.com/watch?v=GnUCnh1CQHI.

37. Joseph Melvin Schafer, interview by Dale Rosengarten and Klyde Robinson, July 11, 1995, transcript, Jewish Heritage Project, Robert Scott Small Library, College of Charleston; Griffin, "South of the Border Turning 50;" "South of the Border (A Short History)" 2000. This document was given to me when I met with Susanne Pelt, head of public relations at South of the Border in 2000. Because the information within the piece reappears in articles on South of the Border that appeared during the past twenty years, the piece appears to be the document given to journalists and other interested parties throughout the years.

38. Bursey, "Meet Alan Schafer;" Joseph Melvin Schafer, Interview, Jewish Heritage Project.

39. "South of the Border (A Short History)"; Earl Swift, "South of the Border is the big enchilada of East Coast tourism," *(Baltimore) Sun*, April 14, 1996.

40. Advertisement, *Dillon Herald*, May 17, 1951.

41. "Council Sets Curfew: Beer Banned in Dillon After Midnight," *Dillon Herald*, July 21, 1949. Dillon County's rules for selling beer were more lax.

42. "The History of South of the Border," *Discover Dillon County: Quietly Progressive South Living*, Dillon County Chamber of Commerce, March 1994.

43. Alan Quick, "Palmetto Trees Now Greet Tourists Who Used to Inquire About Flag," *Dillon Herald*, June 18, 1954.

44. For the effects of the 1954 Supreme Court decision on South Carolina, see Daniel, *Lost Revolutions*, 195–96, 228–50; Edgar, *South Carolina*, 522–29.

45. Jakle, "Motel by the Roadside," 184; Jakle et al. *The Motel in America*, 138–39.

46. Maxa, "South of the Border Down Carolina Way." Schafer made the same claim using almost the same words in the 1991 SCETV video *South of the Border* (dir. Lisa Napoli). He stated, "The only thing we looked at was the color of the money." On page 527 of Edgar's *South Carolina*, similar phrasing is used in a slightly different context: "When whites in Orangeburg applied economic pressure to blacks who petitioned for the desegregation of the city's schools, the black community retaliated in kind . . . blacks in Orangeburg showed whites that the color of money was neither black nor white; it was green."

47. "Sentence Proceedings Before the Court," reprinted in "The Alan Schafer Story," *Dillon Herald*.

48. "Sentence Proceedings Before the Court," reprinted in "The Alan Schafer Story."

49. Carolina Studio (Dillon, SC) Photographs (ca. 1945–90), "South of the Border and Pageants," South Caroliniana Library, University of South Carolina. Furthermore, the photograph shows the workers primarily grouped by race and gender.

50. Evelyn Hechtkopf, interviewed by author, June 11, 2009, at South of the Border, Hamer, South Carolina.

51. Shirley Jones, interviewed by author, June 11, 2009 at South of the Border, Hamer, South Carolina.

52. Mark Cottingham, interviewed by author, June 12, 2009, at Mount Pleasant, South Carolina.

53. Edgar, *South Carolina*, 526–27.

54. W. Horace Carter, *Virus of Fear* (Tabor City, NC: Atlantic Publishing Co.), 1991.

55. Dick Brown, "The Indians who routed the 'Catfish,'" *News and Observer*, January 26, 1958; Charles Craven, "Indians back at peace and the Klan at bay," *Life*, February 3, 1958; "The Robeson County Indian uprising against the Ku Klux Klan," *South Atlantic Quarterly* 57 (Autumn 1958): 433–42; Timothy B. Tyson, *Radio Free Dixie: Robert F. Williams and the Roots of Black Power* (Chapel Hill, NC: University of North Carolina Press, 2001), 79; Daniel, *Lost Revolutions*, 208.

56. Jack Bass and Jack Nelson, *The Orangeburg Massacre* (Macon, GA: Mercer University Press, 1986). Orangeburg, located on the busy 301 tourist corridor, is just under three hours down the road from South of the Border.

57. Karen I. Blu, *The Lumbee Problem: The Making of an American Indian People* (Lincoln, NE: University of Nebraska Press, 1980, 2001), 12. Blu dates these statements made by Lumbees to the 1960s.

58. Maxa, "South of the Border Down Carolina Way."

59. In "Welcome to South Carolina," Hourigan writes on page 152: "Nearly fifteen years after the interstate's completion, Governor McNair would acknowledge that the two states worked together to help the attraction. Dillon County, he rightfully said, depended on South of the Border for employment. In 1966, the kitschy attraction garnered more visitors per year than the Charleston Museum and the Smithsonian's Arts and Industry Museum combined." Robert E. McNair, interview by Cole Blease Graham, August 23, 1982, Tape 14, transcript; and Table, "Attendance at Selected Attractions" 1967, Governor Robert McNair Papers, Box 79, South Carolina Political Collections.

60. Tim Hollis, *Dixie Before Disney: 100 Years of Roadside Fun* (Jackson, MS: University Press of Mississippi, 1999), 15. Writing about his 1961 road trip across America in *Travels with Charley: In Search of America*, John Steinbeck avoided the "superhighways" because they "are wonderful for moving goods but not for the inspection of the countryside." He feared that one would soon be able to drive from New York to California "without seeing a single thing." John Steinbeck, *Travels with Charley: In Search of America* (New York, NY: Penguin, 1962), 89–92.

61. "NC Highway Commission Proposes I-95 Route to SC Line," *Dillon Herald*, December 16, 1964.

62. The June 3, 1965 "Borderlines" appearing in the Dillon Herald announced that while Schafer would have to relocate certain structures to accommodate the interstate, he was beginning a $100,000 improvement project to expand and improve South of the Border.

63. Tim Hollis, *Dixie Before Disney*, 16.

64. Baltimore is below the Mason-Dixon Line. Headlines in the *Dillon Herald* capitalized every word. Editorial, "South's Racial 'Problems' Are In The Minds Of Northerners With Troubles Of Their Own," *Dillon Herald*, February 5, 1960; Editorial, "Proving Case Against Themselves," *Dillon Herald*, February 19, 1960; Editorial, "Reconstruction Rides Again," *Dillon Herald*, March 9, 1960; Editorial, "Civil Rights Bill Would Disenfranchise Voters," *Dillon Herald*, April 20, 1960.

65. Shirley Jones, interviewed by author.

66. *Dillon Herald*, October 9, 1952. There was also a billboard for South of the Border that read "Confederate Cookin' Yankee Style!" The images on the billboard included a Confederate flag and the American flag on the right side, and a sombrero and serape on the left. The image can be found in "South of the Border's Award Weening Billboard," a publication sold in the souvenir shops at South of the Border.

67. "Pedro's Borderlines," *Dillon Herald*, August 23, 1961.

68. "Pedro's Borderlines," *Dillon Herald*, August 13, 1961. Schafer rarely capitalized Pedro's name in his advertisements.

69. "Confederate Battleship Pee Dee Relics Rest At South of the Border," *Dillon Herald*, August 23,1961; "Confederate Gunboat Boiler, War Relic, Is Moved To Dillon," *Dillon Herald*, August 25, 1961.

70. Image, *Dillon Herald*, August 25, 1961.

71. "Pedroland Dedication Monday: Hon. John A. Mays To Make Address And Place Plaque," *Dillon Herald*, August 25, 1961; "Six Thousand Visit Historical Wonderland: Speaker Calls Confederateland Fantastic; Fabulous; Spectacular," September 1, 1961.

72. "Pedroland Dedication Monday: Hon. John A. Mays To Make Address And Place Plaque," *Dillon Herald*, August 25, 1961; "Six Thousand Visit Historical Wonderland: Speaker Calls Confederateland Fantastic; Fabulous; Spectacular," September 1, 1961; "Pedro's Borderlines," *Dillon Herald*, October 11, 1961.

73. Preston, *Dirt Roads to Dixie*, 144. Preston mentions famed western travel stops such as Camp Grande in El Paso, Texas, and Grande Tourist Lodges in Dallas, Texas, as influences on the South's tourism industry.

74. Editorial, "Confederateland And South of the Border Are Tremendous Assets To Dillon County," *Dillon Herald*, September 8, 1961.

75. Mark Cottingham, interviewed by author.

76. Susanne Pelt, interviewed by author, June 9, 2009, South of the Border, Hamer, South Carolina.

77. Schafer cryptically quipped, "With all the wheels around that day, too bad Roger didn't have an axle with him—he could have presented pedro with that bicycle he promised him a couple of years ago!"

78. Ad, *Dillon Herald*, June 10, 1960.

79. "Roger Scott Wins Nomination In Second Primary," *Dillon Herald*, June 29, 1962. For more on Schafer's public attacks on political enemies at this time, see the June 1962 editions of the *Dillon Herald* for extensive political ads and Schafer's attacks in "Borderlines." For example, in the "Borderlines" that appeared on June 13, 1962, "Pedro's thought for the day" touted Pedro's recent political fame. "Whoever won the election (and this is written several days before) pedro won the unique distinction of being the first fictitious character since 'Kilroy' was here to be a political campaign issue!" After the second primary, Dixon Lee was defeated, and Pedro's "good buddy" Roger Scott was elected the new state senator.

80. "Fine Harness Racers Coming to South of the Border: Schafer Plans Track & Stalls With A Racing Season Likely," *Dillon Herald*, June 25, 1962.

81. Ad, *Dillon Herald*, May 15, 1964; "Dillon County Sheriff Hits Back At Campaign Charges," *Dillon Herald*, June 3, 1964; "Sheriff J. D. Rogers Says Senator R. W. Scott Opposes Him In Race," *Dillon Herald*, June 17, 1964.

82. Tall tales of Schafer's extensive political power abound throughout South Carolina, but there is often little hard evidence to substantiate these tales. There is certainly a need for more research into Schafer as a "politician;" yet, I look at this aspect of his identity primarily as it fits with the story of South of the Border. Laura

Koser, "Planned By Pedro," 81–82; Alan Schafer Correspondence to Olin D. Johnston, August 28, 1964, "Legislative, General, 1964," Olin D. Johnson Papers, Modern Political Collections, South Caroliniana Library.

83. The article, "Nation: Where Barry Stands," from the August 2, 1963 edition of *Time* magazine, states: "[Goldwater] was a member of the N.A.A.C.P. in the early 1950s, contributed $400 to the N.A.A.C.P. effort to get the Phoenix school system desegregated. He quit the N.A.A.C.P. several years ago, but he remains a member of the Urban League, which is also dedicated to the advancement of Negroes."

84. "Red" Bethea was an unwavering segregationist, and when he ran for governor of South Carolina in 1962—garnering only 7 percent of the vote—he promised to close the state's schools to African Americans "so tight you can't get a crowbar in it." As a state representative, Bethea potentially threatened peaceful desegregation of schools in South Carolina when Harvey Gantt entered Clemson College (now University). Bethea, himself a Clemson alumnus, was described as "a loose cannon with a well-deserved reputation for fiery and bombastic speeches." He helped Governor George Wallace of Alabama campaign against the national civil rights legislation in Maryland. He hoped to bring Wallace to South Carolina and charged local blacks with selling their votes in 1964. Winfred B. Moore and Orville Vernon Burton, *Toward the Meeting of the Waters: Currents in the Civil Rights Movement of South Carolina During the Twentieth Century* (Columbia, SC: University of South Carolina Press, 2008), 276; Jack Bass and Walter De Vries, *The Transformation of Southern Politics: Social Change & Political Consequence Since 1945* (Athens, GA: University of Georgia Press, 1995), 258; Jack Bass, Marilyn W. Thompson, *Strom: The Complicated Personal and Political Life of Strom Thurmond* (New York, NY: Public Affairs, 2005), 177; "Bethea Alleges Reg. Certificates Being Bought and Sold In County," *Dillon Herald*, May 13, 1964; "Rep. Bethea Wants Gov. Wallace In S.C.," *Dillon Herald*, May 29, 1964. Roger Scott threatened a local black minister with "cutting off free government food" and "upping the text book rental" for local African Americans if the minister did not vote the way Scott wanted in 1964. "Sheriff J. D. Rogers Says Senator R. W. Scott Opposes Him In Race," *Dillon Herald*, June 17, 1964. Rogers claimed Scott and others were working to elect his opponent, Dixon Lee: "Rogers also charged that Scott threatened a Lake View Negro minister with cutting off free government food to them and upping the text book rental from $2 to $16 or $25 next year unless they voted for Lee . . . Scott said these rumors were false but did admit to telling the minister he might cut off the government food and up the textbook rental if Negroes were hauled to the polls in the run-off to vote for either candidate chosen beforehand."

85. The dip that Interstate 95 takes to run by South of the Border is also a lasting material sign of Schafer's power.

86. "Schafer, two others named in indictment," *Columbia Record*, June 29, 1981.

87. United Press International NY, "Schafer unhappy with Carter," *Columbia Record*, August 11, 1980.

88. "Schafer Makes It," *Columbia Record*, February 27, 1980; "Tourist Complex Owner Elected to Commission," *State*, February 21, 1980.

89. Federal agents explored three aspects of the election: "straight buying of votes, civil rights violations," and "use of mail to carry out schemes." Jack L. Truluck, "U. S. Attorney Joins Probe Of Dillon Vote Charges," *State*, June 19, 1980; "Schafer to Learn How Much Prison Time He Must Serve," *Columbia Record*, February 10, 1982; Anne Marshall, "Suspended Councilman Pleads Guilty to Three Counts of Vote Fraud," *Columbia Record*, July 13, 1981; Jack L. Truluck, "Probe Narrowing in Dillon County Vote Buying Saga," *State*, February 2, 1981.

90. Jack L. Truluck, "Judge Says Vote Fraud Verdict Makes S. C. Better Place to Live," *State*, May 17, 1981.

91. "Schafer, 67, and the former Patricia Francis Campbell, 40, were married on October 4 at the Bamberg home of Julius B. Ness, associate justice of the South Carolina Supreme Court . . . Mrs. Schafer has been a secretary at her husband's South of the Border tourist complex in Dillon for many years," "Schafer puts troubles aside to get married," *Columbia Record*, October 16, 1981.

92. The editorial also criticized the ten-year sentence of State Senator Gene Carmichael and the prosecution of Judge Rogers in the vote buying scandal. Using strong language, the editorial posed the question: "Has justice been served in the rape of Dillon County?" Editorial, "Get Off Our Backs," *Dillon Herald*, April 29, 1982.

93. Schafer, "Alan Schafer Story," *Dillon Herald*, April 29, 1982.

94. There is certainly evidence to support Schafer's claims about the tradition of vote buying in the area. Joseph Schafer, Alan's brother, recalled visiting the polls with their father and seeing voters plied with booze by both sides. Joseph Schafer pointed out that "vote buying back then was not as covered up." In 1960, the *Dillon Herald* announced that a group of concerned citizens was forming a group to "curb vote buying." In a statement directed at the county's "Negro population," Rep. A. W. Bethea charged in 1964 that registration certificates were being illegally sold. During a stump speech, the segregationist politician stated, "If you [black voters] have a registration certificate use it, but if you think so little of it that you would sell it, you don't deserve to have one." He said the certificates were being sold for five to seven dollars each. Bethea stated that federal agents would be in the county for the election. He threatened, "If you get caught by the federal men, civil rights will not help you." Joseph Schafer, Interview. "Latta Group Formed to Curb Vote Buying," *Dillon Herald*, June 24, 1960. "Bethea Alleges Reg. Certificates Being Bought and Sold In County," *Dillon Herald*, May 13, 1964.

95. In "Alan Schafer Story," South of the Border's owner explains that Roy Lee's opponent, Greg Rogers, is the son of the probate judge Pete Rodgers, and that "Pete Rogers had already secured the election of his son-in-law, Jack McInnis, to the Dillon County seat in the S.C. House of Representatives." Therefore, Schafer reasoned that the elder Rogers was attempting to become a "one-man dictator" in Dillon County. "If Rogers could win the Sheriff's office, he would control the top three Dillon County

political offices in his immediate family." In the hotly contested election, Rogers received 4,686 votes to Lee's 3,905. However, Lee received 1,265 absentee ballot votes to Roger's 81. Jack Trulock, "Probe Narrowing in Dillon County Vote Buying Scandal," *State*, February 1, 1981.

96. Schafer, "Alan Schafer Story."

97. Bursey, "Meet Alan Schafer."

98. Parks, Recreation, and Tourism Press Release, September 28, 1988, Tourism in South Carolina Vertical Files Collection, South Caroliniana Library, University of South Carolina.

99. Kevin Geddings, a marketing consultant for Schafer who referred to his boss as the "greatest marketing mind" in the twentieth century in South Carolina, explained, "You know Georgia had Coke and North Carolina had Pepsi, [Schafer] didn't want to see the Blenheim brand lost forever." "Roadside Legacy," *St. Petersburg (Florida) Times*, July 21, 2001.

100. Will Moredock, *Banana Republic: A Year in the Heart of Myrtle Beach* (Charleston, SC: Frontline Press, 2003), 45; "S.C. Court Rejects Video Gambling Referendum," *Washington Post*, October 14, 1999.

101. "South of the Border (A Short History)," 1999. After the Silver Slipper, Schafer opened the Golden Eagle in 1997, then The Orient Express and Pedro's Hideaway in 1998. The Golden Eagle was the smallest poker mall (as they were called by the industry) and the only one not open around the clock.

102. A few weeks before the election, Beasley's campaign filed suits against Schafer and another video gaming mogul, Fred Collins, to stop the ads and force the men to divulge how much they had spent on the political advertisements. A judge refused the request, and after the election, which Hodges won, the Beasley campaign dropped the suit. Catherine Pritchard, "North Carolinians Place Their Bets" *Fayetteville Observer-Times*, March 2, 1997; Michael Sponhour, "Ads Break State Law, GOP Says," *State*, August 29, 1998.

103. The legislature passed a Hodges-backed measure requiring that the video gambling issue be decided by popular referendum, to be held in November of 1999. But a month before the vote was to be held, the South Carolina Supreme Court ruled that by holding such a referendum, the legislature would unconstitutionally delegate its lawmaking responsibilities to voters. The court upheld the part of the law stipulating if no referendum were held, video gambling would become illegal as of July 1, 2000—and it did. Michael Sponhour, "Gov.-elect Hodges Wants Final Step in S.C. Video Poker War to be a State Wide Referendum," *State*, November 19, 1998; Cliff LeBlanc and Douglas Pardue, "Video Poker Operators Says Court Will Put Them Out of Business," *State*, April 29, 1999; Cliff LeBlanc, "No Poker Vote, S.C. Supreme Court Decision Halts Games By July 1, 2000," *State*, October 15, 1999; "S.C. Court Rejects Video Gambling Referendum," *Washington Post*, October 15, 1999. David Firestone, "South Carolina High Court Derails Video Poker Games," *New York Times*, October 15, 1999.

104. It was actually Beasley's call for the removal of the Confederate flag from atop the statehouse—after a religiously inflected dream cause him to switch sides on the issue—that led to his defeat in 1998. Video gambling was a big issue, but the Confederate flag issue was bigger.

105. Jack Barth and Doug Kirby, *Roadside America* (New York, NY: Simon & Schuster, 1986), 15–16. South of the Border is also featured in the new and updated *Roadside America* (New York, NY: Simon & Schuster, 1992), 107–10.

106. Eva Zibart et al. "Tack Mentality," *Washington Post*, July 12, 1996.

107. "Talk About Town," *State*, July 24, 1996.

108. "10 Great Places to Stop the Car and Take a Look" *USA Today*, August 3, 2001; John Margolies, "The Best Roadside Attractions," *American Heritage* (April 2001), 18.

109. Anna Griffin, "South of the Border creator Schafer Dies," *Sun News*, July 21, 2001.

110. Swift, "South of the Border is the Big Enchilada of East Coast Tourism;" Griffin, "South of the Border Turns 50."

111. Lisa Napoli, *South of the Border.*

Chapter Three

1. John Brinckerhoff Jackson, "The Word Itself," from *Discovering the Vernacular Landscape* (New Haven, CT: Yale University Press, 1984), 3–8.

2. Maurie D. McInnis, "Little of Artistic Merit? The Problem and Promise of Southern Art History," *American Art*, Vol. 19.2, 2005, 11–18.

3. McInnis, *Little of Artistic Merit?*, 16.

4. Kirshenblatt-Gimblett elaborates: "While the icons of good taste stand the test of time, the emblems of bad taste come and go. Subject to the wild fluctuations of fad and fashion, the will (or suggestibility) of the herd, bad taste spreads rapidly and almost as quickly ends up as a mountain of discards, thus suffering the double stigma of mindless acceptance and mindless rejection. These most debased of commodities are also the most fertile for recoding, because they constitute such abundant trash." *Destination Culture: Tourism, Museums, and Heritage* (Berkeley, CA: University of California Press, 1998), 273.

5. Russell Underwood, "Under the Big Sombrero: Fear and Loathing at South of the Border," *Point*, October 1993.

6. David Grimsted, "The Purple Rose of Popular Culture Theory: An Exploration of Intellectual Kitsch," *American Quarterly* 4 (Dec 1991), 562: "To say that the value of any cultural analysis is related to the thoughtful intensity given to the artifact is both to say the obvious and to say what needs to be said most in the classical and postclassical popular culture debates."

7. Milan Kundera, *The Unbearable Lightness of Being* (New York, NY: Harper Perennial Modern Classics, 1984, 2009); Marita Sturken, *Tourists of History: Memory,*

Kitsch, and Consumerism from Oklahoma City to Ground Zero (Durham, NC: Duke University Press, 2007).

8. Susan Sontag, "Notes on 'Camp,'" in *Against Interpretation* (New York, NY: Anchor Books, 1990, originally published 1964), 275–92; David Bergman, ed., *Camp Grounds: Style and Homosexuality* (Amherst, MA: University of Massachusetts Press, 1993); Moe Meyer, ed. *The Politics and Poetics of Camp* (London, England: Routledge, 1994).

9. Joseph Schafer interview. He describes the early handmade beer signs at South of the Border.

10. For an article on the politics of aesthetics of *Hustler* magazine, see Laura Kipnis, "(Male) Desire and (Female) Disgust: Reading Hustler," *Cultural Studies* (London, England: Routledge, 1992), 373–91.

11. Sontag, 282.

12. "Explosion Wrecks Store Near State Line on Sunday," *Dillon Herald*, September 8, 1949.

13. Sontag, "Notes on 'Camp,'" 288.

14. Sontag, "Notes on 'Camp,'" 291.

15. Ludwig Wittgenstein, *Philosophical Investigations* (Malden, England: Blackwell, 2001, 1953); Marjorie Perloff, *Wittgenstein's Ladder: Poetic Language and the Strangeness of the Ordinary* (Chicago, IL: University of Chicago Press, 1996).

16. Napoli, *Southern Lens: South of the Border*, 1991.

17. Shirley Jones, interviewed by the author.

18. Sontag, "Notes on 'Camp,'" 291.

19. Fredric Jameson, "Is Space Political?," *Rethinking Architecture: A Reader in Cultural Theory*, ed. Neil Leach (London, England: Routledge, 1997), 255–70.

20. Dell Upton, "Architectural History or Landscape History?" *Journal of Architectural Education*, August 1991, 195–99.

21. Robert Venturi, Denise Scott Brown, and Steven Izenour, *Learning From Las Vegas: The Forgotten Symbolism of Architectural Form*, revised edition (Cambridge, MA: MIT Press, 1977, 1972); Thomas Hine, *Populuxe* (New York, NY: Overlook Press, 1986); Alan Hess, *Googie: Fifties Coffee Shop Architecture* (San Francisco, CA: Chronicle Books, 1986) and *Googie Redux: Ultramodern Roadside Architecture* (San Francisco, CA: Chronicle Books, 2004).

22. Earl Swift, "South of the Border is the Big Enchilada of East Coast Tourism," *Virginian-Pilot*, March 25, 1996.

23. Tom Wolfe, *The Kandy-Kolored Tangerine-Flake Streamline Baby* (New York, NY: Farrar, Straus and Giroux, 1965), xiii.

24. Wolfe, xiv.

25. Bursey, "Meet Alan Schafer."

26. Pete Daniel, *Lost Revolutions: The South in the 1950s* (Chapel Hill, NC: University of North Carolina Press, 2000), 91.

27. Shelley Nickles, "More is Better: Mass Consumption, Gender, and Class Identity in Postwar America," *American Quarterly* (December 2002), 582.

28. Deborah Wyrick, editor's introduction to *Jouvert: A Journal of Postcolonial Studies*, vol. 4. Issue 2, 2000. (Note: this journal was produced by the College of Humanities and Social Sciences at North Carolina State University but is no longer published.)

29. Mikhail Bakhtin, *Rabelais and His World* (Bloomington, IN: Indiana University Press, 1941).

30. Helen Delpar, *The Enormous Vogue of Things Mexican: Cultural Relations between the United States and Mexico, 1920–1935* (Tuscaloosa, AL: University of Alabama Press, 1992); also see W. Dirk Raat, *Mexico and the United States: Ambivalent Vistas* (Athens, GA: University of Georgia Press, 1992). John Jakle discusses the use of Latin styles in roadside motels during the 1950s in *The Motel in America*, 45.

31. Tom Kuntz, "Adios Speedy, Not So Fast," *New York Times*, April 7, 2002; "Andale! Andale! Arriba! Arriba!" *Hispanic*, May 2002; "Cartoons si, correctness no," *Report/Newsmagazine*, July 8, 2002.

32. In 1952, C. Vann Woodward discussed the American South's quasi-postcolonial distinction, separated from the rest of the country because of its defeat and "occupation" following the surrender of the Confederacy in the Civil War. C. Vann Woodward, Southern Historical Association presidential address: "The Irony of Southern History," *Journal of Southern History* 19 (February 1953), 3–19. Also see *The Burden of Southern History* (Baton Rouge, LA: Louisiana State University Press, 1989, 1960).

33. For an example of how the transnational forces of tourism work in Mexico, see Rebecca Maria Torres and Janet D. Momsen, "Gringolandia: The Construction of New Tourist Space in Mexico," *Annals of the Association of American Geographers*, Vol. 95.2 (June 2005), 314–35. Torres and Momsen write: "The extravagance and overbuilt nature of Cancun has transformed it into a circuslike spectacle referred to as *Gringolandia* by locals. The term not only reflects the Disneyesque quality of the spectacle that is large-scale mass tourism in Cancun (Torres 2002a), but it also implies the invasion and expropriation of Mexico space by American place," 314. For an exploration of many Souths, see Pippa Holloway, ed., *Other Souths: Diversity and Difference in the U.S. South, Reconstruction to Present* (Athens, GA: University of Georgia Press, 2008).

34. The "Pedro" image is a stock character that appears throughout popular culture, especially to advertise Mexican food or products. I am not suggesting that it originated with South of the Border.

35. Maxa, "South of the Border Down Carolina Way." Schafer's comments express a geographic dislocation because he suggests that workers be sent "down" from Mexico, when they would actually be coming "up" from a more southern location. This mistake shows how Schafer's lifelong location "down" in the American South has clouded his geographic acumen. The common phrase "down South" represents an American construction that is further complicated by a global context.

36. "The road less traveled hits a few bumps," *(Raleigh, North Carolina) News and Observer*, May 25, 2004.

37. Takahama, "Seeing Where Cultures Come Together."

38. Jan Nederveen Pieterse, *White on Black: Images of Africa and Blacks in Western Popular Culture* (New Haven, CT: Yale University Press, 1992), 232–33. Pieterse continues: "Accordingly, images of Africa and of blacks in western cultures must be interpreted primarily in terms of what they say about those cultures, not in terms of what they say about Africa or blacks. It is not that they do not convey any information regarding Africa or blacks, but that information is one-sided and perverse."

39. "Sentence Proceedings Before the Court," reprinted in "The Alan Schafer Story."

40. Shirley Jones, interviewed by author.

41. Jim Goad, *Redneck Manifesto: How Hillbillies, Hicks, and White Trash Became America's Underclass* (New York, NY: Touchstone, 1998, 1997.

42. "Lions Club Annual Minstrel Show at 8pm Tonight," *Dillon Herald*, March 18, 1960; Editorial, "Lions Club Annual Minstrel Show Preserved Only Truly American Theatrical Art Form," *Dillon Herald*, March 23, 1960.

43. "Pedro Presents South of the Border Award Weening Billboards" can be purchased in most of the souvenir shops at South of the Border for fifty cents (marked down from the original one dollar price). No date given. I purchased my copy in 1999.

44. Thanks to Warren Belasco for pointing out that "Jewish trickster" Mel Blanc voiced Speedy Gonzalez and the Frito Bandito (along with many other popular Warner Bros. cartoons). Also see the collection of Jewish folktales, Matilda Koen-Sarano, ed., *Folktales of Joha, Jewish Trickster* (Philadelphia, PA: Jewish Publication Society, 2003). Also see Henry Louis Gates, Jr.'s groundbreaking study of the African American trickster trope, *The Signifying Monkey: A Theory of African-American Literary Criticism* (Oxford, England: Oxford University Press, 1988).

45. G. D. Gearino, "Hasta La Vista, Pedro."

46. "Pedro's Borderline," *Dillon Herald*, February 26, 1965.

47. "Pedro's Borderline," *Dillon Herald*, April 8, 1965. It must be noted that Schafer chose the letters that appeared in "Pedro's Borderline," and his purpose was to promote his business. The letters from tourists are filtered through the owner before becoming part of the public record.

48. Dan Lackey, "South of the Border," *State*, October 11, 1987.

49. Lawrence Toppman, "You're a beeg wiener at Pedro's: You never sausage a place," *Toronto Star*, January 27, 1990.

50. Griffin, "South of the Border turning 50."

51. "South of the Border," http://www.roadsideamerica.com.

52. Evelyn Hechtkopf, interviewed by author.

53. For criticism of Pedro as a racist caricature, see internet blogs such as "Palin' with Chris and Dr. K South of the Border" http://www.the-isb.com/?p=2606; Racialicious, "When Truth is Stranger (and More Racist) Than Fiction" http://www.racialicious.com/2007/08/29/when-truth-is-stranger-and-more-racist-than-fiction-ibeat-blaxx-and-pedroland/; Bruce on the Backroads, "South of the Border bumper sticker: Dillon, SC," http://www.roadsideonline.com/

the-great-us-scavenger-hunt/6462-south-of-the-border-bumper-sticker-dillon-sc; or KinoSport's interesting comment that Pedro is "cute in a racist way" in "You Never Sausage a Place," http://kinosport.tv/american-notes/south-carolina/south-of-the-border/. This is just a sampling taken from the web on March 31, 2010.

54. Maxa, "South of the Border Down Carolina Way."

55. Barth, *Roadside America*, 16.

56. Gearino, "Hasta la vista, Pedro."

57. Gearino, "Hasta la vista, Pedro."

58. Cathy Lynn Grossman, "Bordering on the Absurd: 1,000 Acres of Kitsch on the Road," *USA Today*, June 29, 1994.

59. Gearino, "Hasta la vista, Pedro."

60. Gearino, "Hasta la vista, Pedro."

61. This trend continued from 2000 to 2010. With 148 percent growth, South Carolina's Latino population had the largest growth rate in the United States over the past decade. Nine of the twelve states with the largest increases are located in the South. Pew Hispanic Center Tabulations of the United States Census Bureau, 2010; Chris Kromm, "Latino South Rising," *Facing South*, Institute for Southern Studies, http://www.southernstudies.org.

62. Gearino, "Hasta la vista, Pedro."

63. Catherine Gudis, *Buyways: Billboards, Automobiles, and the American Landscape* (New York, NY: Routledge, 2004; Laura E. Baker, "Public Sites Versus Public Sights: The Progressive Response to Outdoor Advertising and the Commercialization of Public Space," *American Quarterly*, December 2007, 1187–213.

64. Jesse Berger and Nate Mallard, interviewed by author on June 23, 2009, Charleston, South Carolina.

65. Jesse Berger and Nate Mallard, interviewed by author.

66. Jesse Berger and Nate Mallard, interviewed by author.

67. Gearino, "Hasta la vista, Pedro."

68. Charles Hillinger, "The Big Bang; Business Booms All Year Round at the Nation's Biggest Fireworks Stand," *Los Angeles Times*, July 4, 1989.

69. Shirley Jones, interviewed by author.

70. This quote is from a video I took of the sign at the shop's entrance/exit in summer 2000.

71. Lucy R. Lippard, "Turning the Mirrors Around: The Pre-Face," *American Art*, Vol. 5 no. ½ (Winter-Spring 1991), 30–31.

72. Joshua Brockman, "Don't Jeer at the Souvenirs; They May Be the Real Deal," *New York Times*, September 2, 2001.

73. This is a central idea in Nicholas Thomas's book, *Entangled Objects: Exchange, Material Culture, and Colonialism in the Pacific* ([Cambridge, MA: Harvard University Press, 1991], 4). Thomas looks at the "indigenous appropriation of European things" and the "European appropriation of indigenous things" within the context of colonialization.

74. This quote comes from a picture I took inside Pedro's Africa Shop in summer 2000.

75. These observations and the close reading of the artifacts for sale within Pedro's Africa Shop are based on a trip I made to South of the Border on May 16, 2008. The Black Liberation Flag is also called the Pan-African or African Liberation flag.

76. For more extensive analyses of these types of collectables and their cultural significance, see Kenneth E. Goings, *Mammy and Uncle Mose: Black Collectibles and American Stereotyping* (Bloomington, IN: Indiana University Press, 1994); M. M. Manring, *Slave in a Box: The Strange Career of Aunt Jemima* (Charlottesville, VA: University of Virginia Press, 1998). Also see Jan Nederveen Pieterse, *White on Black: Images of Africa and Blacks in Western Popular Culture* (New Haven, CT: Yale University Press, 1992); Diane Roberts, *The Myth of Aunt Jemima: Representation of Race and Region* (New York, NY: Routledge, 1994); Herman S. Gray, *Cultural Moves: African Americans and the Politics of Representation* (Berkeley, CA: University of California Press, 2005); Psyche Williams-Forson, *Building Houses Out of Chicken Legs: Black Women, Food and Power* (Chapel Hill, NC: University of North Carolina Press, 2006).

77. Sally Price's *Primitive Art in Civilized Places*, second edition, addresses the details and argues for the movement of art from non-Western cultures inside the art world and the complexities of such a movement. Deborah Knight, "Why We Enjoy Condemning Sentimentality: A Meta-Aesthetic Perspective," *Journal of Aesthetics and Art Criticism*, Vol. 57 no. 4 (Autumn 1999), 411–20, details the rhetoric against sentimentality in art, turning this position on its head in her conclusion. Knight writes: "The philosophical condemnation of sentimentality can, in short, be a sentimental activity." The work of Price and Knight shows the need for a more inclusive and mobile perspective on aesthetics, with a broader view of what is considered art. My analysis of Pedro's Africa Shop and its combination of various commodities in one equalizing space seeks to show how a souvenir shop that is indeed complex and problematic also serves to dislocate the social strictures we place on meaningful material culture and its aesthetic merits.

78. Patrick Huber, "The Riddle of the Horny Hillbilly," *Dixie Emporium*, 69–86.

79. Evelyn Hechtkopf, interviewed by author, South of the Border.

80. Shirley Jones and Suzanne Pelt, interviewed by author.

81. Shirley Jones, interviewed by author.

82. Jesse Berger and Nate Mallard, interviewed by author.

83. Jesse Berger, Nate Mallard, Mark Cottingham, and Evelyn Hechtkopf, interviewed by author.

84. Belnheim Ginger Ale, "About Us," http://www.blenheimgingerale.com/about-us/. Company Brochure, "We Make Ginger Ale the Old Fashioned Way, Since 1903," Blenheim Bottlers (Hamer, SC, 1999); William Grimes, "A Southern Ginger Ale With a Sting in Its Tail," *New York Times*, February 25, 1998; Paul Lukas, "Surviving by Fizzy Logic," *New York Times*, August 12, 2003.

85. Napoli, *South of the Border* (film), 1991.

86. Earlier in the twenty-first century, South of the Border had a very meager website with little pizazz—the now defunct http://www.pedroland.com/. This website was still full of the "Pedroisms" of an earlier era of South of the Border. While Pedro remains on the new website, the "Pedroisms" have not survived.

87. Inkhaus Creative, http://www.inkhaus.com/.

88. Blog post, "South of the Border Custom Wordpress Website Design," August 4, 2009, http://www.inkhaus.com/.

89. Border Motorsports, "About Us," http://bordermotorsports.com/index.php ?option=com_content&task=view&id=24&Itemid=9.

Chapter Four

1. Thaxton Dixon, interviewed by Angela Hornsby, Greensboro, North Carolina, January 12, 2003, Atlantic Beach Oral History Project, Sherry A Suttles Collection, 1080, Box 4, Avery Research Center for African American History and Culture, College of Charleston, South Carolina.

2. For work on the Jim Crow period in southern history and culture, see C. Vann Woodword, *The Strange Career of Jim Crow*, third revised edition (Oxford, England: Oxford University Press, 1974, 1955); Catherine A. Barnes, *Journey from Jim Crow: The Desegregation of Southern Transit* (New York, NY: Columbia University Press, 1983); John Egerton, *Speak Now Against the Day: The Generation Before the Civil Rights Movement in the South* (Chapel Hill, NC: University of North Carolina Press, 1994); Glenda Elizabeth Gilmore, *Gender and Jim Crow Women and the Politics of White Supremacy in North Carolina, 1896–1920* (Chapel Hill, NC: University of North Carolina Press, 1996), and *Defying Dixie: The Radical Roots of Civil Rights, 1919–1950* (New York, NY: W. W. Norton & Company, 2008); Leon F. Litwack, *Trouble in Mind: Black Southerners in the Age of Jim Crow* (New York, NY: Alfred K. Knopf, 1998); Jane Dailey, Glenda Elizabeth Gilmore, and Bryant Simon, eds., *Jumpin' Jim Crow: Southern Politics From Civil War to Civil Rights* (Princeton, NJ: Princeton University Press, 2000); William H. Chafe, Raymond Gavins, and Robert Korstad, eds., *Remembering Jim Crow: African Americans Tell About Life in the Segregated South* (New York, NY: The New Press, 2001); Charles M. Payne, *Time Longer Than Rope: A Century of African American Activism* (New York, NY: New York University Press, 2003); Steven Hahn, *A Nation under Our Feet: Black Political Struggles in the Rural South from Slavery to the Great Migration* (Cambridge, MA: Harvard University Press, 2003); Michael J. Klarman, *From Jim Crow to Civil Rights: The Supreme Court and the Struggle for Racial Equality* (New York, NY: Oxford University Press, 2004); Allison Dorsey, *To Build Our Lives Together: Community Formation in Black Atlanta, 1875–1906* (Athens, GA: University of Georgia Press, 2004).

3. "Steps Forward And Steps Back," *New York Times*, July 31, 1994.

4. Atlantic Beach was the premiere spot for African American leisure culture on the South Carolina coast, but it was not the only place. Riverside Beach, outside of Charleston, Mosquito Beach, on James Island, and McKenzie Beach, near Pawleys Island, were also beaches reserved for African Americans along the coast during Jim Crow. While not historically black recreational beaches, South Carolina's sea islands, along the southern coast in Beaufort County, and Sandy Island, a federal reserve near Georgetown, South Carolina, are inhabited by Gullah people. The Gullah population has dwindled in recent years, partly due to tourism development. Today, Atlantic Beach remains the only historically black recreational beach on the South Carolina coast that has maintained predominantly black ownership and black governance.

5. W. Fitzhugh Brundage writes: "If characterizations of southern memory are to be meaningful, attention should be given to what kind of history southerners have valued, what in their past they have chosen to remember and forget, how they have disseminated the past they have recalled, and to what uses those memories have been put. We need, in short, a social history of remembering in the South." W. Fitzhugh Brundage, "Introduction: No Deed but Memory," in *Where These Memories Grow: History, Memory, and Southern Identity* (Chapel Hill, NC: University of North Carolina Press, 2000), 3.

6. Tyson owned a successful laundromat and dry cleaner in neighboring Conway, and his wife, Roxie Ballen Tyson (1889–1973), was a talented seamstress. Tyson bought the first forty-seven acre tract of land in Atlantic Beach (29th and 30th avenues) in 1934 from R. V. Ward for $2,000. In 1941, he purchased Pearl Beach (31st and 32nd avenues) from Viola Bell for $600 and the mortgage. This forty-nine acre tract brought Tyson's land holdings and Atlantic Beach to a total of ninety-six acres spanning four blocks. In 2001, Atlantic Beach was listed as 98.85 acres. Horry County Deeds in Sherry A. Suttles, *Atlantic Beach: Images of America* (Charleston, SC: Arcadia Publishing, 2009), 14–15; Town of Atlantic Beach Comprehensive Plan, 2001; Stokes, *Myrtle Beach*, 199.

7. Suttles, *Atlantic Beach*, 14; Chazznet, "Atlantic Beach Story," http://chazznet .net/mday984.html; Emma Lee Vereen Earlene Woods, and Ronald Isom, "The Black Pearl: A History: Atlantic Beach, SC," Sherry A. Suttles Collection 1080, Box 3, Avery Research Center for African American History and Culture, College of Charleston, South Carolina.

8. Mark M. Smith, *How Race is Made: Slavery, Segregation, and the Senses* (Chapel Hill, NC: University of North Carolina Press, 2006), 79. On page 5 of the introduction, Smith explains: "Love and hate regulated southern slavery, and at the center of that perverse intersection stood an intimate, uneven, sensory exchange between the races."

9. Earlene Woods, interviewed by Damon L. Fordham, October 10, 2002, Atlantic Beach Oral History Project, transcript, Sherry A. Suttles Collection, Box 4, Avery Research Center for African American History and Culture, College of Charleston.

10. Upperman explained: "[Tyson] needed someone to take up the mortgage. So, Dr. [Peter Carlisle] Kelly (1911–80) [from Georgetown, SC], along with Dr. Robbie

[Robert Keith] Gordon [from Dillon, SC] (1891–1964), used their influence and contacted some other doctors and college presidents to try to get some money to bail out Tyson in his real estate problems." The president of Fayetteville State University [in North Carolina], James Ward Seabrook, Ph.D. (1886–1974), became the mastermind and president of the company, which originally included Sam Taggard, Charles Baggett, F. L. Atkins, Dr. H. H. Creft, Dr. W. P. DeVane, Dr. J. D. Douglass, and A. J. Henderson, in addition to Upperman, Gordon, and Kelly. Dr. Leroy Upperman, interviewed by Randall A. Wells, August 11, 1995, Horry County Oral History Project, video and transcript, Coastal Carolina University, Conway, South Carolina; Yolanda Jones, "$10,000 started Atlantic Beach: Buyers sought a black haven," Sun News, February 20, 1994; Suttles, Atlantic Beach, 9–17. In 1944, the Atlantic Beach Company donated the land for the First Missionary Baptist Church of Atlantic Beach. The church was completed in 1947.

11. William P. Johnson, Sr., interviewed by Damon L. Fordham, October 29, 2002, Atlantic Beach Oral History Project, transcript, Sherry A. Suttles Collection, 1080, Box 4, Avery Research Center for African American History and Culture, College of Charleston, South Carolina.

12. Yolanda Jones, "$10,000 started Atlantic Beach: Buyers sought a black haven," Sun News, February 20, 1994.

13. Ronald Smothers, "Black Resort in South Splits Over Development," New York Times, August 16, 1989.

14. The town's now defunct website featured a quotation attributed to John Hope Franklin: "Rich in culture and entertainment, Atlantic Beach was one of the most prosperous and popular places for Blacks during the 40s to mid 70s." Town of Atlantic Beach, "Atlantic Beach, South Carolina: Her History," http://www.atlanticbeachsc.com/asps/history.asp. Atlantic Beach's official website is no longer active. The author possesses printouts of the town's website from 2007. The site was last updated in 2003.

15. Dr. Leroy Upperman, Leroy, interviewed by Randall A. Wells, Horry County Oral History Project.

16. William Moredock, Banana Republic: A Year in the Heart of Myrtle Beach (Charleston, SC: Frontline Press, 2003), 63.

17. Carrie Rucker, interviewed by Damon L. Fordham, October 10, 2002, Atlantic Beach Oral History Project, transcript, Sherry A. Suttles Collection, Avery Research Center for African American History and Culture, College of Charleston.

18. Robert Morris, "From back seat to oval office," Sun News, January 18, 2009.

19. Jeremy Korr, "A Proposed Model for Cultural Landscape Study," Material Culture, Fall, 1997.

20. Russell Skeeters, Alice Graham, Carrie Rucker, and Earlene Woods, interviewed by Damon L. Fordham, October 10 and 29, 2002, Atlantic Beach Oral History Project, transcript, Avery Research Center for African American History and Culture, College of Charleston, South Carolina.

21. Earlene Woods, interviewed by Damon L. Fordham, Atlantic Beach Oral History Project.

22. Willie L. Isom, interviewed by Damon L. Fordman, October 29, 2002, Atlantic Beach Oral History Project, transcript, Avery Research Center for African American History and Culture, College of Charleston, Charleston, South Carolina.

23. Stanley D. Coleman, interviewed by Randall A. Wells, October 21, 1993, Horry County Oral History Project, video and transcript, Coastal Carolina University, Conway, South Carolina.

24. Earlene Woods and Carrie Rucker, interviewed by Damon L. Fordham, Atlantic Beach Oral History Project.

25. Suttles, *Atlantic Beach*, 33.

26. George Lipsitz, *How Racism Takes Place* (Philadelphia, PA: Temple University Press, 2011).

27. For pictures of early businesses at Atlantic Beach see Suttles, *Atlantic Beach*, or Sherry A. Suttles Collection, Box 6–7, Avery Research Center for African American History and Culture, College of Charleston.

28. Earlene Woods, interviewed by Damon L. Fordham, Atlantic Beach Oral History Project.

29. Dr. Leroy Upperman, Interviewed by Randall A. Wells, Horry County Oral History Project.

30. "This is Hotel Gordon, the famous beach front hotel at Atlantic Beach, SC. With hot and cold water in every room, with private or semi-private bath, Beautyrest mattresses, and a spacious dining room, offering food second to none. Open the year round." Postcard in Box 7, Sherry A. Suttles Collection, Avery Research Center, and reprinted in Suttles, *Atlantic Beach*, 33.

31. Luegenia Marshall opened Hotel Marshall with her husband Robert Marshall, who published a small newspaper in Atlantic Beach in the 1940s called *The Shadow*. In an interview with the current owner of Hotel Marshall, Brenda Rowell-Bromell, in 2000, Luegenia Marshall stated that her husband was "mysteriously gunned down," perhaps because of something he reported in the newspaper. This is a very intriguing story; however, there do not appear to be any remaining copies of *The Shadow* from this period. Sherry A. Suttles Collection, 1080, Box 4, Avery Research Center for African American History and Culture, College of Charleston, South Carolina.

32. Other motels during the golden era include Smith's Place, Parkview Motel, J & L Motel, L & J Motel, Ida Palms, Sherbert Hotel, the Lodge Hotel, the Evan's Motel, the Woods Apartments, Palms Motel, Gateway Inn, Scotteretta Motel, Idle Hour, Superfine Motel, Riviera Motor Lodge, and the Nylon Motel. These various businesses are discussed in the Atlantic Beach Oral History Project and in Suttles, *Atlantic Beach*. These motels do not constitute an exhaustive list of Atlantic Beach businesses. It is an overview of the most memorable or prominent businesses. For more on the Holiday Motel see Suttles, 43–47.

33. Earlene Woods, interviewed by Damon L. Fordham, Atlantic Beach Oral History Project.

34. Robert Morris, "On 75th anniversary, a fragile peace reigns over the Black Pearl," *Sun News*, March 29, 2009.

35. Alice Graham, interviewed by Damon L. Fordham, October 10, 2002, Atlantic Beach Oral History Project, transcript, Avery Research Center for African American History and Culture, College of Charleston.

36. Earlene Woods, interviewed by Damon L. Fordham, Atlantic Beach Oral History Project.

37. Etrulia Pressley Dozier, interviewed by Damon L. Fordham, Atlantic Beach Oral History Project.

38. Ray Charles, *Brother Ray: Ray Charles' Own Story* (New York, NY: Dial Press, 1978).

39. Woods added, "By sharing this with you [the oral history project]. It will always be here." Earlene Woods, interviewed by Damon L. Fordham, Atlantic Beach Oral History Project.

40. Suttles, *Atlantic Beach*, 57.

41. 'Fessa John Hook, *Shagging in the Carolinas* (Charleston, SC: Arcadia, 2006), 118.

42. Russell Skeeters, interviewed by Damon L. Fordham, Atlantic Beach Oral History Project.

43. Pete Daniel, *Lost Revolutions: South in the 1950s* (Chapel Hill, NC: University of North Carolina Press, 2000).

44. Frank Beacham, "Charlie's Place: The 1950s South Carolina Beach Scene was a Haven for Innovative—and Interracial—Dancing Then the KKK Took Notice," *Oxford American* November/December 2000, 50–62. This article later became the first chapter in Beacham's book, *Whitewashed: A Southern Journey Through Music, Mayhem, and Murder* (New York, NY: Booklocker.com, 2002), 19–60.

45. Stokes, *Myrtle Beach*, 193–96.

46. Stokes, *Myrtle Beach*, 196. In "Welcome to South Carolina," Hourigan writes: "Some historians claim that Fitzgerald and his wife Sarah's decision to register to vote gave impetus to the Klan furor. But in 1948, a full two years before [KKK Grand Dragon] Hamilton's raid, Fitzgerald and his wife took their names off the voter roles in a highly publicized act." "Lone Myrtle Beach Negro Voters Request that Names be Removed," *State*, August 11, 1948. It appears that the registration and even the threat of black voting in 1948— compounded by the Fitzgerald's wealth and power in the community—provoked the violent disapproval of the Klan.

47. Beacham, "Charlie's Place" and *Whitewashed*.

48. Beacham, "Charlie's Place" and *Whitewashed*; W. Horace Carter, *Virus of Fear: Relive the Infamous Resurrection and Demise of the Carolinas' Ku Klux Klan* (Tabor City, NC: Atlantic Publishing Company, 1991). Carter won the Pulitzer Prize for reporting on the Klan violence for the *Tabor City (North Carolina) Tribune*.

49. Suttles, *Atlantic Beach*, 27.

50. Stokes, *Myrtle Beach*, 194; *Sun News*, September 1, 1950.

51. Andrew W. Kahrl discusses such incidences in "'The Slightest Semblance of Unruliness': Steamboat Excursions, Pleasure Resorts, and the Emergence of Segregation Culture on the Potomac River," *Journal of American History*, March 2008, 1108–36.

52. *Sun News*, September 1, 1950.

53. Beacham, "Charlie's Place," *Oxford American*, 62.

54. Thaxton interview, Atlantic Beach Oral History Project.

55. Etrulia Pressley Dozier, interviewed by Damon L. Fordham, Atlantic Beach Oral History Project.

56. Thaxton Dixon interview, Atlantic Beach Oral History Project.

57. Janie Isom, Earlene Woods, and Russell Skeeters, interviewed by Damon L. Fordham, Atlantic Beach Oral History Project.

58. "Atlantic Beach, South Carolina: Her History," town website, 2003–7.

59. Russell Skeeters and William P. Johnson, Sr., interviewed by Damon L. Fordham, Atlantic Beach Oral History Project.

60. Etrulia Pressley Dozier, interviewed by Damon L. Fordham, Atlantic Beach Oral History Project.

61. Etrulia Dozier and Earlene Woods interviews, Atlantic Beach Oral History Project.

62. See W. Fitzhugh Brundage, *Southern Past: A Clash of Race and Memory* (Cambridge, MA: Harvard University Press, 2005) 321–22; "Contentious and Collected: Memory's Future in Southern History," *Journal of Southern History* (August 2009) 751–66; Michelle R. Boyd, *Jim Crow Nostalgia: Reconstructing Race in Bronzeville* (Minneapolis, MN: University Of Minnesota Press, 2008).

63. Toni Morrison, *Love* (New York, NY: Vintage, 2003), 8.

64. Morrison, *Love*, 39.

65. David Fear, "Beachfront property: John Sayles skewers the Sunshine State," *San Francisco Bay Guardian Online*, June 26, 2002, http://www.sfbg.com/36/39/art_sunshine.html.

66. The ways in which the past can live on in the present are apparent in *Lonestar* (1996), another John Sayles film that deals intimately with race, identity, history, and controversy. The camera often pans without a cut from the past to the present while telling the stories of individuals living on the borderland where cultures clash, in a small Texas town called Frontera.

67. Suttles, *Atlantic Beach*, 124.

68. Russ Rymer, *American Beach: A Saga of Race, Wealth, and Memory* (New York, NY: HarperCollins, 1998), 101.

69. Rymer, 105.

70. In the last years of her life, Betsch was widely recognized for her preservation and public history work. An article in *Smithsonian* magazine in 2003 and the cover

of *Preservation* magazine in 2005 both featured her work. The cover article, "Whose Beach Is It, Anyway? One woman fights for a piece of Florida's past," focuses on Betsch's inventive and personal approach to preservation. Michael Parnell, "Beach Lady Dies" *(Fernandina Beach, FL) News-Leader*, September 5, 2005.

71. Phelts's book, *An American Beach for African Americans*, blends the beach's history with her own perspective and her role as local librarian and historian. In the chapter, "The Irony of Civil Rights," Phelts explains how the "American Beach that grew and prospered under segregation vanished with the passage of the Civil Rights Act, July 2, 1964." She ends her book with a plea for preservation of the town, which is facing development from outside: "But I thank God for the chance to try and tell my American Beach story—so you can understand the depth of feeling in our hearts and souls, and why we think it so important that an American Beach for African Americans be preserved for generations to come." Marsha Dean Phelts, *An American Beach for African Americans* (Gainesville, FL: University Press of Florida, 1997), 119, 178.

72. Lyn Riddle, "Around the South: Strand's 'Black Pearl' seeks renewed luster," *Atlanta Journal and Constitution*, November 2, 1997; Will Moredock, *Banana Republic*, 63–64. Upperman, interviewed by Randall A. Wells, Horry County Oral History Project.

73. Suttles, *Atlantic Beach*, 96.

74. Sherry A. Suttles Collection, Avery Research Center, Box 3.

75. Waccamaw Regional Planning and Development Council, "Atlantic Beach Land Use Plan and Housing Element," June 1979, South Caroliniana Library, University of South Carolina.

Journalist Robert Morris used the term "desegregation's diaspora" in a 2009 article on Atlantic Beach. He writes, "Gone are the Ferris wheel and children's rides of its hey day—long lost to desegregation's Diaspora—but the derelict buildings and their criminal inhabitants are also disappearing, leaving only grassy lots." Robert Morris, "On 75th anniversary, a fragile peace reigns over the Black Pearl," *Sun News*, March 29, 2009.

76. Town of Atlantic Beach Comprehensive Plan, 2001, http://www.atlantic beachsc.com/asps/future.asp. This plan was downloaded from the now defunct Atlantic Beach website. A hard copy is in the author's possession. This is not the current plan for development of Atlantic Beach (Zyscovich Architects), but this document was produced with the vision of the town's residents at the beginning of the twenty-first century in mind. Of the various plans, which I discuss later in the chapter, the 2001 plan appears to have had the most input from local residents.

77. Leroy Upperman, interviewed by Randall A. Wells, Horry County Oral History Project.

78. Atlantic Beach Land Use Plan and Housing Element, 1979, 28.

79. Town of Atlantic Beach Comprehensive Plan, 2001, 23.

80. Atlantic Beach Land Use Plan and Housing Element, 1979. The 2000 census shows only 31 percent of Atlantic Beach families below the poverty line, which is quite

an improvement from 1970 (and even the 43 percent recorded in 1990), but which still exceeds regional and state averages.

81. Earlene Woods, interviewed by Damien L. Fordham.

82. Town of Atlantic Beach Comprehensive Plan, 2001, 4.

83. Town of Atlantic Beach Comprehensive Plan, 2001, 5.

84. Suttles, *Atlantic Beach*, 97.

85. Atlantic Beach Land Use Plan and Housing Element, 1979, 68–72.

86. Robert Morris, "Atlantic Beach population drop may be new hurdle," *Sun News*, February 22, 2009; "The latest AB liferaft," *Sun News*, June 19, 2009. Two public housing units have already closed, and the final forty-unit building has been slated to close. A protest against closing public housing in Atlantic Beach took place in July 2010. Rev. Wendy Price and Carolyn Cole organized the rally to allow the voices of public housing residents to be heard "against the injustice that has been done here in Atlantic Beach" and to fight the "civil conspiracy orchestrated in the town of Atlantic Beach through political leaders and policy makers to demise [sic] and to strip the town of its charter." Quotes are from a rally video posted on the *Sun News* website on July 8, 2010, http://www.thesunnews.com/.

87. Atlantic Beach Land Use Plan and Housing Element, 1979, 77.

88. Town of Atlantic Beach Comprehensive Plan, 2001, 16–17.

89. Town of Atlantic Beach Comprehensive Plan, 2001, 11.

90. Kim Hughes, "Memories of Atlantic Beach," *Sun News*, December 9, 2005.

91. Suttles lists other founders of the organization and "outsiders who cared" in her 2009 "Images of America" book about the town: Carolyn Marie Sadler and her husband Thomas "Pop" Sadler from Charlotte, North Carolina; James Goodman and James Williams from Florence, South Carolina; Johanna Martin-Carrington (Jenkins Institute) and James French (*Chronicle*) from Charleston, South Carolina; and locals Betty "Toby" Dixon, Brian Shaw, and Latonia Peterson. Suttles, *Atlantic Beach*, 6.

92. After the publication of the book in 2009, the historical society's collection of photographs and other historical materials were donated to the Avery Research Center for African American History and Culture at the College of Charleston.

93. Suttles, *Atlantic Beach*, 6, 126.

94. Sammy Fretwell, "Atlantic Beach struggles to maintain its identity," *Sun News*, 1987.

95. Margaret A. Shannon with Stephen W. Taylor, "Astride the Plantation Gates: Tourism, Racial Politics, and the Development of Hilton Head Island," in *Southern Journeys*, 177–95. Shannon and Stephen Taylor offer frameworks that can be applied to Atlantic Beach: "Attempts to understand the racial dynamics of southern economic development have often fallen victim to the fallacy that African Americans have never participated in the course of that development." The participation of African Americans is erased from both historical memory and the built environment. In addition, both Hilton Head and Atlantic Beach "illustrate the broader principle that economic identity, not racial identity alone, creates political coalitions, and it is these

economic issues that determine the course of industrial development in general, and tourism development in particular." Also see Michael N. Danielson, *Profits and Politics in Paradise* (Columbia, SC: University of South Carolina Press, 1995)

96. Even though Atlantic Beach did not incorporate into the city of North Myrtle Beach in 1968, North Myrtle Beach currently provides water, wastewater, and fire protection to Atlantic Beach. Town of Atlantic Beach Comprehensive Plan, 2001, 12.

97. Sammy Fretwell, "Atlantic Beach struggles to maintain its identity," *Sun News*, 1987.

98. Earlene Woods, interviewed by Damon L. Fordham, Atlantic Beach Oral History Project.

99. Police protection has been an issue in Atlantic Beach since the 1984 lawsuit. In 1994, Police Chief David Allen pleaded guilty to accepting bribes from the owners of the town's topless bar. Another officer was sentenced to six years in prison after accepting a $3,000 bribe to drop drug charges. In 2001, Benny Webb was removed as police chief after allegedly assaulting an Atlantic Beach landowner. In 2007, Police Chief Juan Lopez resigned. The main reason he cited was concern that the town could not afford to continue to pay him, but recent claims of racism (which were found to be false) lodged against Lopez also soured him on the job. In October 2009, Atlantic Beach's police chief Randy Rizzo was suspended after he was arrested for public intoxication. Crime, corruption, and law enforcement issues all became issues for Atlantic Beach in the 1980s.

100. Sammy Fretwell, "Atlantic Beach struggles to maintain its identity," *Sun News*, 1987.

101. After graduating from Clemson with a degree in architecture, Gantt received a master's degree in planning from MIT. He was also the first black mayor of Charlotte, North Carolina, and unsuccessfully ran as a Democrat against Republican Senator Jesse Helms in 1990 and 1996. Harvey Gantt, interviewed by Lynn Haessly, January 6, 1986, Oral Histories of the American South, University of North Carolina, Chapel Hill, North Carolina; *News & Observer* biography, http://projects.newsobserver.com/under_the_dome/profiles/harvey_gantt.

102. Elizabeth Leland, *The Vanishing Coast* (Winston Salem, NC: John F. Blair Publisher, 1996), 73–75.

103. Ronald Smothers, "Black Resort in South Splits Over Developing," *New York Times*, August 16, 1989.

104. Erin Reed, "A Victim of Indecision?" *Sun News*, February 16, 2003; David Wren, "Five Rivers closed down amid scandal," *Sun News*, November 19, 2006. In 2001, the Atlantic Beach Community Development Corporation merged with the Waccamaw Community Development Corporation to form the Horry County Community Development Corporation. In December of 2001, The Horry County CDC announced it was dropping the development of Atlantic Beach from its mission, because the town's "officials have been difficult to work with in making development happen." Erin Reed, "Development group to turn focus from South Carolina's Atlantic Beach," *Sun News*, December 13, 2001.

105. Robert Morris, "On 75th anniversary, a fragile peace reigns over the Black Pearl," *Sun News*, March 29, 2009.

106. Sammy Fretwell, "Atlantic Beach struggles to maintain its identity," *Sun News*, 1987.

107. Yolanda Jones, "Official urges blacks to keep beach property," *(Rock Hill, South Carolina) Herald*, May 4, 1997.

108. Thaxton Dixon interview, Atlantic Beach Oral History Project.

109. Lyn Riddle, "Strand's 'Black Pearl' seeks renewed luster," *Atlanta Journal and Constitution*, November 2, 1997.

110. Sammy Fretwell, "Atlantic Beach struggles to maintain its identity," *Sun News*, 1987.

111. Chandra McLean, "AB votes to sue for Bikefest, bad trees," *Sun News*, August 24, 2004; Robert Morris, "On 75th anniversary, a fragile peace reigns over the Black Pearl," *Sun News*, March 29, 2009.

112. "Also, the Town does not wish to develop in a hostile manner that pits landowners against the government. Instead, the Town will facilitate development by providing incentives for landowners to participate in development and provide opportunities for landowners to meet in the hopes that they will work together for personal gain and the overall good of the Town." Town of Atlantic Beach Comprehensive Plan, 2001. The redevelopment plan was nebulously based on "input received and data gathered from a variety of sources."

113. Town of Atlantic Beach Comprehensive Plan, 2001, 35–37; Erin Reed, "A victim of indecision?" *Sun News*, February 16, 2003.

114. This "heritage experience" is described in more detail in the 2001 report: "For example, at your family reunion, we'll greet you upon arrival with African and Native American drums, arrange your meeting spaces and meals, plan your leisure activities, supervise activities for children while adults have down time, and invite you to attend an authentic worship service with an excellent gospel choir before your departure with a T-shirt in hand."

115. David Wren, "Town manager prepares to sell land, leave position," *Sun News*, August 8, 2004. Sherry Suttles Collection, Avery Research Center, Box 3. Sherry Suttles, "Letter to the Editor: Town Harasses AB Historical Society," *Sun News*, February 3, 2005.

116. Because she was not being paid as town manager at the time, Montgomery was not convicted on ethics violations. Even after leaving Atlantic Beach, Montgomery continues to spawn controversy. In 2008, Montgomery sued the town of Atlantic Beach for the repayment of $190,000 she loaned the town in 2002; with interest, the sum owed amounted to over $300,000. The loan was granted by the Tyson Beach Group, owned by Montgomery's husband. The lawsuit against Atlantic Beach became intertwined with Montgomery's divorce settlement. Many saw the loan and the development company as conflicts of interest for Montgomery. Pending lawsuits— Montgomery's is one of numerous suits for non-payment—have the potential to bankrupt the town. David Wren, "Town manager prepares to sell land, leave position,"

Sun News, August 8, 2004; Robert Morris, "Questions surround former AB town manager, lawsuit over loan," *Sun News*, April 1, 2009.

117. Joe Montgomery, past mayor of Atlantic Beach, was removed from office due to bribery charges involving the Crazy Horse strip club in Atlantic Beach. Charles Williams, former town manager of Atlantic Beach, spoke publically to the *Sun News* concerning the town's drug problem and was working with police in 2006 to identify and eradicate places of drug infestation. The paper reported: "In a September 8 memo to Williams, former Atlantic Beach Police Capt. Frank Johnson identified the Evans Motel as 'the major facility' where prostitution occurs and said 'some of the people that we believe are [drug] dealers, now and in the past, reside at the Woods Apartments.'" An old and respected Atlantic Beach family owned these businesses. Irene Armstrong, mayor in 2006 and daughter of first generation business owner Earlene Woods, and sister of town councilman Jake Evans, admitted that there were problems with the motels, but said that her family had worked hard to rectify these issues. "You can't pick who you rent to," Armstrong explained. "Whenever it is determined that a person who rented a room is there for a negative element, they were evicted every time." Letters were sent out to all property owners whose businesses were suspected sites of illegal activity. Atlantic Beach has many absentee landowners. When they received the letters, these landlords' responses ranged from appreciation and corrective action, to statements blaming problems on the lack of police enforcement. David Wren, "Safe living: Development's legs tied up by city's crime," *Sun News*, March 26, 2006.

118. The headline for the March 26, 2006, *Sun News* reads: "Solutions in development." The articles, "Atlantic Beach hopes investors can cure its ills," and "Development's legs tied up by city's crime," are both written by David Wren, but they present two different sides of the development issue.

119. Wren, "Atlantic Beach hopes investors can cure its ills."

120. Josh Hoke, "AB vision has hefty price tag," *Sun News*, February 1, 2007; Jonathan Tressler, "AB to pursue master plan with state funds," *Sun News*, November 21, 2007; Editorial: "State grant brightens AB future, Mayor dispute won't hurt town," *Sun News*, November 25, 2007; Robert Morris, "Town's grant disappeared in 6 weeks," *Sun News*, March 28, 2009.

121. Robert Morris, "Ex-property manager of Atlantic Beach developer indicted," *Sun News*, February 8, 2009. In February 2009, Charles DeWayne Washington, ex-property manager at Atlantic Beach, who had been working on a development plan through his firm La Casa Real Estate, was indicted on charges of embezzling more than $700 thousand from the company.

122. Robert Morris, "Atlantic Beach, SLED could team up on drugs: Officers ready for revival in summer," *Sun News*, March 20, 2009.

123. The Federal Bureau of Investigation's Uniform Crime Report is aggregated for most rankings and statistical comparison of crime in the United States. However, as the report's website states, the rankings are "merely a quick choice made by the data user; they provide no insight into the many variables that mold the crime in a particular town, city, county, state, region or other jurisdiction." They list "economic

dependence on nonresidents (such as tourist and convention attendees)" as one of the social factors skewing crime statistics. The FBI points out that ranking "often create misleading perceptions adversely affecting cities and counties." [http://www2.fbi.gov/ucr/cius2009/about/about_ucr.html.]

With this caveat in mind, Tulia.com, a community information site focusing on real estate, compares the crime rates for Myrtle Beach, North Myrtle Beach, and Atlantic Beach with the much lower state averages. Property crime as listed by percentage of the population affected is 18.1 percent for Myrtle Beach, 9.17 percent for North Myrtle Beach, and 8.71 percent for Atlantic Beach. For violent crime, Atlantic Beach is 3.96 percent, 2.06 percent for Myrtle Beach, and 0.42 percent for North Myrtle Beach. However, differences in size must be considered when viewing these statistics. With a population of fewer than 400, Atlantic Beach will experience a major statistical impact from every crime committed in the town. By way of contrast, the city of Myrtle Beach has 30,000 people, and the city of North Myrtle Beach has over 16,000. "South, tourist area hit hard," *USA Today*, 1995; David W. MacDougall, "SC 4th on U.S. danger scale," *Sun News*, April 6, 2010; Tonya Root, "Thefts, assaults and domestics top crime reports in Myrtle Beach area," *Sun News*, March 1, 2011; "Myrtle Beach ranked as dangerous spring break destination," *Sun News*, March 9, 2011. In the Myrtle Beach area in 2010, police responded to 119,329 calls for assistance.

124. Wren, "Atlantic Beach hopes investors can cure its ills."

125. Bailey, "Amid apathy, hope glimmers in town."

126. Janelle Frost, "Atlantic Beach turns over financial duties," *Sun News*, April 8, 2008.

127. Mike Cheney, "Pierce: I did not know I had to stay in the car," *Sun News*, January 2, 2008; Robert Morris, "Grand jury to decide fate of Atlantic Beach mayor's job," *Sun News*, April 12, 2009; Editorial: "Power play or path to progress? stripping AB Mayor of duties," *Sun News*, May 7, 2009.

128. Robert Morris, "Atlantic Beach town meeting ends in walkout," *Sun News*, April 21, 2009.

129. Earlene Woods and Jaine Islom, interviewed by Damon L. Fordham, Atlantic Beach Oral History Project.

130. Thaxton Dixon interview, Atlantic Beach Oral History Project.

131. WROC sent out 245 surveys and received 101 responses. The Atlantic Beach Planning Commission voted three to one to keep the road closed. Janelle Frost, "Atlantic Beach: We don't want Ocean Boulevard open," *Sun News*, October 22, 2010; Janelle Frost, "Atlantic Beach wants Ocean Boulevard open: 62 percent of owners say road should connect to neighbors," *Sun News*, November 19, 2010; Editorial, "Two-Way Traffic," *Sun News*, December 9, 2010.

Chapter Five

1. The concluding paragraph of Stokes's *Myrtle Beach: A History, 1900–1980* introduces the black motorcycle festival as an "event that attracted tens of thousands,

bringing much needed income and life back to the Black Pearl." The Bikefest serves as a conclusion for Stokes's book, which ends in 1980 (the year the Bikefest began). Barbara Stokes, "Atlantic Beach," *The South Carolina Encyclopedia* (Columbia, SC: University of South Carolina Press, 2006), 34–35.

2. "The History of The Carolina Knight Riders," (courtesy of the *Sun News*) http://www.freewebs.com/carolinaknightridermc/history.htm; Rolling Blue Thunder, Inc., "Black Bike Week History," http://www.rollingbluethunder.com/BBW_History.htm; Will Moredock, *Banana Republic*, 66.

3. The attendance numbers are reported with huge discrepancies and, lacking any formal studies, are based on subjective estimations.

4. "The History of Black Bike Week."

5. Kent Bernhard, Jr., "Myrtle Beach, North Myrtle Beach police prepare for weekend visitors," *Sun News*, May 22, 1996.

6. Kent Bernhard, Jr., "Myrtle Beach, North Myrtle Beach police prepare for weekend visitors," *Sun News*, May 22, 1996.

7. Mark Smith, *How Race is Made*, and Andrew W. Kahrl, "'The Slightest Semblance of Unruliness': Steamboat Excursions, Pleasure Resorts, and the Emergence of Segregation Culture on the Potomac River," *Journal of American History*, March 2008, 1125.

8. Yolanda Jones, "Beach town ready to rock: Atlantic Beach set for bikers," *Sun News*, May 23, 1996.

9. Katie Merx, "North Strand struggles with plan for biker fest," *Sun News*, April 8, 1997.

10. Yolanda Jones, "Bikers arrive early in Atlantic Beach," *Sun News*, May 24, 1997

11. Mike Soraghan, "Biker fest ban proposed: MB politician to ask council for referendum," *Sun News*, May 26, 1997. It is interesting to note that the historic Chesterfield Inn, built in 1946 and listed on the National Register of Historic Places, was torn down as part of a six million dollar boardwalk development plan and replaced by a miniature golf course in the spring of 2010. Kent Kimes, "In with the new; what to do with the old?" *Weekly Surge*, October 8, 2009; Lorena Anderson, "Work rips up Ocean Boulevard in Myrtle Beach," *Sun News*, February 1, 2010.

12. Yolanda Jones, "Council gets diverse views on bike fests," *Sun News*, May 28, 1997; Katie Merx, "Council seeks cure to bike woes: But end to fests is not a solution," *Sun News*, May 28, 1997.

13. Katie Merx, "Views on gay pride's purpose," *Sun News*, March 29, 1998.

14. Lyn Riddle, "What Kind of Growth Is in Store for Myrtle Beach?" *New York Times*, December 6, 1998.

15. Anita Brown and Yolanda Jones, "Biker fest precautions spur mixed reactions," *Sun News*, March 20, 1998.

16. Anitra Brown, "Grand Strand readies for Bike Festival," *Sun News*, May 21, 1998.

17. Anitra Brown, "Former air base prepares for bikers," *Sun News*, May 22, 1998.

18. Lauren Leach, "Police say bike fest went well," *Sun News*, May 26, 1998.

19. Craig S. Lovelace, "Bike festival spending prompts Horry County audit," *Sun News*, July 30, 1998; Anitra Brown, "AB approves fest spending," *Sun News*, August 7, 1998; Chandra L. McLean, "AB fest spending cleared by audit," *Sun News*, November 26, 1998.

20. Chandra L. McLean and David Wren, "Veterans to get Memorial festival," *Sun News*, October 15, 1998.

21. Richard Hourigan writes in "Welcome to South Carolina": "By the early 1960s, students comprised 38 percent of those visiting the beach, the most of any occupation," 102.

22. Charbonee LaBelle, "Police Chief: Close stretch of boulevard for Bikefest," *Sun News*, December 10, 1998.

23. In April of 1999, the Horry County Accommodations Tax Advisory Committee only allocated $25,584 to Atlantic Beach for the upcoming festival. This was down from $79,977 in 1998 and much lower than the $122,000 requested by the town. Tax advisory committee chairman Paul Goodrich stated, "We didn't feel that it was fair that the taxpayers pay for something that should pay for itself." Charbonne La Belle, "Police beef up role in bike fest," *Sun News*, March 11, 1999; Chandra L. McLean, "Board advises less funds for bike fest," *Sun News*, April 17, 1999.

24. Chandra L. McLean, "Visitor guide created for Bike Fest," *Sun News*, February 26, 1999.

25. Chandra L. McLean, "Opposition to guard presence for AB fest rises," *Sun News*, February 11, 1999; Charbonne La Belle, "Dog use at bike fest rejected," *Sun News*, March 6, 1999.

26. Chandra L. McLean, "Area planning now for 2000 biker fest," *Sun News*, June 4, 1999; Charbonne LaBelle, "Official commends city on handling of bike festival crowds," *Sun News*, July 9, 1999.

27. Chandra L. McLean, "Conference seeks Bike Fest answers," *Sun News*, September 29, 1999.

28. Professors George Smeaton and Bharath M. Josiam of the University of Wisconsin, and graduate student Holly Sowell of Pennsylvania State University, completed a study comparing the party habits of black and white college students on spring break in 1998. The study analyzed responses from African American students attending Atlanta's controversial and much-maligned Freaknik festival, and those of white students traveling to Panama City, Florida: "The researchers found that thirty-six percent of the predominantly white students in Florida reported being 'drunk every day,' whereas seventy-six percent of the students at Freaknik said they never got drunk during the entire celebration. Nearly one third of the Panama City group said they smoked marijuana compared to eighteen percent of the Freaknik attendees. Just over thirteen percent of the Panama City group engaged in sexual activity with people they had first met at the event compared to ten percent of the Freaknik attendees." More research needs to be done to understand tourists' actual behavior, rather than what they report that behavior to be after the fact. Quantitative and qualitative research

into tourist behavior and point of view is important in negotiating the different ways
of seeing place based on racial identity. George Smeaton and Bharath M. Josiam,
"Comparing the Party Habits of Black and White College Students on Spring Beak,"
The Journal of Blacks in Higher Education, Summer 2000, 18.

29. Chandra L. McLean, "Conference seeks Bike Fest answers," *Sun News*,
September 29, 1999.

30. Morehead, *Banana Republic*, 63.

31. Ned Glascock, "Black bikers debate breaking boycott to attend festival,"
(Raleigh, North Carolina) News & Observer, March 8, 2000; Chandra L. McLean,
"NAACP moves to weaken Bike Fest," *Sun News*, February 10, 2000; Chandra L.
McLean, "NAACP criticizes Atlantic Beach, SC, Mayor for continuing Bike Festival,"
Sun News, February 13, 2000.

32. Chandra L. McLean, "Vendors say business is slow so far," *Sun News*, May 27,
2000.

33. Chandra L. McLean, "Justice to look at bike fest complaints," *Sun News*, May 30,
2000.

34. Crowd estimates in *Sun News* articles range from one to four hundred thousand
attendees at the Bike Fest. Isaac J. Bailey, "Bikers yield profits for small businesses," *Sun
News*, May 17, 2001. Mary-Kathryn Craft, "Residents observe changes over years," *Sun
News*, June 20, 2001. Chandra McLean, "Boycott not expected at forefront this year,"
Sun News, May 24, 2001.

35. After unsuccessful experiences outsourcing festival planning in past years—
especially a failed concert organized by Omega International in 1998, and a lawsuit
for lack of payment from the 2000 organizer—Atlantic Beach put all organization in
the hands of the Bikefest Committee, made up entirely of Atlantic Beach residents.
While there was skepticism about the town running the festival on its own, Atlantic
Beach reportedly raised $90,000. The controversy taught the small town—which
often has intense economic viability issues—how to take control and turn tourists into
dollars. Following the 2001 festival, Sherry Suttles began the process of forming an
Atlantic Beach chamber of commerce to help lobby for the town's specific tourism and
business interests. Chandra McLean, "Atlantic Beach will not give up," *Sun News*, April
3, 2001; Chandra McLean, "Bike Festival plans unclear," *Sun News*, February 3, 2001;
Chandra McLean, "Bike festival inflates AB coffers," *Sun News*, July 11, 2001; Kathleen
Vereen Dayton, "Support solicited for new chamber," *Sun News*, June 22, 2001.

36. Mayor Irene Armstrong challenged the South Carolina Department of
Transportation's plan to close main streets in Atlantic Beach to traffic during the
2002 festival. Erin Reed, "PR firm to earn at least $64,000," *Sun News*, April 6, 2002;
Erin Reed, "AB mayor works to change street closings for bike week," *Sun News*, May
9, 2002; Erin Reed and Tonya Root, "AB bike event in full swing," *Sun News*, May 26,
2002.

37. David Klepper, "MB, county, hotel to face lawsuit," *Sun News*, May 20, 2003.

38. Kenneth A. Gailliard, "Lawsuits allege unfair treatment at Bikefest," and Kevin Wiatrowski, "Officials say NAACP effort won't hurt Strand," *Sun News*, May 21, 2003.

39. Kenneth A. Gaillard, "NAACP sues four MB restaurants," *Sun News*, May 24, 2004.

40. Kweisi Mfume, "Four Myrtle Beach Restaurants Sued for Discrimination," NAACP News Release, May 27, 2004.

41. Kenneth A. Gialliard, "NAACP suit cites letter," *Sun News*, May 29, 2004.

42. Jeffrey Gettleman, "Suit Charges Bias at Rally for Black Bikers," *New York Times*, May 21, 2003; Jeffrey Gentleman, Claims of Bias Cloud an American Dream for Black Bikers," *New York Times*, May 25, 2003; "Black Bikers Sue Myrtle Beach for Discrimination," CNN, aired May 21, 2003, 20:40 ET.

43. David Klepper, "Plaintiffs push for race talks," *Sun News*, May 23, 2003.

44. Emma Ritch, "MB, NAACP still ironing out lawsuit issues," *Sun News*, September 2, 2005; Dawn Bryant, "Bike rallies' many voices meet today," *Sun News*, September 19, 2005; Dawn Bryant, "Bike forum settles only on more talks," *Sun News*, September 20, 2005.

45. Anna-Marie Harris, "South Carolina Hotel Settles Biker Lawsuit," *The Crisis*, November/December 2004, 54–55.

46. Emma Ritch, "Biker will be riding one way," *Sun News*, February 3, 2006; Emma Ritch, "City's conflict with NAACP settled after nearly 3 years," *Sun News*, February 15, 2006.

47. Kenneth A. Gailliard and David Klepper, "Suits move forward as event nears," *Sun News*, May 25, 2004.

48. Kenneth A. Gailliard, "Atlantic Beach Bikefest lawsuits continue," *Sun News*, October 11, 2003; Kenneth A. Gailliard, "NAACP lawyers plan '04 Bikefest injunction," *Sun News*, December 1, 2003.

49. Emma Ritch, "NAACP strives to clog Bikefest traffic patterns," *Sun News*, March 17, 2005.

50. Emma Ritch, "MB resist call to alter Bikefest traffic-flow plan," *Sun News*, March 20, 2005.

51. Emma Ritch, "NAACP: MB readies for event with racial biases," *Sun News*, April 16, 2005.

52. Emma Rich, "NAACP, MB talk Bikefest in court," *Sun News*, April 26, 2005. The empirical data on the bike festivals range widely in their numbers, making reliable attendance figures difficult to determine. A 2001 economic impact study done by Coastal Carolina University, using crowd estimates from the Myrtle Beach Area Chamber of Commerce, found that the Atlantic Beach crowd had a "greater overall impact." The crowd estimates were 80,000 for the Harley Festival (with a $9.14 million daily impact) and 450,000 for the Atlantic Beach Bikefest (with a $34.05 million daily impact). While, the Harley attendees reportedly spent about $40 more per person than Bikefest attendees, the overall economic impact was smaller for the Harley rally

because of the much larger crowd estimates for Bikefest. But these excessively high numbers for the black motorcycle festival seem questionable, especially in comparison with other studies. For example, in early May 2005, Gary Loftus of Coastal Carolina University used local bookings in Horry County to determine that 70 percent of all rooms were booked for the Harley Festival and 50 percent were booked for the Atlantic Beach Bikefest. These numbers were slightly higher than the previous year, when "preliminary estimates put the attendance for the Harley Rally at more than 250,000 and Bikefest at more than 225,000," according to the Loftus figures. In 2003, the *Washington Post* reported: "Each event brings about $34 million to the area, according to the local convention and visitors bureau. They are also nearly equal in the number of violations, criminal charges and police calls, according to the *Sun News*, which used statistics from the Myrtle Beach Area Chamber of Commerce, Coastal Carolina University and the Horry County Public Safety Division." All of these numbers are, however, difficult to verify. The black motorcycle festival is held during Memorial Day weekend, generally a busy weekend and the kickoff of the tourist season. Accommodation taxes, which are used to study the economic impact of tourist spending, do not break down according to race, and not all African American tourists visit the area for the motorcycle festival. Further study of the attendance and economic impact of the two bike festivals is needed to combat many of the preconceived notions and subjective assumptions surrounding motorcycle festivals in the Grand Stand and in other tourist areas. Isaac J. Bailey, "Bikers Yield Profits for Businesses: Studies by Strand institutions reveal spending diversity," *Sun News*, May 14, 2001; Sarah P. Kennedy, "Ready or not, here they come," *Sun News*, May 8, 2005; Darryl Fears, "Hog Heaven for White but Not Black Bikers? Motorcyclists' Destination Accused of Bias," *Washington Post*, May 25, 2003.

53. Age discrimination, often applied in cases of advanced age, is a growing field of civil rights litigation. See The Age Discrimination in Employment Act of 1967 (ADEA), which applies to people over forty, and The Age Discrimination Act of 1975, which applies to public entities. It is apparent that, in many situations, groups of young people are discriminated against in their attempts to access public accommodations.

54. Emma Ritch, "MB rebuffed in bike-traffic fight," *Sun News*, May 10, 2005; Emma Ritch, "NAACP rallies to demand equal treatment of bikers," *Sun News*, May 20, 2005; Jessica Foster, "NAACP rallies Bikefest participants," *Sun News*, May 27, 2005.

55. Emma Ritch, "NAACP, MB talk Bikefest in court," *Sun News*, April 26, 2005.

56. Kenneth A. Gailliard, "Lawsuits allege unfair treatment at Bikefest," and Kevin Wiatrowski, "Officials say NAACP effort won't hurt Strand," *Sun News*, May 21, 2003.

57. Emma Ritch, "MB rebuffed in bike-traffic fight," *Sun News*, May 10, 2005; Emma Ritch, "NAACP rallies to demand equal treatment of bikers," *Sun News*, May 20, 2005; Jessica Foster, "NAACP rallies Bikefest participants," *Sun News*, May 27, 2005.

58. Paul Wachter, "Uneasy Riders: Myrtle Beach's separate and unequal biker rallies," *Legal Affairs: The Magazine at the Intersection of Law and Life*, November/December 2005, http://www.legalaffairs.org/issues/November-December-2005/scene_wachter_novdec05.msp.

59. Emma Ritch, "Bikers will be riding one way," *Sun News*, February 3, 2006; Emma Ritch, "City's conflict with NAACP settled after nearly 3 years," *Sun News*, February 15, 2006.

60. Emma Ritch, "NAACP plans monitoring of 2006 rallies," *Sun News*; May 18, 2006; Paul Nelson and Josh Hoke, "AB readies plan to tame rally traffic," *Sun News*, May 26, 2005; Issac J. Bailey, "Bikefest has its own set of worries," *Sun News*, May 26, 2006; Emma Ritch, "NAACP pledges to monitor Strand during Bikefest," *Sun News*, May 26, 2006.

61. Hebdige explains: "The struggle between powerful and powerless groups was displaced literally onto the surface of things, was transmuted into the 'struggle for the sign', and the 'political' moment of subculture became synonymous with the moment of (conspicuous) consumption." Dick Hebdige, "Traveling Light: One Route Into Material Culture," *RAIN*, December 1983, 11–13. Dick Hebdige's foundational work on postwar subcultures is *Subculture: The Meaning of Style* (New York, NY: Routeledge, 2002, 1979); see also Ken Gelder, *Subcultures: Cultural Histories and Social Practice* (New York, NY: Routledge, 2007), 2, 66–82.

62. John W. Schouten and James M. McAlexander, "Subcultures of Consumption: An Ethnography of the New Bikers," *The Journal of Consumer Research*, June 1995, 43, 49.

63. I only touch on the complex semiotics of the subculture of young black motorcylists. The black biker—an under-analyzed aspect of contemporary subcultures of consumption—is ripe for further academic attention, beyond just the context of the Atlantic Beach Bikefest.

64. Peter Stanfield, "Heritage Design: The Harley-Davison Motor Company," *Journal of Design History*, 5.2 (1992), 141–55.

65. A subculture that is not only different from the dominant culture, but also oppositional to important aspects of dominant culture is classified as a counterculture.

66. Barbara Klinger, "The Road to Dystopia: Landscaping the Nation in *Easy Rider*," p. 181 in Steven Cohan and Ina Rae Hark, eds., *The Road Movie Book* (New York, NY: Routledge, 1997).

67. Brian Alexander, "Now Racing: Black Motorcyclists Move From Street to Track," *New York Times*, October 27, 2004.

68. Alexander, "Now Racing," *New York Times*.

69. Alexander, "Now Racing," *New York Times*.

70. Alexander, "Now Racing," *New York Times*.

71. Another controversial aspect of the subculture involves negative representations of women, like those found at the Atlantic Beach Bikefest. Leslie Estes's article comments on the "usual Biker Weekend T-shirt with a fully dressed man surrounded by bikini-clad women." Leslie F. Estes, "Small town abuzz with big crowd," *Sun News*, May 27, 1996. A great deal of the criticism during the 1990s and subsequent decades centered on the nudity and sexual vulgarity found at the motorcycle festival. In 2007, that criticism came from women, like Patience Suggs, inside the local community of African American bikers, rather than from those outside the community. Suggs, a twenty-two-year-old stay-at-home mother married to a former

US Marine, rides a motorcycle. Her mother and her husband also ride motorcycles. Through her public campaign, Suggs wanted young women to know that they do not have to "expose" their bodies and "defraud" themselves "in the name of black bike week." Issac J. Bailey, "A note to female bikers," May 11, 2007.

72. Patrick Johnson, "A motorcycle mecca stirs up questions of race," *Christian Science Monitor*, May 27, 2005.

73. Christopher T. Shields, "Why Harley Davidson Isn't a Real American Motorcycle," http://www.goingfaster.com/angst/noharley2.html.

74. From a personal video made by the author, "Atlantic Beach Bikefest, 2007."

75. "Atlantic Beach: Her History," town website, 2003–7.

76. Josh Hoke, "AB rally embraces Harley presence," *Sun News*, May 20, 2007.

77. Josh Hoke, "Old notions of race and rallies loosening," *Sun News*, May 27, 2007.

78. Locals often discuss the story of a white biker gang, often referred to as the Hell's Angels, closing down the highway into Myrtle Beach; however, I cannot find a reference to this mythological stand-off published in the local paper during the month of May in the 1970s. Perhaps the story was not covered because it gave the tourist town a bad reputation.

79. Issac A. Bailey, "Company cleans up biker rallies," *Sun News*, May 30, 2007.

80. Issac A. Bailey, "Company cleans up biker rallies," *Sun News*, May 30, 2007.

81. Myrtle Beach's new ordinances include a controversial helmet requirement that applies within city limits. This ordinance contradicts the more lenient state law, which leaves it up to individuals over the age of twenty-one to determine if they will wear a helmet. Other controversial rules include a prohibition of loitering in parking lots, stricter noise and muffler rules, and restrictions on oversized vehicles and trailers parked on public roads. Some rules apply only to young people. There is a curfew lasting from one to six in the morning for anyone under the age of eighteen, and individuals under eighteen cannot check into a hotel without a parent or legal guardian present. Horry County also lowered the number and duration of vendor permits and raised the cost for permits east of the Waccamaw River, where the city of Myrtle Beach begins. The town of Surfside Beach, just south of Myrtle Beach, stopped granting vendor permits for two years. The city of North Myrtle Beach, which surrounds Atlantic Beach, instituted no new laws in 2009. City of Myrtle Beach, http://myrtlebeachbikerinfo.com/faq.html; Lorena Anderson, "Judge doesn't halt Myrtle Beach noise, helmet rules," *Sun News*, December 4, 2008; Lorena Anderson, "Myrtle Beach gets word out on motorcycle rallies," *Sun News*, January 13, 2009.

82. The Carolina Dealers' Association promoted a four-day festival. Eight years ago, Harley-Davidson of Myrtle Beach began to sponsor its own event, trademarked as the "Harley-Davidson Spring Cruisin' the Coast" rally, which lasts for ten days. Mike Shanks, who works promoting the Cruisin' the Coast event, explained that it was a "confluence of things" that pushed organizers to start the longer rally. People began coming to the beach earlier, and most beach house rentals run from Saturday to Saturday. Myrtle Beach also had more motorcycle-oriented businesses that benefited

from the longer rally—not to mention the local rental agencies, hotels, restaurants, and bars that also benefited. Lorena Anderson, "Grand Strand hold on ahead of motorcycle rallies," *Sun News*, May 3, 2009.

83. Lorena Anderson, "Myrtle Beach gets word out on motorcycle rallies," *Sun News*, January 13, 2009. Another justification used by local politicians for the 2009 anti-bike rally campaign in Myrtle Beach was the lethal shooting of a twenty-year-old man in the course of a dispute over a parking space during the Atlantic Beach Bikefest in 2008. Though the incident involved only locals, the man who died was a white student attending Coastal Carolina University in Conway, and the shooter, who was African American, attended Myrtle Beach High School. There were no bikers or tourists involved in the incident; however, this shooting was constantly cited by politicians and anti-biker crusaders as the catalyst for the proactive stance against bike rallies in Myrtle Beach, simply because it took place during the Memorial Day weekend (when the bikefest is held). "Myrtle Beach officials: No more biker rallies (20-year-old student killed over parking spot)," *Sun News*, May 28, 2008.

84. Motorcyclists often serve in the military and have families. Since 1988, Rolling Thunder, a non-profit organization for military veterans and bikers, sponsors an annual Memorial Day ride to the nation's capital in Washington, D.C. The sounds of motorcycles, while annoying to some, are presented as symbols of the sounds of war. The organization explained the plan for the first Memorial Day rally: "Their [bikers'] arrival would be announced by the roar of their motorcycles, a sound not unlike the 1965 bombing campaign against North Vietnam dubbed Operation Rolling Thunder." The annual Memorial Day event draws hundreds of thousands of people and is a well-respected tradition that attracts veterans and their supporters from around the country to the nation's capital. This tribute to American war heroes focuses on remembrance of prisoners of war (POWs) and those missing in action (MIAs). Rolling Thunder, http://www.rollingthunder1.com/index.html; Michael E. Ruane, "Motorcyclists Make Annual Noisy Salute to Veterans in D.C. Parade," *Washington Post*, May 25, 2009.

85. The city's planned expenditures include $70,000 for two hundred "pocket-sized digital video camera[s] and supporting software" to allow officers to "videotape the now-illegal parties in parking lots or other potential noise-ordinance violations and play the tapes back in court if tickets are contested." Four hundred and fifty thousand dollars were set aside to build a new five-member "traffic-enforcement squad," with cars and high-tech equipment. Other expenditures included sending city officials to bike rally conventions to get the word out about the new laws, and "defending the city against lawsuits arising from the anti-rally efforts." Lorena Anderson, "Myrtle Beach motorcycle rally funds up for debate," *Sun News*, February 8, 2009.

86. Mike Shank, head of a Harley Week promotions firm called Festival Promotions, filed two federal lawsuits against the city of Myrtle Beach in early 2009. Bart Viers, who received a ticket for not wearing a helmet, and Business Owners Organized to Support Tourism (BOOST), filed a lawsuit in the South Carolina

Supreme Court contesting the constitutionality of the new laws. In March of 2009, Chief Justice Jean Toal of the South Carolina Supreme Court issued a brief memo to "county and city administrators, attorneys and council leaders," stating that the new ordinances were "repugnant and unconstitutional." Justice Toal opined that the separate administrative hearing system violated the state constitution. Tom Leath, city manager for Myrtle Beach, admitted the South Carolina Supreme Court would most likely decide the constitutionality of the ordinances and the hearing process, but that Toal was simply "stepping out early and giving her opinion." The memo, while not binding, was a positive sign for foes of the ordinances. Numerous special interest groups had also lobbied for and supported the ordinances, such as Take Back May, an anti-bike-rally group headed by Tom Rice, a tax attorney from Myrtle Beach. Lorena Anderson, "Myrtle Beach motorcycle rally funds up for debate," *Sun News*, February 8, 2009; Lorena Anderson, "Judge allows city bike rules to roll on," *Sun News*, February 24, 2009; Lorena Anderson, "City's bike rule process catches flak from court," *Sun News*, March 26, 2009; Lorena Anderson, "Myrtle Beach helmet law gets airing in top court," *Sun News*, June 16, 2009.

87. Charlie Campbell, owner of the Dead Dog Saloon in Murrells Inlet, pushed for a rebranding of the rallies without reference to Myrtle Beach. Possible names included the Grand Strand Rally and the Murrells Inlet Rally. Much of the motorcycle rally business was already moving south of Myrtle Beach around Murrells Inlet and north near Atlantic Beach. Campbell suggested, "Myrtle Beach has taken itself out of the loop on the bike week. Their brand equity is irreparably damaged. If they stay with any kind of association, the bike rallies will ultimately erode and go away." Janelle Frost and Kelly Marshall Fuller, "North Myrtle Beach sees bikers roll in for rally," *Sun News*, May 11, 2009; Mike Cherney and Lorena Anderson, "Myrtle Beach hears pros, cons of motorcycle rally aftermath," *Sun News*, May 27, 2009.

88. Robert Morris, "Bikers unite in defense of rallies," *Sun News*, January 31, 2009.

89. Lorena Anderson, "Laws don't stop Helmet Freedom Ride into Myrtle Beach," *Sun News*, March 1, 2009.

90. Once the city instituted its campaign to end the motorcycle festivals, people scrambled to figure out what this "Newer May" would look like along the Grand Strand. There was general agreement that fewer bikers attended the 2009 rallies but the numbers still seemed high—especially for events staged during an economic recession. The cause of the decline was even more uncertain than the numbers. General reports during the rallies indicated that the number of bikers dropped, but not to tragically low points. Typical headlines include "Motorcycle rally's started low on gas," and "Myrtle Beach rally ranks look thin." Mike Cherney, "Motorcycle rally's started low on gas," *Sun News*, May 9, 2009; Steve Jones "Myrtle Beach rally ranks look thin," *Sun News*, May 15, 2009.

91. In "Welcome to South Carolina," Hourigan writes: "The racy promotions [scantily clad women] soon brought in complimentary businesses that catered to white men, namely strip clubs and golf courses. Today, Myrtle Beach is South Carolina's

home for vice. Fourteen strip clubs call the Grand Strand home; that is roughly one for every one thousand male residents over eighteen years old. Men flock to the area to partake in the steamy nightlife," 10. There are 102 golf courses in Myrtle Beach (http://www.visitmyrtlebeach.com/Media/Fast_Facts.html).

92. Mike Cherney and Lorena Anderson, "City hears pros, cons of rally aftermath," *Sun News*, May 27, 2009.

93. Lorena Anderson, "Former Myrtle Beach mayor McBride running again for city seat," *Sun News*, September 3, 2009.

94. Steve Jones, "Hard feelings in wake of helmet law in Myrtle Beach area biker rally," *Sun News*, October 2, 2010.

95. Lorena Anderson, "Myrtle Beach sends refund checks for motorcycle helmet tickets," *Sun News*, July 13, 2010.

96. "Atlantic Beach, South Carolina: Her Future," town website, 2003–7.

97. Jason M. Rodriguez, "Gullah descendants congregate at festival," *Sun News*, August 19, 2007.

Conclusion

1. John H. Sprinkler, Jr., "'Of Exceptional Importance': The Origins of the 'Fifty-Year Rule' in Historic Preservation," *The Public Historian*, Spring 2007, 29.2, 81–103.

2. Dolores Hayden, "Foreword: In Search of the American Cultural Landscape," in *Preserving Cultural Landscapes in America*, Arnold R. Alanen and Robert Z. Melnick, eds. (Baltimore: Johns Hopkins University Press, 2000), ix.

3. Organizations such as The Society for Commercial Archaeology (SCA), "the oldest national organization devoted to the buildings, artifacts, structures, signs, and symbols of the 20th-century commercial landscape," The Recent Past Preservation Network, the Vernacular Architecture Forum (VAF), and numerous academic and popular books speak to emerging interest in original roadside attractions like South of the Border.

4. Sherry Suttles writes in *Atlantic Beach*: "[T]he state archives declared that not a single building in Atlantic Beach would meet National Register designation requirements" (108).

5. See South of the Border's website: http://www.thesouthoftheborder.com/2009/05/26/the-border-foundation-pedro-helping-our-community/, and Suttles, *Atlantic Beach*, 62–92.

6. Richard Francaviglia, "Selling Heritage Landscapes," in *Preserving Cultural Landscapes in America*, 65.

7. Sherry A. Suttles collection, Box 3, Avery Research Center for African American History and Culture, College of Charleston, Charleston, South Carolina.

8. Ibid.

BIBLIOGRAPHY

Archival Sources

Avery Research Center for African American History and Culture. Charleston,
    South Carolina
    Sherry A. Suttles Collection, 1080, Boxes 3–7.

Chapin Memorial Library. Myrtle Beach, South Carolina
    Motorcycle Festivals. Clipping File.
    NAACP Boycott. Clipping File.
    Atlantic Beach Oral History Project. Transcripts.

Coastal Carolina Library. Conway, South Carolina.
    Horry County Oral History Project. Transcripts. Waccamaw Center for Cultural
        and Historical Studies.
    Tourism in South Carolina. State documents.
    The Waccamaw Room. Waccamaw Region and South Carolina Materials.

Robert Scott Small Library, College of Charleston. Charleston, South Carolina.
    Schafer, Joseph Melvin. Interview with Dale Rosengarten and Klyde Robinson,
        July 11, 1995, Jewish Heritage Project.

South Carolina Historical Society. Charleston, South Carolina.
    Tourism Folders.
    George S. Bliss, "Charleston South Carolina Garden Tour, A Notebook of a trip to
        Charleston and other points, 1941."

South Caroliniana Library, University of South Carolina. Columbia, South Carolina.
    Olin D. Johnston Papers. Modern Political Collections.
    Schafer, Alan. Bibliographical Vertical File and Modern Political Collections.
    Schafer, Alan. *The Story of the South Carolina Low Country.*Herbert Ravenel Sass,
        ed. 3 vols. West Columbia, SC: J.F. Hyer Publishing Company, 1956.
    South of the Border. Box Collection.
    South of the Border. Carolina Studios Photographic Collection.
    Tourism in South Carolina Vertical Files Collection.

Waccamaw Regional Planning and Development Council. Atlantic Beach Land Use Plan and Housing Element. June 1979.

Author Interviews

Berger, Jesse and Nate Mallard. June 23, 2009. Charleston, South Carolina.
Cottingham, Mark. June 12, 2009. Mount Pleasant, South Carolina.
Hechtkopf, Evelyn. June 11, 2009. South of the Border, Hamer, South Carolina.
Jones, Shirley. June 11, 2009. South of the Border, Hamer, South Carolina.
Pelt, Susanne. June 2000 and June 11, 2010. South of the Border, Hamer, South Carolina.

Newspapers

Atlanta Journal and Constitution. Atlanta, Georgia.
Columbia Record. Columbia, South Carolina.
Dillon Herald. Dillon, South Carolina.
Fayetteville Observer-Times. Fayetteville, North Carolina.
Los Angeles Times. Los Angeles, California.
New York Times. New York, New York.
News and Observer. Raleigh, North Carolina.
Point. Columbia, South Carolina (monthly; ceased publication in 2001).
Post and Courier. Charleston, South Carolina.
State. Columbia, South Carolina.
Sun News. Myrtle Beach, South Carolina.
Sun. Baltimore, Maryland.
St. Petersburg Times. St. Petersburg, Florida.
Toronto Star. Toronto, Ontario, Canada.
USA Today. McLean, Virginia.
Washington Post. Washington, D.C.
Weekly Surge. Myrtle Beach, South Carolina.

Secondary Sources

Alanen, Arnold R., and Robert Z. Melnick, eds. *Preserving Cultural Landscape in America*. Baltimore, MD: Johns Hopkins University Press, 2000.
Appadurai, Arjun. "Commodities and the Politics of Value," Introductory essay, *The Social Life of Things: Commodities in Cultural Perspective*. Arjun Appadurai, ed. Cambridge, England: Cambridge University Press, 3–63.

Baker, Houston A. *Turning South Again: Re-thinking Modernism/Re-reading Booker T.* Durham, NC: Duke University Press, 2001.

Baker, Laura E. "Public Sites Versus Public Sights: The Progressive Response to Outdoor Advertising and the Commercialization of Public Space." *American Quarterly*, December 2007, 1187–213.

Bakhtin, Mikhail. *Rabelais and His World.* Bloomington, IN: Indiana University Press, 1941.

Barnes, Catherine A. *Journey from Jim Crow: The Desegregation of Southern Transit.* New York, NY: Columbia University Press, 1983.

Barth, Jack, and Doug Kirby. *Roadside America.* 1986. Reprint, New York, NY: Simon & Schuster, 1992.

Bass, Jack, and Jack Nelson. *The Orangeburg Massacre.* 1984. Reprint, Macon, GA: Mercer University Press, 1996.

Bass, Jack, and Marilyn W. Thompson. *Strom: The Complicated Personal and Political Life of Strom Thurmond.* New York, NY: Public Affairs, 2005.

Bass, Jack, and Walter De Vries. *The Transformation of Southern Politics: Social Change & Political Consequence Since 1945.* Athens, GA: University of Georgia Press, 1995.

Beacham, Frank. *Whitewash: A Southern Journey Through Music, Mayhem, and Murder.* New York, NY: Booklocker.com. Inc., 2002.

Belasco, Warren James. *Americans on the Road: From Autocamp to Motel: 1910–1945.* Baltimore, MD: Johns Hopkins University Press, 1986, 1979.

———. "Commercialized Nostalgia," in David L. Lewis and Laurence Goldstein, eds. *The Automobile and American Culture.* Ann Arbor, MI: University of Michigan Press, 1980.

Bergman, David, ed. *Camp Grounds: Style and Homosexuality.* Amherst, MA: University of Massachusetts Press, 1993.

Blu, Karen I. *The Lumbee Problem: The Making of an American Indian People.* 1980. Reprint, Lincoln, NE: University of Nebraska Press, 2001.

Bone, Martyn. "The transnational turn, Houston Baker's New Southern Studies and Partick Neate's *Twelve Bar Blues*." *Comparative American Studies*, 2.2 (2005): 189–211.

Borden, Edward B. "Tourism: A Top SC Industry." *Sandlapper*, May 1968: 57–61.

Bourdieu, Pierre. *Distinction: The Social Critique of the Judgement of Taste*, trans. Richard Nice. Cambridge, MA: Harvard University Press, 1984 (originally published 1979).

Boyd, Michelle R. *Jim Crow Nostalgia: Reconstructing Race in Bronzeville.* Minneapolis, MN: University Of Minnesota Press, 2008.

Brundage, W. Fitzhugh. "Contentious and Collected: Memory's Future in Southern History." *Journal of Southern History*, August 2009: 751–66.

———. *Southern Past: A Clash of Race and Memory.* Cambridge, MA: Harvard University Press, 2005.

———. *Where These Memories Grow: History, Memory, and Southern Identities*. Chapel Hill, NC: University of North Carolina Press, 2000.

Carlton, David L., and Peter A. Coclanis. *The South, the Nation, and the World: Perspectives on Southern Economic Development*. Charlottesville, VA: University of Virginia Press, 2003.

Carr, Duanne. *A Question of Class: The Redneck Stereotype in Southern Fiction*. Bowling Green, OH: Bowling Green State University Popular Press, 1996.

Carter, W. Horace. *Virus of Fear: The Infamous Resurrection and Demise of the Carolinas' Ku Klux Klan*. Tabor City, NC: W.H. Carter, 1991.

Cash, W. J. *The Mind of the South*. New York, NY: Alfred A. Knopf, 1941.

Castronovo, Russ, and Susan Gillman. *States of Emergency: Object of American Studies*. Chapel Hill, NC: University of North Carolina Press, 2009.

Chafe, William H., Raymond Gavins, and Robert Korstad, eds. *Remembering Jim Crow: African Americans Tell About Life in the Segregated South*. New York, NY: The New Press, 2001.

Chamberlain, Charles. *Victory at Home: Manpower and Race in the American South During World War II*. Athens, GA: University of Georgia Press, 2003.

Cobb, James C. *Away Down South: A History of Southern Identity*. New York, NY: Oxford University Press, 2005.

Cobb, James C., and William Stueck, eds. *Globalization and the American South*. Athens, GA: University of Georgia Press, 2005.

Cochran, Augustus B., III. *Democracy Heading South: National Politics in the Shadow of Dixie*. Lawrence, KS: University Press of Kansas, 2001.

Cohan, Steven, and Ina Rae Hark, eds. *The Road Movie Book*. New York, NY: Routledge, 1997.

Cohen, Lizabeth. *A Consumer's Republic: The Politics of Mass Consumption in Postwar America*. New York, NY: Knopf, 2003.

Cohn, Deborah, ed. *Look Away: The U.S. South in New World Studies*. Durham, NC: Duke University Press, 2004.

Coski, John M. *The Confederate Battle Flag*. Cambridge, MA: Harvard University Press, 2005.

Coté, Richard N. *Redneck Riviera*. Mt. Pleasant, SC: Corinthian Books, 2001.

Cresswell, Tim. *In Place/Out of Place: Geography, Ideology, and Transgression*. Minneapolis, MN: University of Minnesota Press, 1996.

Dailey, Jane, Glenda Elizabeth Gilmore, and Bryant Simon, eds. *Jumpin' Jim Crow: Southern Politics From Civil War to Civil Rights*. Princeton, NJ: Princeton University Press, 2000.

Daniel, Pete. *Lost Revolutions: The South in the 1950s*. Chapel Hill, NC: University of North Carolina Press, 2000.

———. "Going among Strangers: Southern Reactions to World War II." *The Journal of American History*. 77.3 (December 1990): 886–911.

Danielson, Michael N. *Profits and Politics in Paradise*. Columbia, SC: University of South Carolina Press, 1995.

Davidson, Donald et al. *I'll Take My Stand: The South and the Agrarian Tradition*. 75th Anniversary Reprint. Baton Rouge, LA: Louisiana State University Press, 2006, 1930.

Delpar, Helen. *The Enormous Vogue of Things Mexican: Cultural Relations between the United States and Mexico, 1920–1935*. Tuscaloosa, AL: University of Alabama Press, 1992.

Denkler, Ann. *Sustaining Identity, Recapturing Heritage: Exploring Issues of Public History, Tourism, and Race in a Southern Town*. Lanham, MD: Lexington Books, 2007.

Dorsey, Allison. *To Build Our Lives Together: Community Formation in Black Atlanta, 1875–1906*. Athens, GA: University of Georgia Press, 2004.

Duck, Leigh Anne. *The Nation's Region: Southern Modernism, Segregation, and U.S. Nationalism*. Athens, GA: University of Georgia Press, 2006.

Edgar, Walter. *South Carolina: A History*. Columbia, SC: University of South Carolina Press, 1998.

Egerton, John. *The Americanization of Dixie: The Southernization of America*. New York, NY: Harper's Magazine Press, 1974.

———. *Speak Now Against the Day: The Generation Before the Civil Rights Movement in the South*. Chapel Hill, NC: University of North Carolina Press, 1994.

Forman, Seth. *Blacks in the Jewish Mind: A Crisis of Liberalism*. New York, NY: New York University Press, 1998.

Foucault, Michel. *The History of Sexuality: An Introduction*. Volume I. Trans. Robert Hurley. 1968. Reprint, New York, NY: Vintage Books, 1990.

Gabardi, Wayne. *Negotiating Postmodernism*. Minneapolis, MN: University of Minnesota Press, 2000.

Gelder, Ken. *Subcultures: Cultural Histories and Social Practice*. New York, NY: Routledge, 2007.

Gilmore, Glenda Elizabeth. *Gender and Jim Crow Women and the Politics of White Supremacy in North Carolina, 1896–1920*. Chapel Hill, NC: University of North Carolina Press, 1996.

———. *Defying Dixie: The Radical Roots of Civil Rights, 1919–1950*. New York, NY: W. W. Norton & Company, 2008.

Goad, Jim. *Redneck Manifesto: How Hillbillies, Hicks, and White Trash Became America's Underclass*. 1997. New York, NY: Touchstone, 1998.

Goings, Kenneth E. *Mammy and Uncle Moses: Black Collectibles and American Stereotyping*. Bloomington, IN: Indiana University Press, 1994.

Gray, Herman S. *Cultural Moves: African Americans and the Politics of Representation*. Berkeley, CA: University of California Press, 2005.

Grimsted, David. "The Purple Rose of Popular Culture Theory: An Exploration of Intellectual Kitsch." *American Quarterly*, 4, December 1991.

Gudis, Catherine. *Buyways: Billboards, Automobiles, and the American Landscape*. New York, NY: Routledge, 2004.

Hahn, Steven. *A Nation under Our Feet: Black Political Struggles in the Rural South from Slavery to the Great Migration*. Cambridge, MA: Harvard University Press, 2003.

Hale, Grace Elizabeh. *Making Whiteness: The Culture of Segregation in the South, 1890–1940*. New York, NY: Vintage Books, 1998.

Harris, Eddy L. *South of Haunted Dreams: A Ride Through Slavery's Old Backyard*. New York, NY: Simon & Schuster 1993.

Hebdige, Dick. *Subculture: The Meaning of Style*. 1979. New York, NY: Routledge, 2002.

Hess, Alan. *Googie: Fifties Coffee Shop Architecture*. San Francisco, CA: Chronicle Books, 1986.

———. *Googie Redux: Ultramodern Roadside Architecture*. San Francisco, CA: Chronicle Books, 2004.

Hine, Thomas. *Populuxe*. New York, NY: Overlook Press, 1986.

Hollis, Tim. *Dixie Before Disney: 100 Years of Roadside Fun*. Jackson, MS: University Press of Mississippi, 1999.

Hook, 'Fessa John. *Shagging in the Carolinas*. Charleston, SC: Arcadia, 2006.

Hourigan, Richard R. *Welcome to South Carolina: Sex, Race, and Tourism in Myrtle Beach, 1900–1975*. Tuscaloosa, AL: University of Alabama, Dissertation, Department of History, 2009.

Jackson, John Brinckerhoff. *Discovering Vernacular Landscape*. New Haven, CT: Yale University Press, 1984.

———. *Landscape in Sight: Looking at America*. New Haven, CT: Yale University Press, 1997.

———. *A Sense of Place, a Sense of Time*. New Haven, CT: Yale University Press, 1994.

Jakle, John A. "Motel by the Roadside: America's Room for the Night," in *Fast Food, Stock Cars & Rock-n-Roll*, ed. George O. Carney. Boston Way, MD: Rowman & Littlefield, 1995.

———. *The Tourist: Travel in Twentieth-Century North America*. Lincoln, NE: University of Nebraska Press, 1985.

Jakle, John, Keith Sculle, and Jefferson Rogers, eds. *The Motel in America*. Baltimore, MD: Johns Hopkins University Press, 1996.

Jameson, Fredric. "Is Space Political?" *Rethinking Architecture: A Reader in Cultural Theory*. Ed. Neil Leach. London, England: Routledge, 1997. 255–70.

Johnson, Patrik. "A motorcycle mecca stirs up questions of race." *Christian Science Monitor*, May 27, 2005.

Jones, Suzanne W., and Sharon Monteith. *South to a New Place: Region, Literature, and Culture*. Baton Rouge, LA: Louisiana State University Press, 2002.

Kahrl, Andrew W. "'The Slightest Semblance of Unruliness': Steamboat Excursions, Pleasure Resorts, and the Emergence of Segregation Culture on the Potomac River." *Journal of American History*, March 2008, 1108–36.

Ketchell, Aaron. *Holy Hills of the Ozarks: Religion and Tourism in Branson, Missouri*. Baltimore, MD: Johns Hopkins University Press, 2007.

Kirshenblatt-Gimblett, Barbara. *Destination Culture: Tourism, Museums, and Heritage*. Berkeley, CA: University of California Press, 1998.

Klarman, Michael J. *From Jim Crow to Civil Rights: The Supreme Court and the Struggle for Racial Equality*. New York, NY: Oxford University Press, 2004.

Korr, Jeremy. "A Proposed Model for Cultural Landscape Study." *Material Culture*, Fall, 1997, 1-18.

Koen-Sarano, Matilda, ed. *Folktales of Joha, Jewish Trickster*. Philadelphia, PA: Jewish Publication Society, 2003.

Koser, Laura. "Planned by Pedro: South of the Borer, 1950–2001." Masters Thesis, Department of History, University of South Carolina, 2004.

Kundera, Milan. *The Unbearable Lightness of Being*. New York, NY: Harper Perennial Modern Classics 1984, 2009.

Laderman, David. *Driving Visions: Exploring the Road Movie*. Austin, TX: University of Texas Press, 2002.

Lee, Matt, and Ted Lee. *The Lee Bros. Southern Cookbook*. New York, NY: W. W. Norton & Company, 2006.

Leland, Elizabeth. *The Vanishing Coast*. Winston Salem, NC: John F. Blair Publisher, 1996.

Lewis, Catherine H. *Horry County, South Carolina, 1730–1993*. Columbia, SC: University of South Carolina Press, 1998.

Lewis, Peirce F., "Axioms for Reading the Landscapes: Some Guides to the American Scene," in *Material Culture Studies in America*, ed. Thomas J. Schlereth. Nashville, TN: American Association for State and Local History, 1982, 175–82.

Lipsitz, George. *How Racism Takes Place*. Philadelphia, PA: Temple University Press, 2011.

Litwack, Leon F. *Trouble in Mind: Black Southerners in the Age of Jim Crow*. New York, NY: Alfred K. Knopf, 1998.

Long, Alecia P. *The Great Southern Babylon: Sex, Race, And Respectability in New Orleans, 1865–1920*. Baton Rouge, LA: Louisiana State University Press, 2005.

MacCannell, Dean. *The Tourist: A New Theory of the Leisure Class*. Reprint. Berkeley, CA: University of California Press, 1999.

Manring, M. M. *Slave in a Box: The Strange Career of Aunt Jemima*. 1976. Charlottesville, VA: University of Virginia Press, 1998.

Margolies, John. "The Best Roadside Attractions." *American Heritage*, April 2001. http://www.americanheritage.com/content/best-roadside-attractions.

McInnis, Maurie D. "Little of Artistic Merit? The Problem and Promise of Southern Art History." *American Art*, Vol. 19.2, 2005, 11–18.

McMillen, Neil, ed. *Remaking Dixie: The Impact of World War II on the American South*. Jackson, MS: University of Mississippi Press, 1990.

McPherson, Tara. *Reconstructing Dixie: Race, Gender, and Nostalgia in the Imagined South*. Durham, NC: Duke University Press, 2003.

———. "On Wal-Mart and Southern Studies." *American Literature*, Volume 78, Number 4, December 2006, 696–98.

Mechling, Jay. "An American Culture Grid with Texts." *American Studies International*, 27 (1989): 2–12.

Meyer, Moe, ed. *The Politics and Poetics of Camp*. London, England: Routledge, 1994.

Moore, Winfred B., Jr., Kyle S. Sinisi, and David H. White, Jr., eds. *Warm Ashes: Issues in Southern History at the Dawn of the Twenty-first Century*. Columbia, SC: University of South Carolina Press, 2003.

Moore, Winfred B., Jr., and Orville Vernon Burton. *Toward the Meeting of the Waters: Currents in the Civil Rights Movement of South Carolina During the Twentieth Century*. Columbia, SC: University of South Carolina Press, 2008.

Moredock, Will. *Banana Republic: A Year in the Heart of Myrtle Beach*. Charleston, SC: Frontline Press, 2003.

Morrison, Toni. *Love*. New York, NY: Vintage, 2003.

Napoli, Lisa, dir. *Southern Lens: South of the Border*. South Carolina Educational Television (SCETV), 1991.

Newitz, Annalee, and Matt Wray. *White Trash: Race and Class in America*. New York, NY: Routledge, 1997.

Newman, Harvey K. *Southern Hospitality: Tourism and the Growth of Atlanta*. Tuscaloosa, AL: University of Alabama Press, 1999.

Nickles, Shelley. "More is Better: Mass Consumption, Gender, and Class Identity in Postwar America." *American Quarterly*, December 2002, 581–622.

O'Brien, Gail William. *The Color of the Law: Race, Violence, and Justice in the Post–World War II South*. Chapel Hill, NC: University of North Carolina, 1999.

Payne, Charles M. *Time Longer Than Rope: A Century of African American Activism*. New York, NY: New York University Press, 2003.

Peacock, James L. *Grounded Globalism: How the U.S. South Embraces the World*. Athens, GA: University of Georgia Press, 2007.

Peacock, James L., Harry L. Watson, and Carries R. Matthews. *The American South in a Global World*. Chapel Hill, NC: University of North Carolina Press, 2005.

Perloff, Marjorie. *Wittgenstein's Ladder: Poetic Language and the Strangeness of the Ordinary*. Chicago, IL: University of Chicago Press, 1996.

Phelts, Marsha Dean. *An American Beach for African Americans*. Gainesville, FL: University Press of Florida, 1997.

Pieterse, Jan Nederveen. *White on Black: Images of Africa and Blacks in Western Popular Culture*. New Haven, CT: Yale University Press, 1992.

Preston, Howard Lawrence. *Dirt Roads to Dixie: Accessibility and Modernization in the South, 1885–1935*. Knoxville, TN: University of Tennessee Press, 1991.

Price, Sally. *Primitive Art in Civilized Places*. Second edition. Chicago, IL: University of Chicago Press, 2001 (originally published 1989).

Raat, Dirk W. *Mexico and the United States: Ambivalent Vistas*. Athens, GA: University of Georgia Press, 1992.

Reed, John Shelton. *My Tears Spoiled My Aim and Other Reflections on Southern Culture*. Orlando, FL: Harcourt, Inc., 1993.

Roberts, Diane. *The Myth of Aunt Jemima: Representation of Race and Region*. New York, NY: Routledge, 1994.

Romine, Scott. *The Real South: Southern Narrative in the Age of Cultural Reproduction*. Baton Rouge, LA: Louisiana State University Press, 2008.

Rymer, Russ. *American Beach: A Saga of Race, Wealth, and Memory*. New York, NY: HarperCollins, 1998.

Sandoval, Chela. *Methodology of the Oppressed*. Minneapolis, MN, and London, England: University of Minnesota Press, 2000.

Sass, Herbert Ravenel, ed. *The Story of the South Carolina Low Country*. West Columbia, SC: J.F. Hyer Publishing Co., 1956.

Schouten, John W., and James M. McAlexander. "Subcultures of Consumption: An Ethnography of the New Bikers." *The Journal of Consumer Research*, June 1995, 43-61.

Seiler, Cotton. "'So That We as a Race Might Have Something Authentic to Travel By': African American Automobility and Cold-War Liberalism." *American Quarterly*, 58.4, December 2006, 1091–117.

Simon, Bryant. "'We're Almost There': The Drive-By Truckers' Art of Place." *Southern Spaces* (http://southernspaces.org), March 28, 2011.

Smeaton, George, and Bharath M. Josiam. "Comparing the Party Habits of Black and White College Students on Spring Beak." *The Journal of Blacks in Higher Education*, Summer 2000, 18.

Smith, Jon, and Deborah Cohn. *Look Away! The U.S. South in New World Studies*. Durham, NC: Duke University Press, 2004.

Smith, Mark M. *How Race Is Made: Slavery, Segregation, and the Senses*. Chapel Hill, NC: University of North Carolina Press, 2006.

Sokol, Jason. *There Goes My Everything: White Southerners in the Age of Civil Rights, 1945–1975*. New York, NY: Vintage, 2006.

Sontag, Susan. *Against Interpretation*. New York, NY: Anchor Books, 1990.

Sprinkler, John H., Jr. "'Of Exceptional Importance': The Origins of the 'Fifty-Year Rule' in Historic Preservation." *The Public Historian*, Spring 2007, 29.2, 81–103.

Stanfield, Peter. "Heritage Design: The Harley-Davison Motor Company." *Journal of Design History*, 5.2 1992, 141–55.

Stanonis, Anthony. *Creating the Big Easy: New Orleans and the Emergence of Modern Tourism, 1918–1945*. Athens, GA: University of Georgia Press, 2006.

———, ed. *Dixie Emporium: Tourism, Foodways, and Consumer Culture in the American South*. Athens, GA: University of Georgia Press, 2008.

Starnes, Richard, ed. *Creating the Land of the Sky: Tourism and Society in Western North Carolina*. Tuscaloosa, AL: University of Alabama Press, 2005.

———. *Southern Journeys: Tourism, History & Culture in the Modern South*. Tuscaloosa, AL: University of Alabama Press, 2003.

Steinbeck, John. *Travels with Charley: In Search of America*. New York, NY: Penguin Books, 1962.

Stokes, Barbara F. "Atlantic Beach," in *The South Carolina Encyclopedia*. Columbia, SC: University of South Carolina Press, 2006, 34–35.

———. *Myrtle Beach: A History, 1990–1980*. Columbia, SC: University of South
    Carolina Press, 2007.
Stokes, Duward T. *The History of Dillon County, South Carolina*. Columbia, SC:
    University of South Carolina Press, 1978.
Sturken, Marita. *Tourists of History: Memory, Kitsch, and Consumerism from
    Oklahoma City to Ground Zero*. Durham, NC: Duke University Press, 2007.
Suttles, Sherry A. *Atlantic Beach: Images of America*. Charleston, SC: Arcadia
    Publishing, 2009.
Tuan, Yi-Fu. *Place and Space: The Perspective of Experience*. Minneapolis, MN:
    University of Minnesota Press, 1977.
Tyson, Timothy B. *Radio Free Dixie: Robert F. Williams and the Roots of Black Power*.
    Chapel Hill, NC: University of North Carolina Press, 2000.
Upton, Dell. "Architectural History or Landscape History?" *Journal of Architectural
    Education*, August 1991, 195–99.
Urry, John. *The Tourist Gaze*. 1990. London, England: Sage, 2002.
Venturi, Robert, Denise Scott Brown, and Steven Izenour. *Learning From Las Vegas:
    The Forgotten Symbolism of Architectural Form*. 1972. Cambridge, MA: MIT Press,
    1977.
Wachter, Paul. "Uneasy Riders: Myrtle Beach's separate and unequal biker rallies."
    Legal Affairs: The Magazine at the Intersection of Law and Life, November/
    December, 2005. http://www.legalaffairs.org/issues/November-December-2005/
    scene_wachter_novdec05.msp.
Watson, James. *Golden Arches East: McDonald's in East Asia*. Second edition. Palo
    Alto, CA: Stanford University Press, 2006.
Watts, Rebecca Bridges. *Contemporary Southern Identities: Community Through
    Controversy*. Jackson, MS: University Press of Mississippi, 2008.
Williams-Forson, Psyche. *Building Houses Out of Chicken Legs: Black Women, Food &
    Power*. Chapel Hill, NC: University of North Carolina Press, 2006.
Wittgenstein, Ludwig. *Philosophical Investigations*. 1953. Malden, England: Blackwell,
    2001.
Wolfe, Tom. *The Kandy-Kolored Tangerine-Flake Streamline Baby*. New York, NY:
    Farrar, Straus and Giroux, 1965.
Wollen, Peter. *Raiding the Icebox: Reflections on Twentieth-Century Culture*.
    Bloomington, IN: Indiana University Press, 1993.
Woodward, C. Vann. *The Burden of Southern History*. Baton Rouge, LA: Louisiana
    State University Press, 1960.
———. *Origins of the New South, 1877–1913*. 1951. Baton Rouge, LA: Louisiana State
    University Press, 2000.
———. Southern Historical Association presidential address, "The Irony of Southern
    History." *Journal of Southern History*, 19, February 1953, 3–19.
———. *The Strange Career of Jim Crow*. 1955. Oxford, England: Oxford University
    Press, 1974.

Works Progress Administration. *South Carolina: The WPA Guide to the Palmetto State*. Reprint, with new introduction and appendices by Walter B. Edgar. Columbia, SC: University of South Carolina Press, 1988.

Wray, Matt. *Not Quite White: White Trash and the Boundaries of Whiteness*. Durham, NC: Duke University Press, 2006.

Wyrick, Deborah. "Editor's introduction." *Jouvert: A Journal of Postcolonial Studies*, Vol. 4, Issue 2, 2000. http://english.chass.ncsu.edu/jouvert/v4:2/ed4Z.htm.

Young, Robert. "The Linguistic Turn, Materialism and Race." *Callaloo*, Vol. 24, No. 1 (Winter, 2001), 334–45.

INDEX

CPSIA information can be obtained at www.ICGtesting.com
Printed in the USA
BVOW070858080212

282335BV00004B/3/P

9 781617 032516